GRAY BEARDED GREEN BERET'S GUIDE TO SURVIVING THE WILD

GRAY BEARDED GREEN BERET'S GUIDE TO SURVIVING THE WILD

Essential Bushcraft and First Aid Skills for Surviving the Great Outdoors

JOSHUA ENYART

FOREWORD BY DAVID WESCOTT

MIAMI

Copyright © 2025 by Joshua Enyart.
Published by Mango Publishing Group, a division of Mango Media Inc.

Cover Design: Elina Diaz
Cover Photo/illustration: stock.adobe.com/James O'Donnell, stock.adobe.com/PeterAtkins, stock.adobe.com/Chris, stock.adobe.com/DenisVakhrushev, stock.adobe.com/Jonas Sjöblom, stock.adobe.com/zlikovec
Layout & Design: Elina Diaz

Mango is an active supporter of authors' rights to free speech and artistic expression in their books. The purpose of copyright is to encourage authors to produce exceptional works that enrich our culture and our open society.

Uploading or distributing photos, scans or any cotntent from this book without prior permission is theft of the author's intellectual property. Please honor the author's work as you would your own. Thank you in advance for respecting our author's rights.

For permission requests, please contact the publisher at:
Mango Publishing Group
2850 S Douglas Road, 2nd Floor
Coral Gables, FL 33134 USA
info@mango.bz

For special orders, quantity sales, course adoptions and corporate sales, please email the publisher at sales@mango.bz. For trade and wholesale sales, please contact Ingram Publisher Services at customer.service@ingramcontent.com or +1.800.509.4887.

Gray Bearded Green Beret's Guide to Surviving the Wild: Essential Bushcraft and First Aid Skills for Surviving the Great Outdoors

Library of Congress Cataloging-in-Publication number: 2021936119
ISBN: (hc) 978-1-68481-833-4 (pb) 978-1-64250-543-6, (ebook) 978-1-64250-544-3
BISAC category code SPO030000—SPORTS & RECREATION / Outdoor Skills

Disclaimer: The information in this book is meant to supplement, not replace, proper bushcraft training. Like any practice that requires equipment, skill, and ingredients from nature, this practice poses some inherent risk. The author and publisher advise readers to take full responsibility for their safety. Do not take risks beyond your level of experience, aptitude, training, and comfort level.

This book is not intended as a substitute for the medical advice of physicians. The reader should regularly consult a physician in matters relating to his/her health and particularly with respect to any symptoms that may require diagnosis or medical attention. The reader practices the recommendations contained in this book at their own risk.

Printed in the United States of America

To my wife, Lauren, and my children, Luke, Jacob, Abigail, and Madeline. Thank you for all the support you give me. Everything I am able to accomplish is because of you. You are my true legacy and my biggest source of pride.

Table of Contents

Foreword 11

Preface 15

Chapter 1 **The Building Blocks of Survival** 28

Chapter 2 **Tool Selection, Safety, and Use** 53

Chapter 3 **Fire Craft** 99

Chapter 4 **Shelter Craft** 153

Chapter 5 **Water Procurement** 206

Chapter 6 **Food Procurem ent** 237

Chapter 7 **First Aid in the Wilderness** 288

Chapter 8 **Map Reading and Land Navigation** 355

Chapter 9 **Signaling for Rescue** 412

Closing Thoughts 426

FOREWORD

"Good judgment is the result of experience and experience the result of bad judgment."

—Mark Twain

I've been asked to introduce you to Joshua Enyart and his fine book, *Gray Bearded Green Beret's Guide to Surviving the Wild: Essential Bushcraft and First Aid Skills for Surviving the Great Outdoors.* Having spent over fifty years in the field of survival education, running a respected survival school and editing the *Bulletin of Primitive Technology,* I was exposed to the most up-to-date field practices and the world's top primitive skills practitioners. I feel uniquely qualified to assess what is now being offered to the public under the title of "bushcraft skills"—what many define as the blending of both modern and primitive survival arts and science.

"The majority of emergencies happen to people who didn't think anything could or would happen, so they weren't prepared."

—Joshua Enyart

A survival episode is the result of an unanticipated emergency; how you prepare for or respond to that emergency will define the outcome of the episode. Results can range from disorientation to inconvenience and discomfort to injury and even death. Your ability to adapt to your new conditions can be affected by the nature of the emergency itself, but will more likely depend on how you prepare in advance for and react to such an episode.

> *"Approaching the wilderness with theory rather than experience can kill you."*
>
> —Joshua Enyart

Factors affecting the outcome of a survival episode form a three-legged stool: leg one, you and the knowledge you possess; leg two, the resources you bring or those that are provided by the environment; leg three, the tools you carry or can improvise. *Gray Bearded Green Beret's Guide to Surviving the Wild* is your source for the core knowledge you should develop by teaching you universal survival principles: leg one. It also provides field-tested systems that include the best tools and kits you can assemble to help mitigate life-threatening conditions: leg two. Since in this country, the vast majority of survival episodes don't last more than four days, the principles and systems you need to know are not all that sophisticated, so there's no excuse for you not to dive in and see what *Gray Bearded Green Beret's Guide to Surviving the Wild* can teach you.

> *"Without one, the other two don't matter; without the other two, one alone doesn't help you."*
>
> —Joshua Enyart

So, leg three comes through controlled exposure to typical environments you might encounter. For this, you need a professional survival instructor with extensive field experience and qualifications who can teach you about what to expect and refine the skills needed to reduce your dependence on technology. The field today is glutted with "survival instructors" who have gained acclaim through their ability to copy what they have seen online; these people have reduced proper training to dazzling little parlor tricks, lulling the novice into a false sense of security by inflating their confidence. Even more fall victim to gadgets and technologies that, *when* they fail, leave the victim with few alternatives.

I'll spare you the frustration of bad judgment by using my years of experience to help identify someone whose abilities you can trust. If you read the preface to *Gray Bearded Green Beret's Guide to Surviving the Wild*, you'll come to appreciate the breadth and depth of Joshua's qualifications. His passion for teaching is surpassed only by his strong desire to help people safely experience a life outdoors. Use the benefit of Joshua's real-world experiences and training to help you enjoy a world just beyond your doorstep.

I have spent time with Joshua in simple outdoor classroom settings, and I know how he is able to teach principles that will keep you safe and comfortable. I have watched his online content and enjoy his no-nonsense systems approach to skills instruction. But more importantly, I have been with him as he safely trains people under harsh field conditions, giving them a chance to test their limits and newfound abilities. No macho bologna, just good solid mentoring.

However, this book is not the end of your trail. Since the principles can be applied in a variety of settings, it easily translates to daily life. Tools that you can keep in the kitchen junk drawer or in a "go bag" hanging out in the garage can be used to deal with home emergencies as well. You can pack the book as a reminder, but the principles should already be in your head and the skills at your fingertips.

> *"Simply acknowledging that something could go wrong and preparing for that can turn an emergency into nothing more than an inconvenience."*
>
> —Joshua Enyart

Don't underestimate the need to prepare. The old survival adage, "Plan for the worst, but hope for the best," has never been truer than it is today. The statistics prove it...and the numbers are going up. Don't be a statistic. Get outside and train to become "brilliant at the basics."

David Wescott
Owner of Backtracks, LLC; Host of the annual Rabbitstick Primitive Skills Conference; Former owner/director of Boulder Outdoor Survival School; Editor of the *Bulletin of Primitive Technology, Primitive Technology: A Book of Earth Skills*, and *Primitive Technology II: Ancestral Skills*; Author of *Camping in the Old Style*

PREFACE

I would like to first take this opportunity to thank you for your interest in my first book! Hopefully, it will be the first of many. I don't usually like to talk about myself, but if you'll allow it, I would like to tell you who I am and where I came from.

My name is Joshua Enyart. I am a former Army Ranger and Green Beret. When I say "Army Ranger," I mean that I both served in the 75th Ranger Regiment, and also graduated from the prestigious US Army Ranger School.

It is often said that "the tab is just a school, but the scroll is a way of life." In other words, the Army Ranger School is a leadership school that is available to many branches and occupational specialties (what "jobs" are called in the army). You can attend Ranger School, graduate after several weeks of training, and then return to your original job, though certainly with more recognition and distinction (having "earned your tab"). However, if you're a ranger that serves as part of the Ranger Regiment, being an Army Ranger, is your life, day in and day out. It's where you "earn your scroll." Young Rangers have to prove themselves for a period of time in order to earn an opportunity to attend the Ranger School so that they can become leaders within the Ranger Regiment.

During my time in the Rangers, I served during the Cold War, in Haiti for Operation Uphold Democracy, and traveled three times to Panama for training, two of which were to attend the Jungle Operations Training Center. The value of that training—covering jungle survival techniques and gaining experience in such a wild place—cannot be overstated. Although everything in the jungle seemed to want to bite, poke, or poison me, I have to admit I enjoyed it. Killer bees, piranhas, vampire bats, and poo-flinging monkeys…what's not to love?

Aside from overseas, I trained in several other locales. The woodlands and mountains of the eastern United States; the swamps of the southeast; the desert, High Desert, and mountains of the west and southwest—all of which gave me extremely valuable experience across different environments and conditions. These opportunities would continue throughout my career. Those experiences, in no small way, helped shape me into who I am today. After all, in order to teach you how to survive, I myself must have learned to survive in all manner of environments.

After service with the Ranger Regiment, I moved on to be a Pre-Ranger instructor for the 101st Airborne Division. While I had taught before in my role as a leader, this was really my first assignment as a professional instructor. I went to the Army Instructor Training Course and graduated top of that class. Every day for three years was dedicated to learning the principles of instruction and passing knowledge and skills on to future rangers. I would have students come back to me after they successfully earned their ranger tabs, and tell me how my instruction (and that of the other instructors) was a big part of that. I realized that they would then be the ones effectively leading troops in combat and passing on those skills. That, in my opinion, is true legacy.

> *If you are going to leave anything behind,*
> *leave behind knowledge and skills that better*
> *the lives of others.*

That is what I hope to continue doing with this book.

Even after this rewarding experience, the 101st Airborne Division wasn't quite done with me. I later served as an Infantry Scout with a unit nicknamed "Tiger Force." My role as a scout was to sneak around undetected and gather information on the enemy, as well as travel ahead of larger units to make sure the routes were as secure as possible. I also worked closely with snipers to set up blocking positions and ambushes. During that time, I wrote *Scout Handbook*, a short book full of important knowledge and skills that were tailored to smaller scout units. This was really my first go at writing and customizing information that was directly relevant to the end user (in this case, myself and my small unit). Many years later, I ran into a guy that served in Tiger Force after me who told me that *Scout Handbook* was still being used. This again reinforced the value of legacy.

My next adventure was the unique training required to become a Green Beret: Special Forces Assessment and Selection (SFAS). After completing SFAS, I was selected to train as a Special Forces Weapons Sergeant. Basically, I was trained to maintain and use anything that goes *boom* and sends a projectile downrange toward an enemy. This was true for both foreign and domestic weapons systems—I needed to know them inside and out. But I wasn't just responsible for training my own team on them. Part of being a Green Beret means training foreign military forces that we work with on the battlefield. The foreign weapons and language training I did helped with that.

I learned two valuable lessons from teaching people who speak a different language. First, in order for them to understand, everything has to be broken down into the simplest terms. Second, anything can be learned by anyone if you develop a system or template. Both of these lessons are still part of how I approach training others today.

PREFACE

Part of the Special Forces Qualification Course was SERE training, which stands for Survival, Evasion, Resistance, and Escape. I had gotten some basic survival training in the Rangers, but this was really my first taste of actual dedicated survival training. None of my training was easy—just as learning to survive in the wild can be a challenge—but having a systematic approach to developing skills is valuable. This underlying lesson has influenced how I approach training others. The famous college basketball coach John Wooden once said:

"Champions are brilliant at the basics."

One of the most important lessons I've learned and applied to my own system of training is that there is really no such thing as advanced skills, there is only "brilliance in the basics." Having a multitude of fancy or gimmicky skills that you're capable of performing at a mediocre level will never beat being outstanding at the basic skills that just work. Those are the skills you can rely on when the going gets tough, so they should always be the focus. More skill will always be better than less skill, with the understanding that each skill is fully developed in the first place.

After training on the "running and gunning" techniques of room clearing and "close quarters battle," I was fortunate enough to be chosen to train as a sniper on my team. Being a sniper in the army is a secondary job, not a primary occupation. I was still a Weapons Sergeant but would also be one of the snipers for a particular mission if needed. The training for this was several weeks long. Day in and day out, often well into darkness, we learned fieldcraft, ballistics, and long-range shooting. What I enjoyed most about this training was the fieldcraft. We went out with a partner—this was a very small "unit"— and had to rely on ourselves and our own basic skills to provide for our needs while out. This forced us to learn to make do with what we had, to do more with less, and be more self-reliant. A state of mind you'll learn with this book!

Soon after completing all of this training, I deployed with my team to Afghanistan. This was my second combat deployment on active duty. We operated mostly in the provinces of western and northern Afghanistan but also spent quite a bit of time in the south where the majority of the fighting was. The terrain varied from flat desert with high, beautiful, red rocky mountains jutting up in the distance, to very rugged, mountainous terrain with snowy peaks surrounding lush green valleys. Afghanistan is easily one of the most beautiful

PREFACE

places I've been to date, and the local food was outstanding. Later, as a private contractor, I worked all over the country and soaked up even more of its landscape and culture. In addition to the culture, the landscape taught me quite a bit about different environments. What I found most interesting is that familiar plants I knew from the US also grew in Afghanistan along roughly the same latitudes and in the same conditions. This gave me more of a global perspective and appreciation of Mother Nature. Anything can happen based on conditions and the position relative to the sun—Mother Nature knows no political boundaries. Of course, it was a war that came with dangerous times; however, I also saw it as a unique opportunity to enhance my knowledge of different environments and types of terrain.

My first civilian job after I was honorably discharged was as a weapons and tactics instructor for the US Air Force Special Operations command at the Combat Control School. I attended and graduated the Air Force Basic Instructor Course, which was a nice update to the earlier formal instructor training in the Army. This position was another opportunity to be a full-time instructor and develop my own personal skills of delivering information in a way that was easily understood. I enjoyed teaching the basics to fresh faces. During this time, opportunities arose for private military contracting overseas, so I jumped on them. There are a number of jobs overseas that are outsourced to the civilian market, which reduces the workload on soldiers and allows for more specialization. These jobs go out to private military contractors (like me), who can also be referred to as civilian contractors. I was excited about getting back into the mix of what I felt was important overseas work. All of the contracts I worked on were for the Departments of Defense and State, and for all of them I was an "armed" contractor, meaning I actually still carried a carbine and sidearm. I was just limited to self-defense with those because I was technically a civilian on the battlefield. This gave me the opportunity to actually go "outside the wire" alongside military units as an advisor. I was with the boys and girls in uniform again. Basically, the best of both worlds but with better pay—and I didn't have to shave off my beard!

Over the course of my thirteen trips to the Middle East, I had several close calls, as did so many others. I was in several lengthy firefights, dodged more than my fair share of rockets and mortars, and had a few close calls with enemy snipers. One of my contracts was advising military "bomb squads" who responded to every Improvised Explosive Device (IED) and "roadside bomb" that either was found or actually

PREFACE

went off in our particular area. This was a daily occurrence. We were targeted more than others because of our ability to defuse those devices, which apparently went against the insurgents' plans.

As they say, combat is often days, weeks, and months of boredom, with minutes of sheer terror mixed in periodically. That's fairly accurate, although I cannot remember ever actually being scared. Things happen quickly, you react based on your training, and you either come out on top or you don't, often without any actual choice in the matter other than being there and getting lucky. So after spending so much time "pressing my luck" in the Middle East, I decided I needed to move into a profession that might be less hazardous to my health. But the ability to dissemble, reassemble, perform a functions check, and boresight an M40 105mm recoilless rifle wasn't such a marketable skill in the civilian sector. Who knew? So I chalked my weapons and tactics training up to "fun had" and started looking at opportunities to move into the medical field. After all, the only other things I really enjoyed from my service besides the weapons and tactics were being outdoors, learning survival and woodsman skills, instructing, and honing my medical skills.

During one of my last deployments as a private military contractor, I was given the opportunity to attend a civilian Emergency Medical Technician (EMT) course. I jumped at the chance to attend, and thank goodness I did—I ended up meeting my wife there! Another thing that made this experience so special was that the instructor knew my background and allowed me to adapt his teachings to my tactical trauma training in a way that was more applicable to the battlefield. This was, of course, more useful to me, and it set the foundation for how I would adapt all of my medical training to a more applicable remote wilderness emergency. Most EMT courses are black and white and bound by protocol, whereas I (thanks to the instructor) was allowed to think in color and adapt what I knew to situations as they arose. This is the sort of real-life approach you'll find in this book.

As I later pursued being a physician's assistant, I was able to expand on these skills even more. Amid all the medical training, I kept my instructor skills honed by returning to service once again—this time with the Marine Corps Special Operations Command. I took on a contract to be a Sniper and Ground Warfare Instructor, where I and the rest of the team were responsible for the sustainment and pre-deployment training of already qualified Marine Raiders. Basically, we brushed them up on their skills before they went off to war. I also often handled the tactical trauma and medical side of training, which I found particularly satisfying since that was what I was pursuing as a future PA.

While I did this, I continued building a business on the side that captured my other interests: being in the woods, and practicing and teaching survival and woodsman skills. I started a YouTube channel and began releasing videos on wilderness skills. I originally named the channel after myself but found that very few people could pronounce my last name, and even fewer could actually spell it. When I taught smaller seminars, students would ask me for the name of the channel so they could look it up, and I'm reasonably sure many never found it for this reason. That's why I decided to change the name to something more marketable and memorable. It was a toss-up between "Crusty Old Ranger" and "Gray Bearded Green Beret." Both were meant to pay homage to my roots, and to give the impression that I was an older, possibly wiser, version of my younger self.

Although it was hard for me to decide which had a greater impact on me—being a Ranger in my younger days or being a Green Beret in my later years—I was advised by a close friend that civilians consider the Green Beret more prestigious. He also informed me that he thought both were corny, and I couldn't refute either point. Now, I'm probably more commonly known as the Gray Bearded Green Beret, or simply Gray Beard or GB2. In hindsight, I probably should have chosen the Crusty Old Ranger moniker. Now, people can't find me because they don't know whether to type in the British "Grey" or the American "Gray." Not exactly a "problem solved" situation, but still better.

PREFACE

Gray Bearded Green Beret started off pretty slowly. I put in quite a bit of time, money, and effort for two solid years and saw less than a $10 return on that investment. I had about 500 subscribers and considered stopping YouTube altogether because I wasn't reaching the audience I'd hoped for. Not long after that, I had a video go viral and the channel took off. Other companies began to hire me and pay me to do videos for their channels, and I was being invited to teach courses in more and more places.

Over time, this side pursuit would successfully take over all the others, bringing me to where I am today.

Now, I'm a professional wilderness skills instructor that specializes in what I consider a hybrid blend of military survival, emergency survival, and primitive survival—mixed with a heavy dose of bushcraft, disaster preparedness, wilderness medical, and weapons and tactics training. I'm probably outside the norm of those industries in a lot of ways, mainly because I'm not a "product" of any one of those industries. My teaching style and systematic approach to these subjects are a result of where I came from, a blend of a variety of experiences, instructors, training sources, and interests over decades.

So where did this all start? I was born and raised in southern Ohio along with one sister, awfully close to the setting of *The Frontiersman* by Allan W. Eckert. I was a stone's throw away from the Ohio River Valley and the Shawnee State Forest—they were my playground growing up. When I was seven years old, my family moved out to an extremely rural area: Otway, Ohio. For me, that year was the beginning of a lifelong love of the wilderness. I spent most of my time in the forest from then on.

That same year, I also went to visit my father in Divide, Colorado. We were in a little A-frame cabin up in the mountains. Every day after my dad went to work, I'd grab a Zebco 33 fishing rod and head off through the mountains to three ponds that were chock-full of trout. I'd spend all day filling the stringer, and when I returned with my catches, my grandpa and I would clean and cook them. For two months I was alone in the wilderness, wandering around the mountains by myself, all day, every day. That was my first taste of what I considered freedom.

Back then, I was too young to realize the dangers of having no map, no compass, no emergency signals or gear, no idea that the mountains even had mountain lions or bears, and no concept of how far I was going away from home each day. It was just me, a fishing pole, a bad haircut (I got bored, cut my own bangs, could not get a straight line, and eventually ran out of bangs trying to fix it), and the wilderness. I often wonder if I've subconsciously been chasing that same freedom ever since.

I stayed in the woods, obsessed with the idea of joining the military and being outside, counting down the days until I was old enough to join the Army. My parents had to consent to my signing up the summer between my junior and senior year. I left for basic training five days after I turned eighteen. I'm fortunate enough to say that I was and am what I wanted to be when I grew up.

PREFACE

I've spent tens of thousands of hours in the woods developing and teaching the survival skills I've learned over my lifetime. Most people will spend forty hours a week at an office; my office is the woods. I don't tell you any of this to make it sound like I'm a big deal. I'll only tell you this: I was trained by the best, was a member of some of the best units, and have since been fortunate enough to, in turn, train the best.

Being an instructor is not a hobby for me. It's my profession and has been for much of my adult life. Everything in this book is based on field experience, not theory. I know what good is, I know what bad is, and I know what is and is not going to work because I've done it. The only way to teach from experience is to be experienced. Conventional wisdom and what's normally accepted and regurgitated is not always accurate. It either works, or it does not, and the only way to be sure is to test it.

My motto is:

> *Be prepared first, then be prepared to find yourself completely unprepared.*

My training philosophy recognizes that there's an inverse proportion between gear and skill. The lower your skill level, the more you need to rely on gear to keep you safe in the wilderness in an emergency. The higher your skill level, the less you need to rely on gear. My goal as an instructor is to develop your skills and take you from gear-reliance to self- and nature-reliance. The underlying goal of this book is to get folks off the couch and back out into the wilderness, back in touch with their primal selves, and enjoying the journey, hopefully with their family and friends.

I should mentioned that no single book can cover all skills, circumstances, or environments. Principles and systems are what bridge the gap between one area and another, one skill level to the next. My hope is that you take what you learn from me in this book and tailor it to your specific needs in your environment.

I hope to see you in the woods!

CHAPTER 1

THE BUILDING BLOCKS OF SURVIVAL

Each year, millions of people use precious vacation days to pack up their families and head out to one of nature's remote spots on this beautiful earth. The woods and trails are swollen with hikers, backpackers, hunters, trappers, off-road vehicles, and ATV operators, all out seeking fellowship with the wilderness. Regardless of what takes them out into the wild, there are always inherent risks.

The most common emergency situations you might encounter are getting lost, becoming injured, getting caught in extreme weather, or losing conveyance (broken down vehicle, empty fuel tank, capsized canoe or kayak, etc.). I would argue that the majority of emergencies happen to people who didn't think anything could or would happen, so they weren't prepared. Unfortunately, bad things happen whether we imagine them beforehand or not. Simply acknowledging that something could go wrong and preparing for that can turn an emergency into nothing more than an inconvenience. The "Day Hiker" mentality—when a person feels they do not need much because they are only going out for a few hours and returning home—is what gets people in trouble. That mindset works until it doesn't.

Remember: be prepared first, then be prepared to find yourself completely unprepared. This means that you should have a plan and be equipped to provide for your needs in the event that things *don't* go as planned and you're forced to stay out in the wilderness for longer than expected. This should be the baseline for all rendezvous with nature. From there, you should aspire to learn how to source more of what you need from the wilderness. Not only will this allow you to confidently and safely lighten your load, it will also give you the knowledge and skills you need when you find yourself in an emergency.

Mother Nature will punish the specialist and reward the generalist. If you specialize in doing things one way and the conditions are not right for you to do it that way, you will likely fail. If you are generally good at doing things a lot of different ways, then whatever the conditions are, there's a good chance you'll be able to adapt and succeed. This is something to keep in mind as you begin your journey toward being more self- and nature-reliant.

The Definition of Survival

Survival, quite simply, means to stay alive, often despite difficult circumstances. In order to survive, we must meet basic biological needs: we need air to breathe, water to drink, clothing and shelter to maintain our core body temperature, calorie consumption for energy, and rest. In addition to these, we may need medical care to handle life-threatening injuries. Assuming we have adequate air and respiration, we can shorten that list to:

- First Aid for Life Threats
- Core Temperature Control
- Hydration
- Calorie Consumption
- Rest

Understanding those needs allows us to prioritize the tasks we may need to accomplish in order to survive. These are called "Survival Priorities."

I should mention that I personally do not believe that "survival" is a "Break Glass in Case of Emergency" subject, nor do I believe it to be a situation where you're down to nothing and your life depends on your ability to repurpose trash and sticks to suit your needs. Survival "hacks" are generally nothing more than entertainment and far from practical to stake your life on. If you ever find yourself down to needing to use a gum wrapper or cheese puff to start your fire, take a seat, have a moment of quiet reflection, and ask yourself how you possibly failed to prepare for something so simple. Ask yourself why you're counting on a gum wrapper or cheese puff to save your life. Why didn't you just put a lighter in your pocket and carry some emergency tinder? Be prepared first.

So how do you define what is and isn't a survival skill? What should be included in a guide on the subject and what shouldn't? Labels and definitions are the subject of many heated debates. Some folks feel very strongly that certain things are "survival" related, certain things are for "bushcraft," and certain things are for "preppers." I think the labels don't matter as much as people think. They're all intertwined. Skills that I learn in the woods that many consider "bushcraft" are still skills I can rely on in the woods for survival during an emergency, and vice versa. Our needs are our needs, regardless of why we went into the wild. If a tool and/or skill can provide for our needs for one activity, it can do the same for another.

The Survival Priorities

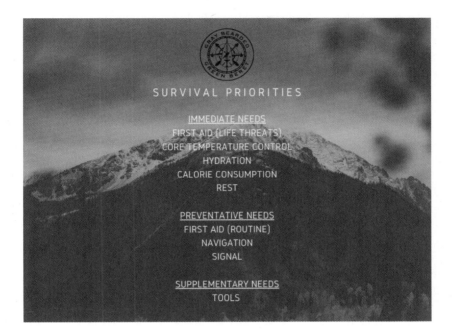

So what's going to kill you first? Learning your survival priorities will help you figure this out. These can differ from one environment to the next, from one situation to another. It's good to know the formula, but the order must be decided by your current situation. They'll normally be prioritized by **Immediate Needs, Preventive Needs, and Supplemental Needs**.

Immediate Needs

First Aid for Life Threats

During one of my EMT courses, my instructor said, "Air goes in and out, blood goes round and round. Any interruption to either of those is a life threat." That may be an oversimplification, but the message is clear: Anything that can stop these things from happening within the next few minutes becomes your priority. Lack of air or blood volume will rob oxygen from our tissues and soon result in death. Minor injuries that are non-life-threatening can wait and are not an "immediate needs" priority. If you have a life-threatening injury, that is obviously priority number one.

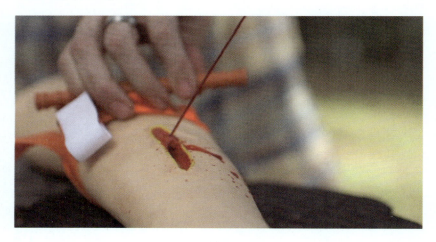

Core Temperature Control

Maintaining your core body temperature will be one of the most important things you do besides handling any immediate life threats. While you may think that shelter is the first thing to set up, that's not always the case. Most think of shelter in the form of a house, cabin, tent, or tarp. We build these to protect us from the elements and maintain our core body temperature. We keep warm in three ways:

Clothing

So long as it is appropriate for the environment, clothing is your first form of "shelter." It's the "first line of defense" against the elements. Your clothing choices should consist of several **layers** that you can put on or take off as needed. Some may be worn, while some may be packed away in case the temperature drops. As a general rule, you should be comfortably cool when moving, and comfortably warm when stationary. Having several layers allows you to do that. Rather than going all out on a huge down jumpsuit you found online, you can always add more layers. But you can only take off so many before it becomes a legality issue.

Fire

Fire also allows us to maintain our core body temperature and, in that way, is a form of "shelter." It can keep us warm and prevent hypothermia. In many environments, a fire can be used without a shelter overhead. In my winter survival course in the Adirondack Mountains of northeastern New York, with temperatures well down into the single digits and below, students have to build a traditional "debris hut" in preparation for a no-gear, no-fire, worst-case scenario. This shelter is constructed from a frame made of logs and sticks and covered by debris. That debris (leaves, pine needles, conifer boughs, etc.) provides insulation and protection from the elements.

The following night, they use an "open air" shelter on a bed made of evergreen boughs next to a "long fire"—a body-length fire, with additional logs stacked behind them to act as a wall and provide fuel through the night—and no overhead cover. When there's no

CHAPTER 1: THE BUILDING BLOCKS OF SURVIVAL

chance of rain or snow, overhead cover isn't always necessary. All the students remarked on how much warmer they were next to a fire compared to inside the debris hut shelter with no fire. Having both a shelter and a fire is the best option, but if you cannot have both, a fire is usually the better choice between the two. I've never heard of anyone dying of hypothermia next to a roaring fire.

In addition, if you somehow become soaked with water, the first thing you need to do is get a roaring fire going and change your clothes (or dry the clothes you have on, if you don't have any spare ones). Taking the time to build a shelter while you're wet, and climbing inside still wet, is not the best option. **Build the fire first.** Dry out and warm up next to your fire as you build your shelter. This is especially useful in winter when hands get cold and lose dexterity for tying knots and lashings. Having a fire going to warm your hands back up is an essential part of shelter construction.

Shelter

Shelter in the form we typically think of (tents, tarps, hammock systems, etc.) will help maintain your core body temperature and protect you from the elements. As a general rule, your shelter should be small in colder weather so that it can trap more body heat in and lose less to the environment, and much larger in hot weather to allow that same heat to escape.

Hydration

Our bodies are made of up to 60 percent water, making it vital for many physical and physiological functions. We cannot go exceptionally long without it. Dehydration can also reduce your ability to regulate your core temperature. Depending on your size, you likely need two to three liters of water per day. Obviously, you'll need more if your activity level is high, you're injured, or if you're in a particularly hot or dry environment. The need for water may outweigh other priorities in those situations.

Calorie Consumption

Although a person can go for long periods of time without food, caloric intake is necessary to maintain energy levels and cognitive function to make sound decisions and physically provide for other needs. Having said that, food would never outweigh First Aid for Life Threats, Core Temperature Control, or Hydration. In addition, consuming food will likely also increase your need for water consumption to digest it. It is said that we can go up to three weeks without food, but who would rely on that fact? After missing just a few meals, food begins to consume a person's thoughts. Three weeks is just how long it takes for us to slowly starve to death. We'd be functioning at a reduced rate well before that.

Rest

This priority is left off most lists, but it shouldn't be. Rest is imperative for your health and well-being. Lack of adequate rest results in poor physical performance and mental functioning. From a survival perspective, our immediate priorities are First Aid for Life Threats, Core Temperature Control, Hydration, Calorie Consumption, and Rest. These are the things that we'll need to address if we are to survive, especially in the short-term.

Preventive Needs

In addition to our biological needs, there are what I call **Preventive Needs**. As you might expect, these priorities may prevent a bad situation from happening in the first place, or at the very least may enable you to get out of the situation if it does happen. These priorities are First Aid for Routine (non-life-threatening) Injuries, Navigation, and Signaling.

First Aid for Routine Injuries

In addition to the life threats stated earlier, other, more minor medical concerns may hinder your ability to survive. While you may not die from them immediately, you should take care of them as soon as your immediate needs are met. For example, losing mobility from an injury to a lower extremity like your knees or ankles can force you to stay overnight in conditions you were not prepared for. The resulting exposure to the elements is the real threat to your survival. Being able to "fix" that injury so you can make it out prevents a potentially life-threatening situation from happening.

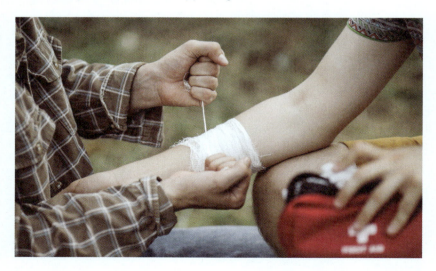

Navigation

Too much reliance on technology over navigational skills is the leading contributor to situations that require Search and Rescue. If your tools require batteries and/or cell or GPS signal, they should be backed up by gear and skills that do not require them. Using a GPS unit or your phone is fine when it works, but when it doesn't, you can no longer help yourself.

Having a solid foundation in basic map reading and land navigation may prevent that "lost hiker" scenario of spending an unplanned night or two exposed to the elements. Solid navigational skills are vitally important to self-rescue rather than sitting and waiting for others to come to your aid. If you don't have good navigational skills, you should sit and wait rather than try to self-rescue. Wandering around the woods aimlessly can make it more difficult for Search and Rescue teams to find you.

Signaling

If you're injured and cannot "fix what's broken" medically to regain your mobility, or cannot navigate to self-rescue, you should stay put and signal for rescue. Making yourself as visible as possible so that Search and Rescue teams can quickly find you decreases the amount of time you must spend exposed to the elements, thus increasing your chances of surviving.

Statistically, most people are found within forty-eight to seventy-two hours of becoming lost (and having someone realize that they're missing). It can take longer, however, so don't allow yourself to be comforted by any statistical scenario that says you only have to make it a certain length of time. You must be able to make it for as long as necessary. Statistics matter very little, and offer little comfort, if you're one of those outliers.

Supplemental Needs

Lastly, there are what I would consider **Supplemental Needs**: Tools, Gear Repair, and Maintenance. These enable you to provide for your other needs.

Tools

For a survival tool kit at the basic level, most tasks (with few exceptions) can be accomplished with a fixed blade belt knife and a good folding saw. One of the most dangerous tools we use in the wilderness is the hatchet or axe. Crosscutting or "bucking"—cutting a piece of wood against the grain—can be more efficiently and safely accomplished with a saw. It's typically not necessary to drop large trees, buck, limb, and split them for firewood, and haul it all back to camp, not to mention the loss of energy that results from doing so. The risks far outweigh the benefits of using a hatchet or axe at the basic level.

A good multi-tool can be an effective backup to your primary tools and puts a few more useful tools at your disposal in a small, lightweight package. It's important that, regardless which tool you choose, it has at minimum a good blade, saw blade, and awl.

Gear Repair

The ability repair gear as needed is also important. Clothing and gear can only perform at their best, and as designed, if they're in good repair. This is often an overlooked need. We focus on making sure we have what we need on hand but often do not use items enough to realize that even the most durable equipment will wear over time, and can sometimes fail. The need for repair in the field can be lessened by care of equipment and inspection prior to going out, but even that is not always enough. Things happen, so be prepared to handle them if needed. Most field-expedient gear repair can be accomplished by adding some duct tape and a large sail needle to your existing kit. Those can be used for patching and mending if the need arises.

Maintenance

This need pertains mostly to the tools that you're using on a daily basis for tasks that must be accomplished. In particular, the sharp edges of knives and axes will dull with use, making them less effective and more dangerous to use. A dull knife is a dangerous knife. It forces you to exert too much pressure to make a cut, and often the cut gives way in an uncontrolled slice and catches you as it does. In addition, steel must be oiled to prevent rusting, wood must be oiled to prevent drying, and leather must be oiled to prevent cracking and breaking.

Survival Kit Planning

I've often heard that all a person needs to do is go out into the wilderness and Mother Nature will teach them everything they need to know. It sounds really easy when you put it that way, but allow me to offer a rebuttal: Mother Nature is neither for you, nor against you. She just is. If you travel out into the wilderness with nothing—no knowledge, skills, or resources—you are completely at her mercy. If you make it out alive, it'll be because conditions were favorable for you to do so. If the conditions are not favorable, you won't make it. Yes, you'll certainly learn some things, but this is a foolish and irresponsible way to go about doing so.

You will, of course, have the instinct to seek shelter, and you may find one in nature or be able to produce one with natural resources. But nature isn't going to teach you how to create fire from the landscape using natural materials. Mother Nature doesn't know how to use a bow drill or a hand drill, and neither do you. She cannot teach you that. There is nothing at all wrong with seeking fellowship with the wilderness, pursuing those primitive skills, and nourishing that connection. But that can all be done in a way that allows you to safely learn those things over time.

Be prepared first, *then* be prepared to find yourself completely unprepared.

When it comes to providing for your needs in a wilderness setting, the need for gear is inversely proportional to your skill level. In the beginning, you are much more gear-reliant because you have not yet learned how to provide for your needs from nature. As skills and experience develop, you can choose what gear you do and don't need, and what you can use from nature to replace what you don't bring. This allows you to shed unnecessary gear and carry something much lighter: knowledge. Gear-reliance is the safety net that is used while learning to become more self-reliant.

When we put together our "survival" kits, we need to think about and understand the needs we're trying to provide for and pack accordingly. Going back to the Survival Priorities, we need to plan and prepare for fire, shelter, water, food, first aid, navigation, signal, and tools. To make things easy, I categorize packing in terms of essential kits, with each kit corresponding to a survival priority. I call my approach "Seven Essential Kits and a Good Knife." This is an easy way for me to remember to pack for my specific needs.

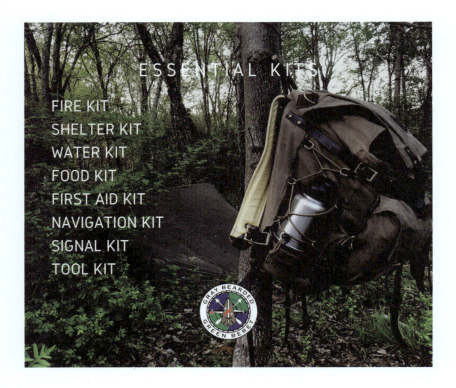

When putting together your survival kit, it's important to take a layered and redundant approach. Don't put all your eggs in one basket. Place some items in your pockets, some on your belt, and some in your pack. For example, I'll usually carry a lighter in my pocket, a ferrocerium rod in my belt pouch, and matches and a magnifying lens in my pack. By doing this, even if for some reason I'm separated from my pack, I still have the means to get a fire going in an emergency.

I call it a "survival kit" because it's catchy and you'd use it for survival. However, it isn't only for "survival" or emergencies—it's just a kit that will provide for your needs in the wilderness. It's not much different than what I pack for activities like hiking, backpacking, and camping.

We will discuss more on each specific kit, and how to use the items within each, in later chapters.

The Psychology of Survival

Is survival more physical or more mental? We often hear that survival is "99 percent mental," and that you must have the "will to live" or the "will to survive" to make it. All these statements are too vague to be useful. They're catchy enough to make a person sound like they gave an answer but offer nothing quantifiable to questioner. These are canned answers with an easy-open lid and an easy-pour spout that spill out effortlessly when the subject of survival psychology comes up.

What do they mean? There are twenty-four hours in a day, so does survival being "99 percent mental" mean that I only need to do physical tasks for 1 percent of the day—less than fifteen minutes—and all should go well? Does "will to live" mean that all I must do is want to stay alive? Got it, I am there. Now what? How can I put that into action to save the lives of my family or myself?

CHAPTER 1: THE BUILDING BLOCKS OF SURVIVAL

Your ability to survive depends on your willingness to adapt to your new environment and provide for your own needs, despite the conditions you face, for as long as necessary.

As a species, we have "progressed" so far that we often don't even think about what our needs are and how they're being provided for daily. Thermoregulation is maintained by a closet full of clothes, a three-bedroom/two-bathroom house, a pile of blankets, and a digital thermostat on the wall. Water comes at the turn of a faucet knob or twisting of a cap. Food is stockpiled in the fridge, cabinets, and freezer, and, when that runs short, the grocery store is never far away—delivery is even an option.

We never really allow ourselves to be even remotely uncomfortable, and many cannot fathom a situation in which they would ever be. Our ability to provide for our needs has adapted to the availability of those modern comforts. Many no longer see the need to know how to start a fire; construct a shelter; procure water off the land and make it safe to drink; or trap, hunt, and fish for food, let alone clean, dress, and prepare it. We've been reduced to the end-user consumer in that process.

So why *wouldn't* we struggle in an emergency? We're taken out of the environment that we've adapted to over a long period of time, and are forced to quickly adapt to a new, often hostile environment, requiring skills we may not have. Thermoregulation is no longer controlled by that thermostat on the wall of your house. There is no tap for water. The grocery store is not around the corner and nobody delivers out in the wilderness. There are no GPS or road signs to lead you back. The emergency room is not right down the road. Your cell phone is either dead or dying, if you even have a signal to begin with. Your needs have not changed, but your circumstances certainly have. Living is going to be a lot harder for you and dying will be a lot easier, so easy that you'll have to dedicate your whole focus to preventing that from happening. It's a race against time, and the clock has already started.

You must *want* to adapt to your new reality. That's what is meant by having the "will to survive." You must maintain that will despite physical, mental, and environmental hardships. "Will" in this context is defined as the "power of choosing one's own actions." It's not enough to just choose to live, however. One must also choose to take the actions necessary to facilitate life. Those actions are physical. The opposite is also true: a person who chooses inaction, who physically lays down and stops providing for their own needs, will succumb if not rescued.

Knowledge of self, knowing what you are made of, is a valuable lesson that can only be truly learned through facing challenges.

When you're cold, wet, tired, hungry, and scared, that's when you meet the real you. So how can we be better prepared? Realistic training and repetition of basic survival skills, under stress and in less-than-ideal conditions beforehand, will lessen the demand on you to adapt in such a condensed period later. You need to fail during training until you get it right so that you don't fail during an actual emergency. This philosophy exists in nearly all aspects of life, with survival being the most important.

A true lesson in survival psychology cannot be taught by a PowerPoint presentation, it can only be learned in the field. It doesn't matter what most people do or how they react under certain circumstances, it matters what *you* do and how *you* react under those circumstances. How do you react to extreme temperatures, dehydration, lack of food, and sleep deprivation? Do you lay down, quit, and stop providing for your needs? Do you get angry and frustrated, clouding your judgment? Or do you dig down deep and do what you must do to stay alive?

If you've never physically been tested in these conditions, then you may be approaching your wilderness encounter with theory rather than experience, and that may very easily get you killed. Seek out training courses that take you out of your comfort zone, so that you can be tested under supervision with a safety net. Find courses that are designed to teach you valuable skills, as well as give you valuable experience. Above all, the unspoken lesson will be knowledge of self. It's one of the most valuable lessons you can possibly learn, and Mother Nature is the best teacher. Find courses that set the conditions for you to meet her and you'll be introduced to the real you in the process.

GRAY BEARDED GREEN BERET'S GUIDE TO SURVIVING THE WILD

Some common reactions to emergencies you should know up front are fear, anxiety, anger, frustration, depression, loneliness, boredom, and often guilt for having ended up in the situation to begin with. You can be better prepared to handle those things if you have that "knowledge of self," anticipate those fears, are realistic, adopt a positive attitude, always remind yourself what is at stake, and train *now* for skills you may need later.

The Triangle of Survival

It's often said that when it comes to survival, knowledge is most important. I must respectfully disagree. There are three things that work together in the **Triangle of Survival**: knowledge, skills, and resources. Without one, the other two do not matter; and without the other two, one alone doesn't help you.

CHAPTER 1: THE BUILDING BLOCKS OF SURVIVAL

"Knowledge" in this context is the theoretical understanding of a given subject. It is more academic. "Skills" are physical applications of that knowledge. They are more practical. "Resources" are materials onto which knowledge and skills are applied to make something happen. These are limited to what you have in your pack or what you can find in nature.

Let's look at fire-making as an example of using the Triangle of Survival. Perhaps I know the theory and practical steps to lighting a fire. But am I skilled at using a spark-producing tool like a ferrocerium rod (ferro rod for short)? And do I have the resources to build a proper tinder bundle to accept the heat from one, get a fire going, and keep it going for my needs?

My goal with this book is to give you the academic knowledge you may need in a backcountry emergency. You must still take this knowledge and go out and physically develop the skills through practical application. Take the time to learn the natural resources in your area so that you can supplement or replace some of the gear you pack, and build confidence in your ability to handle what comes.

If you're out there in the wilderness right now and simply have this book tucked away in your pack, assuming that you can just pick it up and learn the skills necessary to survive without any preparation or practice, then you've already failed. Knowledge, skills, and resources are all extremely important, and you cannot rely on one without the others.

So You're Lost or Injured—Now What?

Every plan works until it doesn't. You're lost, hurt, it's getting dark, a storm is rolling in, you name it—when things don't go as planned, what should you do? Murphy's Law states that anything that can go wrong, will go wrong. We can only control what we can control. For everything else, we can only control how we react. When should you stay put and wait for rescue, and when should you tighten up your boot laces and get moving?

CHAPTER 1: THE BUILDING BLOCKS OF SURVIVAL

You should stay put and signal if...	You should self-rescue if...
You are injured and cannot administer aid	You are injured and can administer aid
You cannot navigate	You can navigate confidently
You informed others of your plans/location prior to setting out, or SAR teams are on their way	No one is looking for you, nor did you tell anyone your plans

CHAPTER 2

TOOL SELECTION, SAFETY, AND USE

Tool Kit

Tools are to be used in conjunction with other resources from your gear or from nature to facilitate your survival priorities. They help you process resources for your fire, build your shelter, process food, and make tasks easier in general.

At a minimum, I recommend a fixed blade belt knife. This is the latter part of my motto "Seven Essential Kits and a Good Knife." However, you are by no means limited to just taking a knife. I would also recommend that a good folding saw be added to your bare minimum essential tool list. There are a number of things you can do with your belt knife, some better than others. Crosscutting wood into smaller, more manageable sizes for your fire and taking down saplings for shelter-building material are not really on that list. A simple folding saw is extremely useful for those tasks. Lastly, having a good multi-tool is a great idea. In addition to having an extra knife blade and saw, it should have an awl, which is useful for crafting and sewing.

Recommended Tool Kit

- Belt Knife
- Multi-Tool
- Folding Saw
- Duct Tape
- Leather Needle
- Leather Paddle Strop
- Honing Compound
- Protective Oil or Wax

Now that you know what tools you should bring, let's discuss why you should bring them. Before you purchase these tools, it's important to understand what they could be used for. As you might expect, I like to organize things within the survival priority framework. If you remember, we defined tools as supplemental needs because they're meant to facilitate the accomplishment of the other priorities.

I should also address some things that we do not need tools for. The market seems to be saturated with what I would consider "sharpened crowbar" knives that are extremely heavy duty, for a market that thinks heavy duty is somehow necessary in the field. A good knife should stand up to normal use in the field with no issues. It's when folks misuse it or have unrealistic expectations for what it should be able to do that they have problems. Rather than accept that they are the reason a perfectly good knife has failed, they demand a heavier duty knife in the name of "reliability."

I suppose suppliers must produce what the market thinks it needs. Well, you don't need a knife to open a steel drum. I have never found one sealed in the forest, and if I did, I'd have no reason to open it. I don't need it to support my bodyweight. In all my years in the forest, using a knife to help me climb a tree has never come up. You don't need the tip to pry anything away except soft pine sap or even softer punk wood to get at grubs. You don't need to be able to pry open a door with it or use it as a screwdriver.

I don't believe there's a difference between a "bushcraft" or a "survival" knife. I don't subscribe to the belief that a "survival" knife needs to be larger or thicker material. A knife is a sharp edge with a handle, and it either does what you need or it doesn't, regardless of the situation. If I'm in the woods for camping, hiking, backpacking, or bushcraft, the materials available and the needs I'm trying to provide for during my time in the woods are no different than in a dire survival situation in that same patch of woods.

You're also not necessarily looking for a "one tool option" or expecting one tool to provide for all of your possible needs in the wilderness. There are many tools that could be considered multi-functional and at least adequate (but not necessarily the best) for the majority of tasks you need it to do, but why would you purposely limit yourself to one tool when you don't have to? For the personal challenge to do more with less? Possibly.

You can use a belt knife for almost everything you need to accomplish, but it's less efficient than another tool that's made specifically for that function. None of this is to say that a single tool cannot be used for everything, for someone that has gained experience with using that single tool. Bottom line: choose your tools based on what they'll do for you realistically, and carry as many or as little as you want, so long as they facilitate your needs.

CHAPTER 2: TOOL SELECTION, SAFETY, AND USE

Knowing what you need tools to actually accomplish will help you choose which tools you'll want to carry to meet those needs.

Tool Selection

With that in mind, let's take a closer look at what you should consider when choosing these basic tools:

1. Belt Knife

I use a belt knife primarily for cutting, slicing, scraping, carving, and shaping material. In some cases, I may also use it to cut down small saplings and process fuel resources like tinder and kindling (softer woods), or to create a friction fire set (also softer woods). Here are the things I look for when selecting a good belt knife:

High Carbon Steel

I personally like a high carbon steel knife. This is a bit of a misnomer, as many stainless steels also have an exceedingly high carbon content. I think a better term for my preference may be a "naked" high carbon steel—I don't want any sort of coating, painting, or additive that prevents or inhibits oxidation (corrosion). The act of "throwing a spark" off the back of the knife with natural stone is a rapid oxidation reaction, and corrosion resistance prevents or inhibits that reaction. Admittedly, the need for this may be a very deep contingency, but I still prefer to have more options when it comes to fire. Nobody's life was ever saved by having to do less maintenance in the field, but being able to start a fire with nothing but a knife and a found stone just might do it.

One exception to this "coating" rule is the black coating used on Morakniv blades like the Bushcraft Black and the Carbon Garberg. This is a DLC (Diamond-Like Carbon) coating that inhibits corrosion well but doesn't hinder the ability of the knife to create sparks with natural stone.

CHAPTER 2: TOOL SELECTION, SAFETY, AND USE

"Naked" high carbon steel is also much easier to maintain the edge in the field in my experience. There are several choices for steel types, but I've found the simple 1095 steel to be more than adequate. "Super steels" are more expensive and while they often retain the edge longer, it is more difficult to sharpen that edge once it's lost, especially in the field. I've found this to be true with stainless steels as well.

Should you use stainless steel if you live on the coast? In my opinion, it isn't necessary unless you plan on either maintaining your knife or storing it for long periods of time without using it. I lived on the coast for several years and teach classes there, and have never found it to be necessary, but I also use and maintain my knives daily. If you do choose to carry stainless steel, I recommend adding a ferro rod to the sheath to make up for its inability to spark with natural stone.

I often see people confused over which steel type can be used with ferrocerium rods. The answer is either one. The only requirement for the "striker," or in this case "scraper" material, is that it needs be harder than the ferro rod. The striker removes pyrophoric material from the rod, so the type of steel is irrelevant. Where it does matter is with percussion ignition (traditional flint and steel). The harder rock removes pyrophoric material from the spine of the knife, and a stainless steel is going to prevent or reduce that ability, as are many coated or painted blades.

Blade Length

For my primary belt knife, I like a blade that's somewhere between four and five inches. I've found this to be the most useful length for most tasks that I need a knife to do. Any larger than that, and you start to lose some of the agility and dexterity for the finer carving tasks. All you really gain is the ability to split larger-diameter woods. I've found a 4-inch diameter to be more than adequate for fire and shelter purposes, so it isn't worth the trade-off for me.

You can only expect a knife to split a diameter that is one inch smaller than the length of the knife itself, so a 5-inch blade will easily split 4-inch diameter material, and a 4-inch blade will easily split up to 3-inch diameter material. For splitting wood that's a larger diameter than the blade length, you can simply split a quick wedge off the side of the piece and drive the wedge through with a billet (baton). If you expect to be processing larger material, you may want to consider carrying a "chopper" that'll be more efficient for the task.

Blade Thickness

I've also found that the thicker the blade, the less agile and dexterous it is. The closer you get to that "sharpened crowbar," the less useful you'll find your blade for the finer (and much more commonly used) tasks. I like knives that are ⅛-inch thick or less.

Tang

The tang is the rear portion of the blade that either protrudes from the handle or becomes part of the handle. There are several different types, including full, partial, and rat tail. When using a correctly made knife under normal circumstances for tasks it was designed to do, almost any tang style can be adequate. Of course, there will be some exceptions with material, production, and quality control from the manufacturer, as well as poor skill level and abuse from some end users. However, a good knife from a reputable brand that's used properly will rarely, if ever, break on you, regardless of the tang.

Some people do like the added (or at a minimum, perceived) additional strength provided by a full tang blade. I cannot disagree that a full tang might be stronger than other styles. It's a single piece of steel for the entire blade and handle. With that said, one tang design being stronger than another doesn't mean that the other is not also strong enough. Which one you choose for your primary belt knife is up to you in the end. Most often, I personally choose full tang with a protruding tang. I don't feel the full tang is needed, but I do think the protruding tang that I gain from it on some knife designs is extremely useful.

Sharpened 90-Degree Spine

This is essential for using your knife as an effective striker for a ferro rod. This also opens a variety of techniques for processing tinder resources, as well as shaving and shaping wood, while saving your edge for actual cutting and slicing tasks. This will reduce the amount of times you have to maintain the edge of the knife in the field.

Grind

The grind is the reduction of material that makes it thin enough to be sharp. There are a few different grinds that are used for the knife edge. Some of the most common and most popular within the outdoor community are convex, Scandinavian, saber, and flat.

Flat grinds are tapered to the full height of the blade. The thinnest portion is, of course, the edge, and it maintains a specific angle all the way to the spine, resulting in a flat surface on each side. This grind is extremely sharp and relatively easy to sharpen in the field.

A **Scandinavian**, or Scandi grind, is a single angle on each side that begins at the edge. That taper does not extend up the full height of the blade. This creates a "single bevel" that's extremely sharp and quite easy to maintain. The bevel is the surface (or surfaces) of the blade that has been removed to form the angles that come together on the edge and make it sharp.

Think of a **saber** grind as a Scandi grind with a secondary bevel. It's also known as a "compound grind" because there are two grinds creating the edge. The secondary bevel offers more strength to the edge as compared to a Scandi. The trade-off is that it's not as easy to maintain due to the angle difference.

The **convex** grind is extraordinarily strong, if not the strongest. However, convex grinds are not as straightforward as other flatter grinds that can be indexed against a strop or stone. Both sides are rounded as they come toward a single edge. They require a little more skill to be maintained effectively. This is another example of something being stronger not necessarily meaning that the others are not also strong enough.

Grind choice is another personal preference. I personally choose a Scandi grind because it is extremely sharp and extremely easy to maintain in the field.

2. Multi-Tool

I typically carry a multi-tool so that I have an additional knife blade and a few more options for different needs that may arise. I personally like the Swiss Army Knife (SAK) style over the style that has pliers. I've found that outside of trapping when I need to cut snare wire or the like, or fishing when removing a deep hook, the pliers are of little use in the field. The SAK is more comfortable for use on more common tasks.

Regardless of what you choose to carry, the three most important tools on it are the blade, the awl, and the saw. These are typically smaller but do provide some redundancy on those three categories of tools.

It should be noted that a true "backup knife" should be capable of accomplishing the same tasks for which you are carrying the belt knife. If it doesn't, it's not an adequate backup that could replace it; it's simply a secondary or supplemental knife.

3. Saw

Primarily, I use a saw to cut down saplings and trees, and to cut material to length. Depending on the size of the material and the amount I expect to process given the conditions, I have several different sizes of folding saws. I also have both dry and green wood bucksaw blades that I can make a frame for in the field, and a collapsible bucksaw that packs well and goes together easier.

My favorite folding saws are Silky brand saws. I have several models but have found the GomBoy 210 to be the most useful size in the most environments. There are different blades for these, and they change out very quickly and easily in the field. The large teeth are more aggressive and great for taking down or breaking down wood. The fine teeth are much less aggressive and useful for finer tasks and working with smaller material. Silky saws are pull saws, meaning they only cut on the pull portion of the stroke. Take care to let up on the downward pressure as you push forward, or you could bend or break the blade. Some people have managed to break them, but from what I've seen it's always been user error and not the saw itself.

Silky saws also have a nice, sharp 90-degree spine that works as well as a knife for scraping tinder, shaving or shaping wood, and striking a ferro rod. In addition, they are a martensitic stainless steel, so they have the anti-corrosion properties of a stainless steel, but act like a high carbon steel that will throw a great spark with natural stone.

The Bahco Folding Saw is a good saw that cuts on the forward and back stroke, but its finer teeth are less aggressive, so it cuts noticeably slower and less efficiently than the Silky. Having said that, it's still an adequate saw that many choose to carry.

When choosing a folding saw, it's important to estimate the diameter of the material you expect to be cutting. For ease of use and efficiency, you want your saw blade to be double the size of the material you're cutting. If your saw blade length is the same as the diameter of the wood you want to cut, there's no room to use it in a sawing motion across the material. However, if you have 4-inch material and an 8-inch saw blade, you have plenty to work with to get through the cut efficiently. The Silky GomBoy 210 that I choose most often has a blade length of 210mm (8.268 inches), which is plenty of saw for the 4-inch or less material that I plan to use.

Knife Safety

Anytime you use a knife—or anything with a sharp edge, for that matter—there is a risk of cutting yourself or another person. It is extremely important to practice good knife safety to prevent injury. There are a few main concepts that you should understand and observe.

First and foremost, always leave your knife (or other sharp tool) in its sheath until you're ready to use it, and always place it back in its sheath when you're finished. Don't get in the habit of placing it down on a table or on the ground with the sharp edge still exposed, or continuing to hold it in your hand while you've moved on (and also shifted your focus) to other tasks that it isn't needed for.

Pay attention to your "**blood circle**" and ensure that nobody is within it. Your blood circle extends to the tip of a knife held at arm's length. Think of this circle as the area in which your knife, while unsheathed and in your hand, could potentially cause an injury to anyone within reach. Take care as the user of the knife to ensure that nobody is within this circle, and continue to watch so that nobody comes into your circle while you're using it. It is also especially important that you not walk into another person's circle while they're focused on using the knife for tasks since they may not see you right away.

CHAPTER 2: TOOL SELECTION, SAFETY, AND USE

The **"Triangle of Death"** is another name for your groin and the inside of your thighs. Imagine a triangle being formed with the apex being your groin, the inside of your thighs being legs of the triangle, and an imaginary line from one knee to the other being the triangle's base. It's important that you never carve or use your knife (or another sharp tool) within that triangle. There is an extremely high risk of cutting major arteries and causing a life-threatening bleed should you have an accident within this triangle. Always carve forward from your knees or off to the side of your thighs.

Understand what a **backstop** is and make sure that backstop is not you or another person. This ties in with the blood circle but expands on it a bit. When you are using a knife, understand in which direction you are cutting and look at where the knife stroke will end once it's through the cut. The backstop is where that cut will end. For the most part, you want this to end on an anvil, a stop cut, or in the air within an empty blood circle, away from you and everyone else. As a general rule, you should never carve toward yourself, always away from yourself.

There are some very safe intermediate and advanced techniques that carve in a controlled manner toward oneself, but those are not recommended for beginners and beyond the scope of this book. A common mistake I see is a person holding the material in their hand or placing it on top of their thigh to carve or shape. Always ask yourself where the cut will end once it's through the material, and where it will stop if you slip when making that cut. If the answer is in your hand or in your thigh (or in those of another person), you need to adjust yourself.

If you must hand your knife to someone else, your best bet is to hand it to them sheathed (or closed) when possible. This is not always practical if you're handing it to them for just a quick cut and your sheath is attached to your belt. For those instances when you do pass an exposed knife to a person, always orient the knife handle toward them, not the blade. Once they physically have control of the knife, they should verbally say "I have it" or "thank you." This verbal acceptance of responsibility for that knife lets you know it's safe to let go of the knife yourself. If you don't take the time to ensure that the other person has taken control and responsibility for the knife, you risk it dropping to the ground, which could damage the knife or cause injury to yourself or them.

Lastly, I want to reiterate something from earlier: a dull knife is a dangerous knife. Seems counterintuitive, I know. It does not mean that a sharp knife is less able to cut you—not at all. A sharp knife is just easier to control and requires less application pressure to make a smooth cut. A dull knife is still capable of cutting you, but because it's not sharp, it will force you to apply more pressure than needed to make a cut, and the tendency to slip and blow through material in an uncontrolled manner increases.

Knife Grips

I should start by stating that there are knife grips, and there are knife techniques. A knife "grip" is a particular way of holding the knife, while a knife "technique" is a method of using the knife in a particular grip. Many techniques use the same grip. To prevent the confusion that can come from mixing the name of a grip with a technique that uses that grip, I prefer to keep them separate.

Having complete control of the knife and safely orienting the sharp edge in a way that is useful for cutting and carving is an essential skill that is sometimes overlooked, resulting in poor knife habits and inefficient use of the tool. Let's establish a baseline for safe and effective knife handling skills so that we can build good habits from the start.

The **forehand grip** could also be referred to as the "hammer grip." The handle of the knife is securely in your closed hand, much like if you were holding the handle of a hammer. For this grip, the sharp edge of the blade is forward (away from your wrist).

The **backhand grip** is like the forehand grip, except that the sharp edge of the blade is facing backward (toward you). This technique is not often used, but more likely than not you have used it in the past to cut a bight of cordage.

With the **side grip**, the knife is more on its side, with your thumb placed on the face of the blade for guidance and control. The sharp edge of the blade is facing forward (away from you).

Knife Techniques

Slicing and Shaping

Now that we understand a few different grips, we need to look at how they're used. Knives are made for slicing. This slicing motion removes material. They are not meant for pushing through material, a common mistake I often see. The highest "point of leverage" on the blade edge will be closest to the handle, and leverage decreases the farther you go out toward the tip. With this in mind, your slicing motion should begin close to the handle, and end closer to the tip as the cut is completed. Therefore, I prefer the **puukko design**. Its straight spine is great for leverage, and the continuous curve of the blade edge matches this slicing action extremely well.

Long story short, if the edge's geometry does not somewhat match your anatomy during this slicing motion, the edge will not maintain contact with the material and the cut will be short and inefficient. This is the main reason I dislike multiple angles and cutting surfaces on the same tool. They're not necessary, cause inefficiency, and are more difficult to sharpen with all the different angles.

If your "cut" starts and ends at the same part of the edge of your knife, you are trying to push the blade through the material rather than cut it with a slicing motion. This does not take advantage of the full cutting surface, nor does it create the slicing effect for which the knife is most efficient.

There are a few basic techniques that you should know when using your knife. The first technique is what I call the "**forward slice**." This is a simple slicing motion used with a forehand grip. The material is held stationary and the knife is sliced through the cut.

The second basic technique I call the "**pull slice**." It is also used with the forehand grip and while holding the knife stationary, but the material is pulled against the edge to create the same slicing motion. Note that the word "pull" in this context refers to pulling the material, not pulling the knife.

A "**combination slice**," as you may have guessed, uses a combination of those two techniques. The knife is sliced forward as the material is pulled back. This can also be referred to as a "**power slice**" because it is particularly good at removing larger amounts of material.

CHAPTER 2: TOOL SELECTION, SAFETY, AND USE

There are a couple more techniques that offer a lot of power when removing material. These are called the "knee lever," "thigh lever," and the "chest lever."

The **knee lever** and the **thigh lever** share similarities with the pull slice: in both techniques, the forehand grip is used, the knife is held stationary, and the material is pulled against the edge of the knife for removal. With the knee lever, the knife hand is braced against the knee. With the thigh lever, it's braced against the outside of the thigh. Both techniques are strong and great for removing large amounts of material. They are also both extremely safe because the knife is stationary and braced forward of the knee or outside the thigh.

The **chest lever** uses the side grip, which is why the names are often used synonymously. It's useful for removing large amounts of material with a shorter slice. With the chest lever, the knife is braced against the chest in one hand, and the material is braced against the chest with the other. The cut is made by combining a slight slicing motion of the knife and a slight pull of the material (a small scale combination slice). Power is given to the cut by expanding the chest cavity while inhaling a deep breath. The knife and the material remain braced against the chest, so it is a noticeably short stroke, but the leverage gained from this coupled with the expanded chest can generate an immensely powerful stroke.

Lastly, there are a couple of reinforced grips and techniques that I recommend you learn to use for finer carving tasks. Both are very controlled, but care must be taken to determine the follow-through of the cut and ensure the backstop is not your fingers or thumb.

The first reinforced grip I call the **"finger-assisted**." It's similar to the side grip, but the fingers of the opposite hand are placed on the spine of the knife to assist in making and controlling the cut. The thumb of the hand gripping the knife can be placed on the end of the material to offer more strength and control to the cut with a slight pulling motion.

The second is the "**thumb-assisted**." This is a reinforced modification of the forehand grip. Rather than having the entire hand gripping the handle of the knife, the thumb of the hand gripping the knife is extended onto the spine. The opposite hand is gripping the material, and the thumb of that hand is placed on the spine of the knife closer to the tip. This offers more strength and control to the cut. The hand holding the material can also pull the material slightly to give the cut more strength.

Splitting

There is much debate on the use of a knife with a billet or baton. I will say this on the subject: there are absolutely times when it is completely appropriate (and just as safe, maybe even safer) to use an axe or hatchet for the same purpose. Again, choppers are some of the most dangerous tools we can use in the field—a heavy sharp edge with momentum. Placing a knife directly on relatively soft material and billeting it through with a baton is more controlled. If the strength of your knife is a matter of concern, I'd encourage you to get a knife you can trust for such a task. You're simply using it as a sharp wedge to split or score softer wood. To explain what I mean, here is some info on the two valuable techniques of splitting and truncating.

When using a billet with your knife, it's important to understand its limitations. First off, your knife is not meant to handle the burden of putting away a face cord of firewood for the night, so don't expect to use it for that. It's not meant to take down large trees. It should not be used to split hardwoods. However, splitting kindling, making friction fire sets, and taking down small saplings are absolutely reasonable expectations for a field knife.

Kindling and friction fire sets should be softer wood because they catch fire more quickly than dense hardwood. You should not be

CHAPTER 2: TOOL SELECTION, SAFETY, AND USE

choosing hardwood for kindling or friction fire sets, so there should be no reason to baton your knife through a dense hardwood. In short, if someone is worried about splitting wood with a knife, I am worried about what type of wood they are selecting and for what purpose. I've had no issue splitting wood with knives that are not full tang, like the Mora Companion and Mora Classic, so I have to wonder why someone else is either breaking a knife or worried about breaking a knife by doing this. Any good fixed blade should be capable of splitting a softer wood. However, a folding knife is one that I would never use with a billet. There is a good chance of breaking one of those at the pivot point.

When **splitting** wood with your knife, ensure first that it's a reasonably softer wood that is appropriate for what you need (typically kindling or a friction fire set). The diameter of the wood you intend to split should also be at least one inch smaller than the length of your blade. This will ensure that you're not billeting too close to the tip of the knife and will reduce the chance that it'll get stuck in the wood with nothing exposed to finish the split. Next, look for any natural cracks in the wood that you can use to your advantage. If you have a good split started, place the knife along that split. If not, start the split in the center of the wood.

It's important to start in the center. If you start to one side or the other, the knife tends to run off to the side and you'll often knock off a small wedge instead of splitting the wood in half. If you do knock off a wedge, you may choose to use that wedge to split the wood instead of your knife. At times when the diameter of the wood is larger than what I expect my knife will be able to split, I will purposely start off-center and split a wedge or two off the piece to use for splitting.

Place the wood to be split on an anvil. You don't want the knife to go all the way through and into the ground where the edge can be damaged. Place the knife directly in contact with the wood where you intend to split it. Keep a firm grip on the knife and control it by keeping it level. Use a billet to hit the spine of the knife toward the front. Use the grip hand to continue to try and keep the blade level. Continue this process until it splits.

If the blade gets stuck and you cannot continue through the split, stop what you're doing and make a wedge. Drive the wedge in to split the wood far apart enough to recover your knife. They can easily get stuck in locations that have knots, so be mindful of that and avoid knots when you can.

Crosscutting/Truncating

Whereas splitting follows the natural grain of the wood, truncating cuts against the grain. Truncating means to make shorter by cutting, so in this context we're cutting to length (shortening) by cutting across the grain. This technique is valuable for notching, producing stop cuts, and even bringing down small saplings.

Place the knife directly against the material you wish to cut at the angle you wish to cut it. It's important to note that cutting across the grain at a slight angle will be much easier than cutting directly perpendicular to the grain. Cutting at an angle tends to follow the grain a bit more while still cutting it, rather than going directly against it. Hit the spine of the knife with a billet and drive it through the material.

The Try Stick

I first learned about the **"try stick"** from an article written by the late Mors Kochanski. The beauty of the try stick is that it can be used to teach basic knife skills, and anyone can use it to practice anytime, anywhere. Every notch and technique on a try stick directly applies to an actual technique that would be used in the field for bushcraft and/or survival. All you need is your knife and a suitable stick to carve on. Even if you cannot get to the woods, you can still practice your knife skills.

I recommend you start with a stick that's reasonably easy to carve. For many of the tasks that this is meant to replicate, softer woods are most appropriate anyway, so don't make it harder on yourself than it needs to be. Some great choices are willow, cottonwood, aspen, and tulip poplar.

Start with a 3.5-foot section of material to work with that's roughly as thick as your thumb. It's important that the stick be at least 6 inches longer than you want the finished product to be. A 3.5-foot section will finish at around 3 feet. It can be green, or it can be dead and dry. You should practice with both, but it matters very little in the beginning. What's important now is producing the various notches and techniques. My version of the try stick may not exactly match the original, but it works as a baseline teaching tool for the techniques that I use most often in the field at the basic level.

Square Reduction

Place one end of the stick on your chest or abdomen to brace the upper end. The lower end should be placed against an anvil on the ground. Choose a 6- to 8-inch section of the lower half of the stick to do a **square reduction**. A reduction is just as it sounds: you're reducing the amount of material in a given area, shaping it in a way to make it more useful. The square reduction reduces the diameter of a section and leaves it with 90-degree edges on all four sides (which will be square in a cross section).

Using a forehand grip, index (lay) the cutting bevel of your knife flat against the surface of the stick and increase the angle slightly so that the edge "bites" into the material.

Use a controlled slicing motion, starting at the highest point of leverage (toward the handle) and ending at the tip, and keep it all within the desired section of the reduction. For best results, keep your arm fully extended and your wrist locked, and use your body weight leaning forward to complete the slice. At the end of each slice, return to the top of the section and continue cutting along that same plane. Rotate the material and repeat the process on the second, third, and fourth planes, paying close attention to the end shape that you're trying to accomplish.

Round Reduction

A **round reduction** is similar to the square reduction, but the end result we're looking for this time is a reduction of material that's round instead of square.

Flip the stick over end-to-end so that you can work on another section of the try stick. Focus on a noticeably light touch with a shallow angle that barely bites into the material. Repeat this process until the section is reduced and you're left with a round area.

Pot Hanger Notch

Start the **pot hanger notch** approximately 8 inches down from what will be the top of your try stick. Place the stick securely on an anvil. Using a billet, score an "X" shape into the try stick. This technique is similar to truncating, but here you're only scoring the material, not actually going all the way through. Essentially, you're making an X-shaped stop cut. You should be going no more than one-third to one-half of the way through. I recommend erring toward the side of more shallow. It's easy to remove more material if needed but impossible to add it back.

Orient the top of the try stick away from you. Starting at the bottom of the "X," begin carving in toward the middle of the "X." It's important not to go past the center on this. Once you get to the center of the "X," use that as a pivot point and carve the sides out toward the top of the "X." With the center of your blade at the center of the "X," turn and carve toward one side of the top of the "X" with one side of your knife, and then pivot and carve toward the other side. Trim those off as necessary to maintain the desired shape.

Continue carving in this manner until you can see the center pith (smallest concentric circle in the center) of your try stick, indicating that you're halfway through. Once you can see the center pith, do not go any deeper. Instead, undercut behind the center of the "X" to form a curved lip that the bail of a bush pot will sit in without coming off. The thumb-assisted technique works well for this step.

You may have noticed, but this is one of the reasons we chose a stick that was 6 inches longer than needed, and we started this notch at least 6-8 inches down. Since we're carving multiple angles with this notch, we need that handle so that we never have to carve toward ourselves. We'll trim that off later.

The true test of this notch is to place a bail on it from a bush pot and give it a little twist back and forth. If properly carved, the bail will not fall off. If it does fall off, you still have some work to do. You'll get better at this notch over time. This is probably the most difficult skill on the entire try stick.

GRAY BEARDED GREEN BERET'S GUIDE TO SURVIVING THE WILD

Square Notch

Before carving the **square notch**, you want to rotate the stick 180 degrees and move farther down, at least the width of your knife. This reduces the chances of breaking it. Each notch will be away from and on the opposite side of the previous notch.

Once you've found your placement, I recommend scoring two lines that will mark the top and bottom of the notch. The notch width should be at least as wide as the knife blade so that you can maneuver it inside the notch while carving it, but not so wide that you're taking up all the real estate you need for the other notches.

Create stop cuts at the scored lines. You can do this with the knife, but it will be much easier to use the truncating technique with a billet (or even a saw) to produce the stop cuts. Either way, remember not to go any farther than halfway.

To remove the material out of the center, you can simply place your knife inside the stop cut at the point of leverage and give it a little twist toward the other stop cut. This will pop the material out right along the grain and leave you with very little to clean up by carving. Clean up the notch and ensure that it's square.

Saddle Notch

Rotate the stick 180 degrees and start at least a blade's width away from the previous notch. For the **saddle notch**, I like to use the thumb-assisted grip and technique. Mark the width that you want the notch to be. From one mark, carve in a curving motion toward the center of the notch. After a couple of curved slices, turn the stick around and carve from the other mark toward the center, meeting the other curves in the middle. This will trim them off as well. Continue "scooping" that out until you just see the center pith and your saddle notch is complete.

V-Notch

The **V-notch** is another simple notch that is extremely useful. To make it, simply mark the width of the notch (top and bottom). Then, create a stop cut in the middle of those marks no more than halfway through the material. Starting at one mark, carve at an angle toward the center stop cut. Flip the stick around and carve from the other mark toward the center stop cut. Continue this until both angles meet in the middle of the stop cut in the shape of a "V."

Stake Notch

To make a **stake notch**, simply make a stop cut at the top and carve at an angle up to that stop cut. The stake notch is sometimes referred to as a "#7 notch" because the end result looks a bit like the number seven.

Latch Notch

The **latch notch** is a modification of the stake notch. It is sometimes referred to as a 90-degree latch notch. To make it, simply make a stop cut at the top again, and rather than carving an angle directly to the stop cut, you want to carve down to the center pith. From there, create a flat plane that leads up the stop cut and forms a 90-degree angle at that point. Think of this notch as an elongated stake notch or a combination of the stake and square notches.

Hole-Through

The next skill to learn is the **hole-through**, which teaches you to use the tip of your knife in an appropriate way. This creates a hole through the material that you're working with. This skill has actual field applications, unlike the ridiculous torture "tip tests" on the internet. You want to reduce the amount of material you have to get through to achieve this hole through the material, so I like to apply this technique to the square reduction I have already done on the try stick.

Place the try stick on an anvil. Find the center of your square reduction. Push the tip of your knife into the material slightly left of center as you are looking at it. If you're using a knife without a finger guard, be careful to place your palm or the heel of your hand on the butt of the knife to prevent slipping forward onto the cutting edge. This is one of few techniques that you will be pushing forward instead of pulling in a slicing motion. The indentation that you've made will be wider at the top where the spine of the knife was and more narrow at the bottom where the edge of the knife went in.

Rotate the stick 180 degrees. Now push the tip of the knife in again. You'll notice that the wide portions of the cut are now opposing, as well as the narrow. Rotate the stick 90 degrees and push the tip of the knife through again. You want the wide portions of the cut to connect with the narrow portions of the cut. Repeat this until you have a rectangular shape started.

Using the edge of your knife, score around the square reduction to transfer the mark for the top and bottom of the hole through from the other side. Repeat the same process on this side, attempting to connect the rectangular shape all the way through the material. You may have to trim bits and pieces out of it from both sides to achieve a nice square hole through. To finish it off, I like to place a sliver of wood through the hole to show that it is a complete and functional hole.

Pointed End

The simplest "notch" is probably the **pointed end**. With this, we are simply removing material as we rotate the stick around and forming a point at the end. The goal is to remove the material uniformly, so that the point remains centered on the try stick and not off to one side or the other.

Rose Cut/Beaver Chew

Now let's remove that extra handle material on the other end and practice a couple of other skills while doing so. For the **rose cut**, simply use your knife to cut in at an angle toward the tip of the stick. Rotate the stick and continue these angled cuts all the way around. For larger-diameter material, you may need to go around a second or third time, cutting in deeper each time. Once you're nearly all the way through, it's quite easy to break the end off and clean it up. If you look at the end of the piece you cut off, it looks a bit like a rose, and that is where this cut gets its name.

CHAPTER 2: TOOL SELECTION, SAFETY, AND USE

The **beaver chew** is similar to the rose cut. Rather than cutting at the same angle all the way around until you are through, you cut all the way around at that angle, then flip the stick and cut at an angle back toward those cuts, similar to how you made the V-notch.

Pommel End (Crown)

With the newly trimmed end, you want to practice what is called a **pommel end** or **crown**. Essentially, you're cleaning up and rounding off the tip of the stick. This is another technique where I find the thumb-assisted grip and technique to be most useful. Use your knife to shape the end of the wood into a rounded crown, or "pommel."

Continue to practice these skills on a try stick, or practically apply them in the field. As a gauge to see how well you're progressing, a good goal is for each skill/notch to take you one minute or less. In the beginning, don't try to race to meet that goal. It matters little in practical application, and there's no reason to progress quicker than you're ready to do so safely. The important thing is to give yourself a tool to develop safe knife handling skills and practical uses that are directly applicable to the field.

Knife Maintenance

Your knife should come very sharp when you first get it. With use, it will of course begin to dull. Knowing how to maintain your knife is an important skill that I've noticed is often lacking. Let's look at some definitions as I understand them so that we're on the same page.

- **Sharpening** is the process of resetting or changing the angle by removing material, typically with a low grit stone.
- **Honing** is the process of straightening the edge while removing little to no material, and is typically done with an exceedingly high grit stone, ceramic rod, or steel.
- **Stropping** is the process of straightening and polishing the edge while removing no material. It's typically done with leather or wood, with or without polishing compound.

Personally, I rarely (if ever) "sharpen" or "hone" my knives. So long as they were sharp from the start, after normal use with no damage, a simple leather strop will return them back to working order. Sharpening removes material, which over time can really start to add up. The only time I use stones is if my knife was dull to begin with, or if the edge somehow gets damaged and I need to remove material to fix it. After the abrasiveness of that sharpening process, I will hone and strop the edge to finish it, and will maintain that by stropping often to keep my edge in working order.

I use and recommend a paddle strop with a leather covering. I also use a polishing compound on the strop. Since I use Scandinavian grinds almost exclusively, they're quite easy to strop as they have a single bevel on each side. I simply index that bevel flat on the strop and use a pulling motion from the rear of the blade to the tip, being careful to keep the bevel flat on the strop as the blade curves. Typically, I perform ten strokes on one side, then flip it over and do the other side. When it comes to maintaining a symmetrical and sharp edge, remember that whatever you do to one side you must also do to the other.

For the next round I do nine strokes per side, then eight, then seven, and so on until I get down to one. I usually finish the series off by alternating one stroke per side for 10–20 total strokes. This takes less than five minutes and is usually plenty to keep my blade as good as new and ready for use the next time I need it.

Carbon steel blades, as well as leather sheaths and wood handles as applicable, should be oiled to prevent corrosion, cracking, and drying.

Saw Safety

The same rules that apply to knife safety also apply to saw safety:

- Keep your folding saw closed unless you're using it.
- Make sure your blood circle is clear.
- Do not cut inside the Triangle of Death.
- Do not use any part of your body as a backstop.

In addition, saws can deliver a nasty, jagged cut if you're not careful. One of the most dangerous times is when you're first starting a cut. If your opposite hand is in the wrong place and the blade jumps out of the kerf (the groove cut by the blade), an injury can occur.

The Plumber's Vice

The safest and quickest way to use a saw is called the **plumber's vice**. My guess is that it got its name from plumbers cutting pipes on the job. I will warn you, electricians may take offense to you calling it the plumber's vice, since they apparently use it, too. Maybe we should rename it the bushcrafter's vice?

CHAPTER 2: TOOL SELECTION, SAFETY, AND USE

With the side of the log or pole that you want to cut toward your dominant side, step over the material with your dominant leg and place it on the back of that knee. Pull the other side of the material up and onto the thigh of your non-dominant leg and squat down. This creates a vice that secures the material and allows you to make the cut on the outside of your dominant thigh. To make multiple cuts, simply loosen the "vice" and slide more material out to the side to be cut off.

The plumber's vice is great for crosscutting smaller-diameter material. You may find that you can't use it for larger material or material that's still attached to a larger tree. Other times, you may be using a "bucking station" (essentially a saw horse), or you may be forced to cut the limb or material as is, however you found it in the wild. For those times, keep your supporting hand well away from the saw until it establishes a fairly deep kerf. If you're using a bucksaw or a bow saw, place your hand through the saw frame so that it's out of the way but still able to support the material.

CHAPTER 3
FIRE CRAFT

Fire Kit

When putting together a fire kit, it's important to understand the components of the commonly known **Fire Triangle**: heat, fuel, and air. Knowing and understanding the fire triangle allows us to build our kits appropriately. For emergencies, we need to carry resources that are capable of producing heat, as well as an emergency fuel source to accept that heat. Mother Nature will provide the air.

Pack Redundant Fire Sources: The ability to make fire is critical. Never go out with only one method of making fire, and never rely on one method working in all conditions. For me, it's wise to have different types of ignition sources that work under a variety of conditions. If the weather is not good for a lighter, I have windproof and stormproof matches. If neither of those work, I have a ferro rod. For more routine fires that aren't an emergency, I can use my ferro rod if it's overcast, and a magnifying lens if it's sunny out. This allows me to conserve the emergency open flame resources as the situation permits.

Gather As You Go: As soon as you hit the woods, you should start gathering **natural tinder** to use for your first fire. This is a resource you shouldn't pass up as you're walking. You don't know how scarce or abundant it will be where you end up, you only know what's in front of you right now. It's too valuable a resource to risk it. With that in mind, you also can't completely rely on finding dry natural tinder quickly in an emergency, so you should carry emergency tinder in your kit.

Emergency tinder is just that—to be saved for an actual emergency (just like a lighter and matches). Otherwise, you should use natural tinder resources that you find along the way and can replenish in the wild. You can use a **beeswax candle** as a "lighter extender." If you use the lighter to quickly light the candle, and then use the candle to light your tinder (which often takes longer to ignite than the candle), you conserve more fuel and extend the life of your lighter.

Fun fact: I once did an experiment on the burn time of a beeswax candle. It burned for twenty-two minutes. A normal Bic lighter is said to be good for up to 3,000 1.5-second lights. That comes out to 4,500 seconds of actual flame. Each beeswax birthday candle burns for 1,320 seconds. That tells me that carrying 4 beeswax birthday candles will give me more burn time (5,280 seconds) than a second lighter will, and I can use the beeswax for other purposes.

In order to gather natural tinder, you'll need something to store it in as you find it. A simple **mesh bag** or other form of "tinder pouch" that can be attached to your belt is a very convenient way to do this.

Lastly, for your fire kit, you want to have a method of **charring material** to make all of your fires easier to start. You're not just preparing for your first fire, but for all that follow. This can be as simple as having a small tin that can be placed in the fire to not only make charred material, but to store it afterward and keep it dry. You can also use other items from your water kit, which we'll cover later.

It should go without saying, but there's no need to put an empty tin in your kit for charring material. Why not fill the tin with charred material before putting it in your kit to make your first fire even easier as well?

Recommended Fire Kit

- Bic lighter
- Windproof/stormproof matches
- Ferrocerium rod
- Magnifying lens
- Emergency tinder
- Beeswax candle(s)
- Tinder pouch
- Charring and storage tin (like an Altoids tin)

The Principles of Fire

The ability to quickly make and sustain a fire is arguably one of the most important survival skills because it is often necessary for so many other survival priorities. It is, of course, needed for maintaining your core body temperature by drying out clothing and warming you up to prevent hypothermia. In many situations, it's more important than shelter for this same reason. For example, if it's raining or you got dumped from your canoe or kayak and are soaking wet, the priority becomes getting out of your wet clothes and drying them (and yourself) as quickly as possible. A large warming and drying fire can be made quicker than a shelter, and although your body heat will likely begin to dry you out, it won't nearly be as fast (and you're still losing body heat all the while). Even when your shelter is complete, you'll likely still be wet when you crawl into it—unless you also build a fire to go with that shelter. I would recommend building the fire first, getting warm and dry as quickly as possible, and then constructing your shelter.

Fire is also my preferred method of disinfecting water to make it safe to drink when I'm stationary. I do use a filter when I'm on the move, but that does have some limitations (much like many other methods) that we will discuss in a later chapter. In that same vein, fire is also essential in cooking food and making it safe to eat. For first aid, fire may be necessary for anything from disinfecting cotton material for bandages, to preparing medical plants for use. Fire makes one of the best emergency signals, too. It has visual and olfactory aspects that really set it apart from other signals. Lastly, fire is useful for making tools, utensils, and implements that may be needed.

It's important, however, to take a deep dive into the subject of fire craft. It isn't enough to just know how to produce it. It's necessary to understand the conditions that allow it to happen, to understand the "why." Understanding the "why" is what allows you to troubleshoot problems when conditions aren't ideal. The more deeply you understand fire craft, the greater your ability to create and sustain it when needed will be.

Fire Safety

As important as fire is, it can also be dangerous. **Duff** (leaf litter and sticks) surrounding your immediate area should be cleared away at a minimum radius of three feet from the center of the fire. Clear the area right down to the bare dirt if possible. Look overhead to make sure there are no low-lying branches full of dry leaves that could catch and spread. You should clear an even larger area on windy days or in especially dry areas. Keep in mind that a small ember can travel great distances and ignite a fire elsewhere, especially in those dry areas. If you're already lost, injured, and trying to survive on scant resources, the last thing you want to do is make it worse and risk injury by setting your area and resources on fire.

That brings up the question: do fire rings work, and are they worth the effort? In my experience, I have found that a fire ring is best suited for keeping the coal bed in one place. It prevents fuel from rolling out of and away from the fire, and potentially into the area around the fire that I haven't cleared. In my opinion, they are worth the time and effort, and I tend to do them. In the areas that I frequent, it's easy enough to make a quick circle out of some rocks. Of course, it won't prevent embers from going up in the air or keep fire from "jumping" and spreading on a windy day, but that isn't an expectation I have for it.

Since we're talking about fire safety and rock rings, an important thing to understand is that the heat from the fire will cause any moisture trapped in a rock to expand, and may cause it to crack. Sometimes it will do so rather explosively, scattering coals and sending sharp little fragments of rock everywhere. As a general rule of thumb, don't use rocks that are pulled out of or near a stream bed because it's highly likely that they contain a lot of moisture. Taking it a step further, rock selection has a lot to do with how porous the rock is. For example, sandstone is very porous and should be avoided in wet areas. Granite, however, is not very porous at all, so there's little chance of it containing any moisture. Regardless, I don't like to use rocks for my base platform under the **fire lay** (the structure of wood, sticks, and other fuel). You will usually always have enough fuel to spare to make this platform.

Having a fire inside your shelter can be a very appealing thing, especially on particularly cold days when you're struggling to maintain warmth and stave off hypothermia. Be overly cautious when doing so, especially with natural shelters. Over time, the natural material will dry out and begin to heat, and your entire shelter will eventually catch. Soot and creosote can also build up over time, and both are flammable and increase that risk. Another undetectable danger that is a product of burning fuels (even wood fuel) is carbon monoxide (CO). If you plan to have a fire inside your shelter, it needs to be well ventilated to prevent CO poisoning.

From an injury perspective, burns are extremely dangerous if you cannot get medical care rather quickly. Larger burns negatively affect your ability to thermoregulate and make you more susceptible to hypothermia. All burns, large or small, tend to get infected easily. This can be a real problem in a remote wilderness emergency. Be incredibly careful when tending your fire or removing things like water bottles and cook pots, so that you don't make a dangerous situation worse.

The Fire Train

The Fire Train is a simple analogy to visualize what you're trying to accomplish when making a fire. Much like a train that starts from a full stop and gradually gathers speed and momentum over time, your fire gradually gains its own momentum when done correctly. There is no shortcut to getting a train up to speed, much like there is no shortcut to getting a sustainable fire going (with the rather dangerous exception of using gasoline, which I don't recommend). You must go through all the steps.

Heat is created with an ignition source, be it a lighter, matches, ferro rod, what have you. That ignition source transfers heat to the fuel starting with the finest, most combustible material available. That material burns long enough to transfer the heat to fuel that is larger in size, but still small enough to readily accept the heat. This transfer of heat continues through fuel that is gradually increasing in size, and therefore burns longer once lit, until the fire is sustainable.

Types of Fuel

Fuel consists of **tinder, kindling,** and **sustaining fuel**. It is especially important that the heat can transfer from the smallest, most finely processed fuels to gradually larger sizes. Trying to shortcut this transfer of heat ("fire train") will result in incomplete or lack of combustion. Doing it right from the start will save you time.

Tinder is where the heat meets the fuel. It is dry, highly combustible material that's processed down as finely as possible so that it readily accepts heat from an ignition source. A good descriptive term for tinder is "fluffy." It's meant to burn long enough to transfer that heat to the larger kindling. Tinder is such a valuable resource that you should always collect enough for one or more fires. When you think of tinder, think of "**coarse, medium, and fine**," as it takes all three types to make a good **tinder bundle**.

Natural Tinder

Specific tinder resources will vary from region to region. It would be as difficult to list all of them as it would be to list even one that could be found everywhere. What *is* possible is listing some categorically and giving a couple of examples that are commonly found in a lot of different areas. The takeaway from this shouldn't be the name of a specific resource so much as the properties of that resource. Knowing what properties to look for should help you identify similar resources in your area. Here are some basic tinder resource categories and examples of each:

- Dried leaves and needles
- Dried grass and wildflowers
- Inner and outer bark
- Wet-weather tinder
- Flash tinder
- Punkwood

Before diving too deeply into this discussion, keep in mind many land plants have a **cuticle**—a plant's waxy outer layer that prevents the loss of water to the environment. In the context of fire, that is problematic in two ways. For one, cuticles trap moisture inside plant material. Second, the coating is a solid wax. While wax is good fuel, it must first be melted into liquid form to really be combustible. Think of how a candle works: the heat from the flame is actually melting the solid wax body of the candle, and the cotton wick is pulling (or wicking) that liquid wax up to be burned for fuel. Knowing these characteristics up front will allow you to arrange your tinder bundle correctly, choose the appropriate ignition source for your tinder, and save you a lot of frustration.

Dried leaves from deciduous trees and **dried needles** from various conifer species are often abundant in most forests. Having said that, most tend to have very heavy cuticles. Anything with a heavy cuticle is only suited for the coarse outer layer of any tinder bundle. You can often get away with using these as tinder only if you're using an open flame ignition source like a lighter, matches, or a candle, but even then it may take some time to really take off. The heat must last long enough to melt the waxy cuticle into a liquid. Even the hot sparks from a ferrocerium rod will often go out well before you achieve that, as the sparks are so short-lived. I rarely, if ever, use either.

If you do find yourself in a situation where these are your only source of tinder, it's best to try and avoid leaves that are mostly intact from the most recent autumn. Look for leaves that are **"skeletonized"** from the season prior to that. I say skeletonized because most of the leaf has decomposed away, including a lot of the cuticle, and what's left is the framework of the leaf.

The best ignition source to use for this tinder resource is either a lighter, matches, or a candle; otherwise, you should only use it as the outermost coarse layer of your tinder bundle. The heat from the fine and medium layers within your tinder bundle will have enough burn time to get this coarse layer going.

Dried grass and the tops and small stems of **dried wildflowers** are another abundant resource that can be found most anywhere. When I say wildflower, I mean any plant in the wild that reproduces by flowering, and that is an overly broad category. Flowering plants are the most dominant form of plants on land. Grasses are also quite common, and both can be excellent tinder resources.

These may or may not have heavy cuticles that you have to contend with. In my experience, many grasses have a heavy cuticle, especially the stems. If you've ever felt the straw in a bale you'll know exactly what that feels like. However, the heads of those grasses when seeded out have very little cuticle. Wildflower tops and stems don't typically have much of a cuticle to worry about when they are dead and dry. The dried conifer leaves and needles rule applies here, too: anything with a heavy cuticle should be limited to the coarse outer layer of the tinder bundle. If it doesn't have one, it's probably suitable for the medium and fine inner layers. As far as ignition sources, an open flame will likely work for any of these. If you plan to use the

CHAPTER 3: FIRE CRAFT

spark from a ferro rod, you'll have better success with some medium and fine layers that have little to no cuticle.

One rather abundant resource from the dried grass category that grows all over the United States is **broomsedge**. This is a very tall grass with long stems that seed out rather heavily. It grows in bundles, so it's quite easy to spot and quite easy to harvest. Because it's so tall, it can be found in the winter sticking up above the snow, high and dry, when most other resources are covered and won't be seen again until spring. This resource is particularly useful because an entire tinder bundle, including coarse, medium, and fine material, can be made from this alone.

Goldenrod is a great example from the wildflower category that grows all over the southeastern US. It's a large "weed" that has delicate, little yellow flowers. Once it's dead and dry, you're left with an abundance of brittle stems, leaves, and flower tops with almost no cuticle to deal with. This plant and others like it are well-suited for a tinder bundle. The stems make a great coarse outer layer, the leaves are great for the medium layer, and the small flowers are excellent for the fine, innermost layer.

I want to reiterate the point that it is more important to learn properties and categories than it is to learn names of specific plants. Regionally, you'll have additional choices like **dog fennel**. It has similar properties to goldenrod and grows all over the southeastern United States. Even if you cannot positively identify it as dog fennel, you'll be able to recognize that it is a wildflower with dry brittle stems, an abundance of small, dry leaves, and flowers. Identification of plants and learning their common and scientific names is a worthy venture, but it should be second to simply understanding the properties that make them worth learning to begin with.

CHAPTER 3: FIRE CRAFT

Dried bark that is suitable for tinder can be found on a variety of different tree species, as the outer barks of some and the inner barks of others. Of course, these need to be dead and dry, not "green" (living). You aren't looking for large, chunky, or scaly barks. What you're looking for are barks composed of fine fibers that can be broken down easily by hand.

Trees like **cedar, juniper, and cypress** are excellent sources of outer bark that can easily be harvested from a dead standing tree, or even one that has fallen. Look for bark that hangs off in what looks like shreds. Even trees that are still living may have some dead outer bark, oftentimes hanging off them and just begging to be harvested. Don't be afraid to take what the tree is offering in that way, but take care and don't take everything from one tree. And never take bark in a ring all the way around a living tree—taking a little bit from several different trees is a better idea and won't harm them. We owe it to the wilderness to be good stewards of the forest.

Outer bark that is hanging can just be pulled off the tree by hand. When it can't, you can use the spine of your knife or folding saw to scrape it off so that it can be gathered. Using the spine preserves the cutting edge of this tool for other tasks. A lot of these barks will come off finely shredded already, but some may require further processing to really break them down and make them fine.

Some trees will have outer bark that isn't suitable for tinder, but directly underneath that layer you'll find inner bark with excellent tinder properties. Some great examples are **cottonwood, aspen, and tulip poplar**. These need to be harvested from dead, dry trees and branches. The valuable inner bark is easy to separate from the outer bark by either pulling it apart by hand or scraping it off with the sharp spine of your knife or saw. This inner bark can be further processed into finer and finer material by twisting and pulling it apart with your hands.

Barks with these properties can be used to make your entire tinder bundle. They only require different levels of processing. Coarse material for the outer layer takes the least amount of effort; more will be required to produce the medium and fine material for your bundle. Most of these barks work well with open flame and spark ignition, and with the right technique, they are excellent for solar as well.

The first three categories are what I would consider your baseline tinder resources. If conditions are right and they are processed correctly, they're all you'll need to produce a great tinder bundle and get your fire going easily. The list is not all-inclusive by any means, but it is a solid starting point and foundation that can be built on as your knowledge and skills develop.

In addition to the baseline categories, there are what I would consider more specialized categories. These are still basic in that they are useful with basic ignition sources, so I feel they are important to cover. They are not always necessary but can be helpful for certain situations. They're typically used in addition to the baseline tinder bundle to make them more effective for certain conditions.

If it's raining or your tinder is damp, you could benefit from adding a **wet-weather tinder** to your basic tinder bundle. Wet-weather tinder

GRAY BEARDED GREEN BERET'S GUIDE TO SURVIVING THE WILD

will still light under these conditions and often burn long enough to dry out and ignite the rest of the tinder bundle. Saps and resins from conifers like **pine, spruce, and fir** work well. Mixing them in with your fine tinder is a great way to get a marginal tinder bundle lit more easily. These are often found on the outside of the tree where it has been damaged, or in small pockets that look like blisters just under the bark for species like the fir. All of these are highly flammable and work well with open flame or spark ignition.

You'll often need more than just these to make a good tinder bundle. These are meant be used in addition to other suitable resources to make a full wet-weather tinder bundle. If conditions are in fact wet, that can be a challenge, but it certainly isn't impossible. Look for dry resources on the undersides of trees and hanging on branches up off the ground. These will often be more dry than anything directly on the ground.

Fatwood is an excellent, naturally occurring wet-weather tinder resource. Other common names for it, depending on what region you're in, are "lighter knot," "lighter pine," and "fat lighter." It is resin-soaked pine that's commonly found in the junctions where limbs meet the trunk of the tree, and in pine stumps after the trees die and all the sap settles in those areas. This resin preserves the wood. You'll notice that even when most, if not all, of the tree has decomposed, the resin-soaked fatwood will remain.

You can find anything preserved in resin, from an entire stump or log to a simple branch junction (which would be a knot in the wood if it were made into lumber, probably why they call it lighter knot in some areas). The larger parts are easy to spot because the rest of the sapwood will have decomposed away, and you'll probably notice sharp ridges on the log or stump. While the outside may be weathered and gray, once you get past that layer you'll notice a sticky, deep orange color that looks waxy or glossy and smells like a pine-based household cleaner. What you're smelling are the terpenes. Pine sap is further refined into turpentine, which is highly flammable.

The value of fatwood is that it is plentiful in many areas so it can be replenished in the wild. And because of the resin, it lights well with open flame and spark ignition sources, even when it's wet. If you're in an area where fatwood can be found, once you learn to find it, you'll see it everywhere. It's most common in red and yellow pines, but it can be found in white pine as well, just in a much smaller amount and less frequently. Resin-soaked wood can also be found in other species like cypress, which I've personally found it in. I've heard that it can be found in spruce and fir, but I have yet to find any in those species myself.

Bark from birch trees should also be included in this category. It's an outer bark, but it also contains a very flammable oil that works well when wet. Birch sheds its outer bark as it grows, so even living trees almost always have shreds of bark hanging off them that can be readily harvested. These shreds will easily light with an open flame ignition source, and many are fine enough to take a spark from a ferrocerium rod. Birch is a little more limited in where it grows, but there are several different species of birch, and one or more could be growing in your area.

Flash tinder is a rather appropriate name for this type of resource. Flash tinder is extremely light and fluffy. Imagine something that is so light, it could be carried by a breeze (and often is). Some common examples are **cattail fluff, thistledown, and milkweed fluff**. As the name suggests, it catches extremely quickly, but also burns up just as fast. Flash tinder on its own is rarely going to help you get a fire going, let alone a sustainable one. The real value of flash tinder is when it's added to a baseline tinder bundle. Think of it as a "super fine" layer that accepts heat even more readily than the already fine layer of the bundle. It doesn't burn long, but it burns long enough to easily transfer the heat to the fine layer and start that fire train. It's a great resource to use for something like catching the spark from a ferrocerium rod. Where it might take three to five strikes from a ferro rod to get your fine tinder lit, it may only take one to get a good flash tinder going.

Punkwood is wood that's slowly decomposing away. It's an extremely valuable tinder resource, especially when dry. You'll often find it in varying stages of decomposition depending on how long the tree has been dead and the local conditions. The most valuable punkwood is soft and spongy, with texture like a kitchen sponge. Because of this, it

CHAPTER 3: FIRE CRAFT

tends to soak up rain and moisture from the air and ground, so it will often be wet when you find it. To use it as a tinder, it will first need to be dried. Once dry, it can be lit easily with an open flame, ferro rod, or solar. It comes off in chunks, and only the outside is exposed to the heat, so it will smolder rather than burn. Think of it as an ember that must be transferred to a tinder bundle and then blown to flame. The heat will be transferred from the smoldering punkwood to other tinder that's airier and more open, and that will burn and produce flame. Many species can and will produce useable punk, but in my experience, **aspen** produces some of the best. Punkwood has an additional benefit to fire-starting that we will discuss in more detail in the section "Follow-On Fires."

Man-Made Tinder

For emergency kits, it's always a good idea to carry **emergency tinder**. It's typically man-made and good for that "Right Now Fire"— an emergency warming and drying fire that you need immediately, or you very well could die. It can be homemade, like cotton balls soaked in petroleum jelly, or already packaged. There are many different types available commercially and they're essentially cotton that has been soaked in a fuel like wax. They are lightweight, don't take up much space, and burn for quite a long time. Pro tip: I use natural tinder when available so that I can save this for that literal "rainy day" or emergency.

Another great resource for any kit is **candles**. I like to think of candles as "lighter extenders." When using a lighter, I don't like to use more than five seconds of fuel to get tinder started. If the tinder is processed properly and isn't damp, that should be plenty of time to get it going. If it takes longer than that, and the tinder is optimal, address this rather than continuing to waste the fuel in your lighter. With that said, there are some instances when I've had tinder as finely processed as possible, but it was still a bit damp. If I have a candle, I can use a few seconds of fuel from my lighter to get the candle lit, and then use the flame from the candle to dry out and ignite that marginal tinder. Once it's lit, I can simply put out the candle and still have it available for the next time. By doing this, I reduce the amount of fuel I have to use out of my lighter, essentially extending its life.

Tip for the Unexpected

Other items in your kit can often be used as a tinder resource in an emergency. Plastics and rubber will burn well, as will duct tape. But you must weigh the value of the item you're about to burn against the value it originally had. Does your need for this fire outweigh the need for this item as it was intended to be used? For example, is it wise to use this bandage to start a fire if you have an injury that you'll need the bandage for later? You will always be limited when it comes to any resource that you pack that can't be replenished from the wild, so it's important to consider.

Kindling

Kindling is the next stop on the fire train. It is dry, combustible material that's not as finely processed as tinder. It's a larger-diameter fuel than the tinder, and it therefore burns longer so that it can transfer that heat to the even larger sustaining fuel. When you think of kindling, think of three sizes: **matchsticks, pencils, and markers**. This is an easy way to remember to gather all three sizes so that heat can continue to be transferred from smaller to larger fuels.

The best wood choices for kindling are ones that will catch quickly. It doesn't necessarily need to burn for an extended period of time, it just needs to burn long enough to get the sustaining fuel going. Some examples are softer woods like most conifers (**pine, spruce, fir, cedar**), and deciduous trees that I would consider a soft-medium density (**cottonwood, willow, aspen, birch, tulip poplar**). Species that contain resins or oils like pines and birch are a welcome bonus when it comes to catching quickly, especially in wet conditions.

Sustaining Fuel

Sustaining fuel is the final stop on the fire train. Sustaining fuel is meant to accept the heat from the kindling and sustain your fire as long as you continue to add fuel, so it's large enough to burn for some time. When you think of sustaining fuel, think thumb-size to wrist-size before going larger.

Sustaining fuel needs to burn longer so that you can efficiently sustain your fire. The best choices for this are often deciduous hardwoods like **hickory, oak, maple, ash, walnut, and cherry**. Hardwoods take longer to ignite but burn slower once lit. These wood choices often put off more heat comparatively, and create a good, long-lasting coal bed.

An exception to this that I should mention—since I live in and frequent the woodlands of the northeastern US—is **birch**. I'd consider birch to be a comparatively soft to medium "hardwood," but the bark contains betulin and betulinic acid, which are highly flammable. The bark can be used as tinder, even in wet weather. The wood catches quickly, so it's suitable for kindling, and it burns hotter than many hardwood species, so it's suitable for sustaining fuel. This species is like a one-stop shop when it comes to fire.

> **Tip for the Unexpected**
>
> **How much sustaining fuel do you need to get through the night?**
>
> Well, that depends largely on the species you choose and the diameter of that sustaining fuel. That, and whether you're relying on your fire to keep warm. It takes time and energy to gather and process fuel. It can be tempting to get the bare minimum that you think you can get by with. When you're tired, cold, wet, and hungry, it's pretty easy to convince yourself that you have plenty to get you through until morning. I'm guilty of that from time to time myself. What I've learned from personal experience is this: when you think you have enough, you need five times more than that. You can either gather enough before you bed down for the night, or you'll have to get up during the night to gather more when you run out.

Creating a Tinder Bundle

Now that you're more familiar with the various types of tinder, let's discuss how to shape them into a bundle. A **tinder bundle** is nothing more than a certain arrangement of tinder resources that maximizes its effectiveness and ease of use. This arrangement is mostly dependent on the planned ignition source. There are three basic types:

- Tinder ball
- Grass or twig bundle
- Bird's nest

The **tinder ball** is just like it sounds: a ball of coarse, medium, and fine material. It's quite simple to construct and is primarily used with either an open flame or a spark from a ferro rod. Because it is mixed, there's little need for precision—a flame or a shower of sparks from a ferro rod will ignite it easily. A fair-weather tinder ball should be about the size of a softball. This should burn plenty long enough to get dry kindling going. For poor weather when it needs to burn a little longer, this should be doubled to about the size of a miniature basketball. Having too small a tinder ball can result in a failure to get a fire going.

A **grass bundle** can also be referred to as a stick or twig bundle, it just depends on what makes up the bundle. For a grass bundle, you simply place the stems together with all the seeded heads toward one end. This arranges it in such a way that all the fine, readily combustible material is at one end, and all the coarse stems are at the other. This type of bundle works best with open flame, but it can also be used with a ferro rod. You simply orient the seeded heads in a downward direction with the stems facing up, and light the bottom. The flame will take on the fine seed heads at the bottom and climb through the medium and coarse material.

If you're using sticks or twigs, keep in mind that they are coarse material so you'll need to place some sort of medium and fine material toward the center. This is a great technique to use when good tinder resources like dried grasses, wildflowers, and barks are less abundant. You can use what little you do have to make up the innermost layers that will accept the heat from your ignition source easily, and your coarse outer layer can be supplemented with more abundant sticks and twigs. Remember that the smallest sized kindling is only as thick as a matchstick, so you want your sticks and twigs to be thinner than that for best results.

Depending on the composition of your grass bundle, you may even be able to use it for **ember transfer**, which is typically reserved for the next tinder bundle we'll discuss (bird's nest). To do this, simply:

1. Make a small cone out of your grasses, sticks, or twigs.
2. Place a layer of medium material inside that cone.
3. Place an inner layer of fine material that you can transfer your ember onto. Picture an ice cream cone: the sticks or twigs are the cone, and the medium and fine material are the ice cream inside.

CHAPTER 3: FIRE CRAFT

For fair weather, the grass bundle should be big enough at the base so that your finger and thumb can just make a circle around the bundle of stems, like an "okay" sign. For poor weather, you'll want a bundle that's at least twice that size at the base. If the tinder is available, you should try and get enough so that it takes both hands make a circle around the base.

A **bird's nest** is a circular arrangement of tinder with a recess in the middle that allows you to securely place an ember inside it. The outer layer is coarse, the middle layer is medium, and the innermost layer is fine material. It can be used with any ignition source, but it takes longer to construct and is really only necessary for transferring an ember that was produced by solar, percussion, or friction ignition, or when an ember is created with charred material, which we will discuss later.

Fire Lays

A fire lay is the arrangement of your fuel that's meant to achieve and sustain a fire. A good fire lay sets the conditions for the entire fire train to happen efficiently. Fire loves chaos, yet it also loves structure to easily climb. It needs all sides of the fire triangle in the correct ratio to consume fuel that gradually increases in size from the smallest tinder to the largest sustaining fuel. With this in mind, you can build a structure of "organized chaos" to set these conditions and be more successful with your fire-making.

An additional consideration for a good fire lay is its ability to dry out larger sustaining fuel that may be damp or wet. Typically, this is accomplished in one of two ways. Smaller-diameter sustaining fuel that will dry rather quickly can be incorporated into the fire lay, arranged in such a way that it is meant to catch last in the fire train. This puts it in close proximity to the fire and takes advantage of that heat to quickly dry it out until it catches flame. The second method is typically used for larger sustaining fuel that may take longer to dry out before it can be used. You can simply arrange the larger fuel around the main fire so that once it's dry, it's ready to use and won't make your fire struggle in the meantime.

CHAPTER 3: FIRE CRAFT

> **Tip for the Unexpected**
>
> **If the ground is wet**, and that includes ice or snow, you need to establish a base for the fire to sit on. If you place dry fuel on wet ground, the fuel will absorb the moisture and become difficult to light. If you do get it lit, the heat from the fire is going to evaporate all the moisture from the ground and pull it up through your fire lay. That will cause the fire to struggle and may put it out. For wet conditions, make a simple platform out of sustaining fuel (thumb-size or a larger diameter) by placing them side by side to prevent this from happening.

The Tipi

The **tipi** fire lay is probably one of the most used arrangements. The tipi shape gives it that airy, chaotic structure that fire loves to climb of fuel gradually increasing in size. This arrangement is temporary—it will probably fall over as it burns, and if it doesn't, it will settle into a nice bed of coals. The structure is only important to set the conditions for the initial fire train to happen. Once you have coals, you can simply add sustaining fuel as needed to keep it going. This fire lay is especially useful for emergency survival situations. If done correctly, you can easily establish a large fire that will quickly dry out clothes and warm you up. It's also a quick and easy fire lay to use for boiling water to make it safe to drink and to charr material for subsequent fires. In addition, this structure is great for drying out damp sustaining fuel.

How to Build

1. Build a base for the fire lay to sit on (if needed).
2. Place a bundle of mixed kindling (matchsticks, pencils, markers) on the base.
3. Place more kindling around this first bundle to form the tipi structure.
4. Leave an opening in the center to allow for placement of your tinder bundle.
5. Place the largest kindling/smallest sustaining fuel around the outside of the fire lay.

Depending on the ignition source you're using, you can either place the tinder bundle inside the fire lay (in the space you left in the initial bundle), or you can light the tinder and place it inside once its burning. The tinder will transfer the heat to the mix of kindling from smallest to largest, and that heat will transfer to the thumb-sized sustaining fuel, which will burn longer and establish a nice bed of coals. Once you have that, it's as easy as adding sustaining fuel to keep it going. The rule of thumb is that once your flames are climbing above the level of fuel in the fire lay, it's safe to add more fuel without smothering it.

The Elevator

My favorite fire lay is what I call the **elevator**. Of course, it also incorporates all the aforementioned principles. This fire lay has the added benefit of allowing you to introduce more air as needed without having to blow on the coals. Men can think of it as a "beard saver," since you don't have to get your whiskers close to the flames.

How to Build

1. Place a large piece of sustaining fuel toward the back of the fire lay to act as a fulcrum.
2. Form a triangle with long pieces of thumb-sized sustaining fuel.
3. Place a bundle of kindling on each side and a third bundle at the apex.
4. Leave the center open to allow for placement of your tinder bundle.

CHAPTER 3: FIRE CRAFT

To Get It Lit

1. Light your tinder bundle and place it in the center of the fire lay.

2. Pull the top bundle of kindling down over the burning tinder bundle. The heat will be transferred from the tinder to the kindling. If you see a lot of smoke (indicating incomplete combustion), rather than huffing and puffing and blowing all over it, simply use the corner of the triangle and lift up the fire lay to introduce air.

3. Once you have better, more complete combustion, you can lower the triangle again, start taking kindling from the outside that isn't burning, and place it toward the center.

4. Add larger and larger sustaining fuel as needed.

Ignition Sources

At a considerably basic level, there are three categories of ignition sources that we should be familiar with: **open flame, spark, and solar**. There are other categories like percussion and friction that I consider more intermediate to advanced, so they're outside the scope of this book for beginners. You could also use chemicals, gunpowder, or electrical means to start a fire, but I personally feel those are more of a gimmick and what I refer to as "Gee-Wizardry"—as in, "gee whiz, did you know that you can mix this with this and start a fire? It's like magic!" It's good information to have (more knowledge and skill always being better than less), but it's not a place to start learning the basics of fire craft in my opinion. I recommend you save the hacks, gimmicks, and Gee-Wizardry for after you have a solid foundation in basic skills.

Open Flame

Open flame ignition sources are exactly that: they produce an open flame that easily transfers heat to a tinder resource. Technically, a **lighter** does use a spark to ignite fuel , but they are self-contained and the result is an open flame. Similarly, **matches** require friction to ignite. However, it's the ignition of the oxidizing agents contained in the match head that results in an open flame without the introduction of another resource.

Open flame ignition is often the best choice in an emergency. Open flame will work with most any tinder resource and bundle. It's exceptionally reliable and easy to use, often called "sure flame" because of its reliability. Notice I didn't say "sure fire"? You can get the flame but still not get the fire if the rest of the fire triangle is not correct.

Bic-Style Lighters

If you follow the five-second rule of thumb, you can expect to get at least 900 fires started with each lighter. The spark you produce with your finger ignites the vapor within, and you have a flame as long as the button is pressed and the environmental conditions are favorable. Lighters are not without limitations, however. The lighter body that contains the fuel is only plastic, and they have a lot of small, cheap parts that can break if not protected.

Some other obvious limitations are that it will be susceptible to wind, water, and temperature. If it's too **windy**, the flame continues to be blown out, so the lighter must be shielded from the wind. If the lighter gets **wet**, there are two issues. First, the metallic housing around the top of the lighter will hold water and need to be cleared out. Second, while the ferro rod is not affected by water, the steel rotary striker will lose the friction it needs to remove the pyrophoric metal from the ferro rod. Both need to be addressed for the lighter to function again. As the **temperature** drops, so does the pressure inside the lighter. If it doesn't have adequate pressure, it will not vaporize when the button is pressed, and the lighter will have no fuel to burn. Care should be taken in extremely cold weather to keep the lighter in a pocket or close to your body to keep it warm.

To rescue a wet lighter, shake the lighter vigorously several times to get rid of the bulk of the water in the housing. Next, blow forcefully down into the housing to get even more water out. Do this several times. If you have dry cotton, be it your clothing or a piece from your kit, use it to dry the rotary wheel striker. When one part is dry, carefully rotate the striker and continue until it is completely dry. Once you can get it sparking again, it should be dry enough to light. You should remove the small metal comfort guard that covers the rotary striker to allow for this. This can be done prior to ever going into the field.

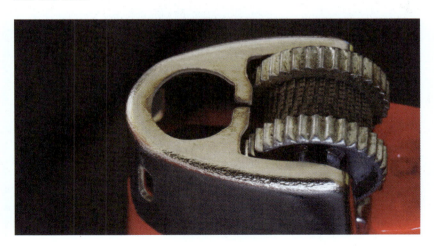

CHAPTER 3: FIRE CRAFT

When it eventually runs out, the lighter is not necessarily useless. It will still create a useable spark, albeit it a small one. Oftentimes, when you find a lighter that has been discarded, it will be out of fuel but still create a spark. That can be used to light certain resources in an emergency, like flash tinder and charred material.

To make it last longer—since its ability to spark will far outlast its ability to flame—you can take steps to restrict the flow of fuel and only create a spark to light your tinder. This will conserve the fuel even longer and make your lighter that much more useful. You can restrict the flow of fuel by tightly wrapping or tying a small piece of cordage under the button, or using a cable tie that you can slide under it when needed—anything that prevents the button from being pressed.

Matches

I've often read (and sometimes heard) that matches are not worth carrying, or that some would rather carry two lighters than one lighter and some matches. I personally feel that matches are worth carrying, and here's why: you always want a backup for something you're relying on in a life-or-death situation. In an actual emergency, when I'm cold and wet and going hypothermic, I'm going to use the easiest and most reliable method to get my "Right Now Fire" going. You shouldn't improvise, nor rely on just one method. For something that is life-or-death critical, set yourself up for the best chance of success and bring a reliable backup. As far as carrying two lighters instead of a lighter and matches, if the conditions are not good for the first lighter to work, they aren't going to be good for the second one either. You want another open flame ignition source that will perform differently in those conditions.

When it comes to matches, you should choose windproof/stormproof matches that burn for as long as possible. Most windproof/stormproof matches have wooden matchsticks and will burn both in high winds and in rainy, wet conditions—times when I would expect a lighter to fail. Paper kitchen matches have no place in an emergency kit.

Matches are limited in that they're only good for one strike, and you can only carry so many of them. Of course, all matches are not created equal, but the average minimum amount of time it takes to ignite a damp tinder bundle (in my personal experience and experimentation) is fifteen seconds. Look for matches that burn at least that long, or at an absolute minimum, long enough for you to light a candle that can then be used to dry out and ignite the bundle.

Spark

Ferrocerium Rods

Spark ignition is produced by a **ferrocerium rod**. "Ferro rods" are remarkably simple with no moving parts, durable, and long-lasting. They're also not susceptible to wet and cold conditions.

To use a ferro rod, you scrape it with a harder object, which removes pyrophoric material from the rod. That object is often the steel "striker" that is supplied with most rods, the spine of your knife, or even flint, chert, quartzite, or glass. Once that material is scraped off and exposed to oxygen, it combusts and produces a spark. Ferro rods differ slightly in composition, but for the most part they all produce sparks that are approximately 5,500 degrees F (3,000 degrees C). This is considered a "hot spark" that works well with a variety of tinder resources.

Larger rods are often better choices than smaller; they allow you to remove more material with each scraping motion. These sparks are short-lived, however, so you want to produce as many hot sparks as possible each time. The larger rods are also easier to use when your hands are cold. You should choose a rod that is approximately a ½-inch thick, and 5–6 inches long.

Ferro rods do involve bit of technique, which takes a little practice, but they're quite easy to use and reliable once you get the hang of them. A person with experience can easily light a tinder resource with a ferro rod within three "strikes." Any more than that, and something is either wrong with your technique or your tinder. One or both of those should be addressed before continuing to waste the resource by scraping it with no real chance of success.

Pin and Pull Technique

The best technique for larger ferro rods is the "pin and pull." This is best done with the sharp 90-degree spine of your knife or folding saw. To use this method:

1. Kneel and place your non-dominant foot next to the tinder bundle.

2. With a secure grip on your striker, pin the striker to the top of that foot. If you're using a knife, the sharp edge should be oriented away from you. The sparks will originate from the edge

of the striker and scatter forward and down, so orient your striker over your tinder for them to fall on the bundle.

3. Grip the ferro rod securely in your dominant hand.
4. Place it in contact with the underside of the striker at the correct angle. It should be in contact with the forward edge at an approximate 45-degree angle.
5. While keeping the striker firmly in place, pull the rod in a scraping motion away from the tinder bundle to create sparks. Again, make the necessary adjustments in your positioning to ensure that most of the sparks hit the tinder bundle.

* * *

When using your knife as a striker, it's important to use the 90-degree spine of the knife to not dull your edge unnecessarily. Since the spine of your knife is removing material from the ferro rod, it doesn't matter if your blade is carbon steel or stainless. It simply must be harder than the rod and have a sharp spine. If your knife doesn't have a sharp spine, it's easy enough to do with a file if you want. If your knife doesn't have a 90-degree spine, consider conserving the edge by using the sharp edge of another piece of gear, like your saw blade or multi-tool. If you absolutely must use the edge of your knife, use the portion toward the tip of the blade edge, since this is often less useful than the edge closer to the handle and the belly of the knife.

Remember the rule of thumb: if it takes you more than three strikes with a ferro rod, something is wrong with your technique, your tinder, or both. Stop and adjust instead of continuing to waste the resource.

Solar

Solar ignition harnesses the power of the sun and magnifies it to transfer heat to a tinder resource. It's the most renewable resource because it consumes nothing from your kit. Of course, it does have its one limitation of needing sunny weather, but when conditions are right and you're not in an emergency, you should always go with this easy and reliable method.

Rather than try to light an entire tinder bundle with the sun, it's best to **create a small ember** that can be transferred into a bird's nest tinder bundle and blown to flame. It'll be much easier to focus the sun on a smaller piece of tinder. One of the best tinder resources for solar is dung from lagomorphs (rabbits, hares, and pikas). These are hind-gut digesters that leave behind pellets that are little more than compressed plant fiber. When these pellets are dry, they make excellent tinder for solar. Of course, this isn't all you can use. You can create a similar "pellet" by taking some of your fine material like an inner or outer bark, rolling it, and compressing it into a tight ball with your hands. Your goal is to create an ember that smolders rather than burns, so you remove air (or at least restrict it) from the fire triangle

CHAPTER 3: FIRE CRAFT

by compressing the tinder. Another good tinder resource for solar is a small piece of dry punkwood.

There are really two things that you need to pay attention to **when using solar as an ignition source**:

1. **The angle of the lens in relation to the sun.** When you look at the light that's passing through the lens and landing on either the ground or the tinder, it should be centered. That is, the light should be centered within the shadow made by the rest of the lens. This gives you the best possible angle in relation to the sun.

2. **The size of the circle of light that you are focusing.** While maintaining the correct angle, move the lens forward or back until the light is as focused and pinpointed as possible. This will give you the most heat. If you focus that spot on your tinder pellet, it should begin to smoke almost immediately. Once smoking, make slow, very tight circles with the light on the tinder to increase the surface area that you're applying heat to with the lens. This process should take twenty to thirty seconds with good sun. You'll know it's lit when you can take away the ignition source and the pellet still smolders. Once smoldering, simply transfer the ember into the bird's nest and reintroduce air to the fire triangle by blowing it to flame.

Tip for the Unexpected

Solar is best during the summer months from ten in the morning to two in the afternoon, but it can still be done at other times. All it takes is full sun and clear skies with no obstructions. Shadows from trees and clouds partially blocking the sun will reduce your ability to get a fire going using this technique. Keep in mind that the larger your lens, the greater its ability to gather and focus light. Double convex lenses work extremely well, as do Fresnel lenses.

Another thing to consider with tinder for solar: stay away from anything that is waxy, oily, or resinous. They don't work well at all with solar because you end up heating the wax, resin, or oil instead of the tinder, and that makes it wet rather than dry. You want tinder that's as dry as possible.

CHAPTER 3: FIRE CRAFT

Follow-On Fires

Charred material is material that has been heated in an anaerobic environment (one without oxygen). This method pushes out impurities and leaves you with what is essentially carbon that readily accepts heat from nearly any ignition source. It's basically a manipulation of the fire triangle. You'll remember that the fire triangle is heat, fuel, and air. What we're doing is finishing two sides and leaving out the third to prevent combustion. We place fuel inside a metal container and add heat, but in the absence of air, this pushes out impurities in the fuel and takes it right up to the point of combustion without going over. What we're left with is carbon that's ready to go with the slightest spark.

Charred material makes achieving ignition extremely easy. If you don't already have charred material for your initial fire, using that fire to produce char will make every subsequent fire that much easier.

Nearly any natural material can be charred and made more useful as a tinder resource. Cotton, more specifically cotton cloth, is often used to make what is called "charcloth." However, cotton is not the only material that can be charred. There are several other natural materials that are readily available and that can be replenished in the wild without sacrificing your clothing or bandages. In earlier times, cotton material would have been scarcer and much more valuable than it is today, so natural materials like punkwood were more than likely to have been charred.

Back then, charred material would also not have been made in a tin. It would've been roasted by the fire and tended to so that it didn't combust and just burn up. The results wouldn't have been perfect, but they would have still been useable. Today, we have the luxury of creating an anaerobic environment by using tins that can survive being placed directly in the fire. We can easily create perfect charred material.

Many will carry a tin and extra cotton material with the intent of charring it with their first fire in the field. To me, this makes little sense. Why not char the material at home and carry it out to the field in the tin you plan to use instead of carrying an empty tin and extra cotton? Once in the field, you can replenish your supply with natural material and save your cotton for other purposes. Most tinder resources, excluding oily or resinous wet-weather tinder, will char well. Punkwood makes the best charred natural material, particularly punkwood from an aspen tree (although others work well, too). Choose punkwood that's as dry as possible and completely spongy with no hard spots. If it's wet, as punkwood often is, you should gather it anyway. The heating process will take longer, but it will push the moisture out, dry it, and then begin to char.

How to Build

1. Leave the natural material in relatively large portions.
2. Place material to be charred loosely in a single-walled metal container.
3. Place a lid on the container to restrict airflow. This lid cannot be completely airtight.
4. Place the container inside the fire and cover it completely with fire.
5. Heat it for 15–20 minutes if the material is dry, 45–60 minutes if it's wet.
6. Remove the container from the fire but do not open until it is cool.

If you don't have a tin, you could also use a single-walled metal water bottle with a nesting cup, or a nesting cup with a lid, both of which would work just as well. You can place the material loosely in the empty water bottle and place the nesting cup over that to act as a lid, or you could place the material in the nesting cup if you have a lid for that. It's worth mentioning that if you don't have a source of water to resupply, emptying your water bottle to make char is likely not the best idea. This is another reason to have multiple options and multifunctional gear when possible.

Do not open it until it's cool to the touch. Introducing air back into the triangle when heat and fuel are present will cause combustion. Before you can add air back into the mix, heat must be taken out of the equation.

It's important to check and test your char while you still have a fire going. When cool, open it up and check it. It should be completely black and delicate, almost fragile to the touch. You'll also notice that it has shrunk to about a quarter of its original size. This is normal, so keep that in mind when loosely filling your container to char. Make sure that it will easily accept a spark and continue to smolder. If it hasn't turned completely black, it needs more charring, so close it up and put it back on the fire. If it is completely black but won't accept a spark, it's possible that the material you started with wasn't ideal, or that too much air was allowed in and it burned rather than charred.

To dispel a couple of myths out there: you cannot "overcook" charred material, but you can undercook it. And while it does need to be vented to allow gases to escape, it's a myth that you must make a small pinhole in the tin. I've actually had great success with much larger holes. A hinged tin already has enough ventilation through the hinges, and nesting cup lids have huge holes in them for straining liquids. The only thing I've ever added a hole to was a screw top tin that had no other way to vent. The heat will forcefully push the gases out, and while that's happening, any ventilation hole is a one-way street. As it cools, yes, air and humidity can get in. With the nesting cup, I just flip it over so the lid is down on the ground, and it seals it off plenty well enough.

Charred material will, of course, accept open flame, hot spark from a ferro rod, and solar. You can also use a variety of less-than-ideal ignition sources like sparks from a lighter that's out of fuel, or from small ferro rods like those you'd keep on necklaces, lanyards, and bracelets. You can even use the small magnifying glass on a compass to light it. Although I don't discuss percussion techniques in this book, char will readily accept the cooler spark of flint or steel, and even from a natural stone like chert or quartzite when scraped on the spine of a carbon steel knife or any other carbon steel source that you might find. The smoldering char can then be placed in a bird's nest tinder bundle and blown to flame. Any char that is lit that you're not using can be snuffed out by putting the lid back on your storage tin. If you're not already carrying char, you should always make some with your first fire to make every subsequent fire easier, and replenish it with natural materials when you get the chance.

CHAPTER 4
SHELTER CRAFT

Shelter Kit

Clothing is your first form of shelter, so the first part of putting together your shelter "kit" is choosing appropriate clothing for the environment you're going to be in (and the worst conditions you expect to face). Don't look at the weather forecast for a final say in what you pack. Plan for the worst conditions you could face in that environment for that season, regardless of the forecast. Weather can change on a dime.

After clothing, being able to build a shelter is next. You need **something to sleep under, something to sleep on, and something to sleep in**. Additionally, you need some **cordage** to "tie" it all together. Cordage comes in a variety of diameters and tensile strengths. Parachute cord, or "paracord," has the reputation of being the #1 cordage for survival, mainly because it was abundantly available to the military where a lot of "survival" training originated. There's also bank line or tarred mariners line, my preferred cordage. Keep in mind that most braided cordage can be broken down into separate strands. Pay close attention to the breaking strength for your needs. You may or may not choose to also carry **stakes** to secure your shelter. These can be made fairly easily if you don't want to carry them.

Recommended Shelter Kit

- Appropriate clothing
- Tarp, poncho, or tent
- Sleeping bag or blanket
- Sleeping mat
- Cordage
- Tent stakes (optional)

Principles of Shelter

How Body Heat Is Lost

Shelter is your first line of defense when you're exposed to the elements and need to maintain your core body temperature—normally 98.6 degrees Fahrenheit—despite the environmental conditions you may find yourself in.

Hyperthermia is when your body temperature is too high, and hypothermia is when your body temperature drops too low. Understanding how body heat is lost to the environment will let you know what you should keep doing in hot weather, and what to avoid in cold weather to stave off hypothermia. There are five main ways your body heat is lost to the environment:

- Conduction
- Convection
- Evaporation
- Radiation
- Respiration

CHAPTER 4: SHELTER CRAFT

Without getting too far into the weeds of thermodynamics, it's still useful to understand some basic concepts. The most important point is that heat normally moves along a temperature gradient from a warmer object or environment to a colder object or environment. In essence, there's no such thing as cold, there's only an absence of heat. Anything that is or feels "cold" is so because the heat has been transferred elsewhere, either to another object or the environment. In other words, if you feel cold, it's because you have lost (transferred) your body heat to a colder environment or object at a faster pace than it can be regenerated. If you're overheating, it's because you're absorbing heat from the environment (you are the "colder object" that the heat is being transferred to) at a faster rate than you can dissipate or release it.

Conduction is the transfer of heat from a warmer object to a colder object through direct contact. For example, if you touch a colder object with your hand, the heat from your hand will transfer to the colder object. This is the same thing that happens when you lie directly on the ground without any sort of insulation.

Convection is the transfer of heat to a moving current. Body heat is transferred to colder water or air as it flows across and around the body. Even a slight loss of heat in this transfer can overwhelm the body's ability to rewarm if the current is constantly flowing. For example, a cold gust of wind may sap your body heat for a moment, but it quickly regenerates and rewarms you even though you were chilled to the bone during the gust. With a more persistent wind, the heat transfer is continual, and your body cannot keep up.

Evaporation—more specifically "evaporative cooling"—is when a liquid absorbs enough heat to turn into a vapor. When it vaporizes and leaves the surface it was on, it takes the heat with it, leaving the surface cooler. This is essentially how sweating works to reduce your body temperature when you're too hot.

Radiation—in this context, "thermal radiation"—is the emission of heat (energy) by electromagnetic waves from all matter that is warmer than "absolute zero." Absolute zero is the lowest temperature that is theoretically possible. When you feel warmth on your face as the sun hits it, that's radiation. When you stand close to a fire and feel that heat, that's also radiation. Everything radiates heat, including your body.

Respiration is the process by which we breathe. Air from the environment is brought into our respiratory system, where gases are exchanged before we exhale the air back into the environment. When we breathe in cold air, our respiratory tract immediately begins warming the air through heat transfer. Once we exhale, our breath takes that warmth with it.

Clothing Choices: How to Get It Right

Stay Warm with This Checklist

Your best defense against the elements and your first form of shelter is your clothing system. It's extremely important to choose clothing that is appropriate for the environment you're in, and to plan for the worst conditions possible given the season.

Follow the **COLDER** Principle:

Clean: Keep your clothing as clean as possible so that it functions as designed. Clothing needs to breathe to not trap moisture against your body.

Overheating: Avoid overheating so that you don't sweat and open yourself up to other forms of heat loss.

Loose Layers: Easily adjust to the conditions by adding or removing layers as needed. Loose layers will allow for air space that can trap warmth and keep it near your body.

Dry: Keep your clothing dry. Wet clothing—whether it's from sweat, water, rain, or snow—will lose much of its insulating properties.

Examine: Look for rips, tears, holes, etc.

Repair: Mend clothing as needed so that it can perform as optimally as possible.

CHAPTER 4: SHELTER CRAFT

Many of these same principles apply to hot weather environments. You still want to keep your clothing clean and free of any damage. However, you may want to take advantage of evaporative cooling and not worry so much about sweating, which is your body's natural reaction to help keep you from overheating. Layering is still important so that you're ready for temperature changes that can occur. I have often found that in some desert environments, the temperature can drop as much as 30 degrees once the sun goes down. This makes for a cold night if you're not prepared.

Additional Considerations

Cover Up: A danger that is more prominent in hot environments but can also be a concern in the cold is protecting yourself from the sun's radiation. You may be tempted to wear shorts and a short-sleeved shirt when it's hot out. Something to consider is that those offer you little protection from sharp sticks, plants, and briars, and open you up to sunburn. I recommend long sleeves and pants whenever you go out into your wilderness of choice. Obviously, warmer layers for cold weather, and more airy, lightweight layers that still protect you from the sun for hot weather. Choosing lighter colors to help reflect some of the sun, rather than absorbing it like dark colors will, is also effective.

Get Some Shades: Protecting your eyes from the sun is another thing to consider in both hot and cold weather environments. And not only the sun—protect your eyes from the sun reflecting up from the ground, snow, or water, too. Sunglasses are something that should be considered when thinking about gearing up for the outdoors.

Cover Your Head: Head coverings are also important. In cold weather, much of your body heat can be lost through your head and neck, so it's always a good idea to wear a hat and scarf. In hot weather, head coverings are still important to protect from the sun beating down on you, but they should be lightweight and still allow heat to escape. For cold weather, gloves are important to have as well.

Material Choices

There's a large variety of material choices available on the market. Plant-based materials like cotton used to be the most prominent raw material for the industry, but that has since given way to synthetics like polyester. Less common are animal-based materials like wool. So which is the better choice? This is a complicated question. I'll try to answer it through the lens of an outdoorsman and keep it very general.

With all the advances in synthetic outdoor clothing and its seeming advantages, the fact is that most synthetics will melt to your skin if you're not careful around a fire. Granted, you'll sustain burn injuries no matter what you're wearing if you're not careful around a fire. But do you want to compound that injury by melting your clothing into your skin as well?

There's a saying that is often repeated in the survival industry: "**Cotton** kills." Well, no, it doesn't. Wet cotton, if you cannot get dry, can kill you in cold (or even cool) temperatures. Dry cotton is actually a very good thermal insulator. Wet cotton, on the other hand, is a terrible insulator and it dries quite slowly—a recipe for disaster in cold weather. However, those same properties may make it an excellent choice for hotter weather. It really comes down to knowing its properties and how they're going to affect you in any environment. Keep in mind that any fabric, cotton, or synthetic can kill you if it gets wet in a cold environment and you cannot get dry.

What about **wool**? It is often said that wool is the best choice because it retains a lot of its insulating value even when wet. The percentage that is often stated is in the ballpark of 70. It may be true that wool insulates better when wet, especially when compared to cotton or synthetics, but wet wool does not insulate better than dry wool by

CHAPTER 4: SHELTER CRAFT

any stretch of the imagination. Wet wool does not keep you warm, it just keeps you warmer than wet cotton or wet synthetics would. Think about it this way: if you're dressed appropriately to maintain your body temperature well in cold temperatures, stay comfortably warm when stationary, and comfortably cool without sweating when moving, imagine a 30 percent loss of the layering's effectiveness that makes that possible. Thirty percent is significant! You are going to be cold. Wool is still a better choice in cold weather because it will be less affected if it does get wet, but you should strive to keep your wool dry so that it can insulate at peak value.

Layered Clothing System

I recommend a layered approach to your clothing system. This layering system can be easily adjusted to weather conditions. It consists of four categories:

- Wicking layer
- Insulating layer
- Durable layer
- Wind/waterproof layer

The inner most **wicking layer** is in direct contact with your skin. It is typically lightweight, and its purpose is to wick moisture away from your skin to prevent heat loss from conduction and evaporation in cold weather. Synthetics like polyester, as well as animal fibers like wool, are good choices for this layer since they both wick well. Cotton is a poor choice for this layer in cold weather because it is highly absorbent.

The next layer, or layers, are **insulating layers**. These are typically thicker and heavier in weight than the wicking base layer. These layers are primarily meant to trap radiating body heat close to your body, as well as offer some protection from convection. Loft (insulating fabric) and the ability to create dead air space that can be warmed by (and kept close to) the body are key. This can be one or more layers, depending on the temperature and the insulation needed. Synthetics like polyester fleece work well, as do thicker wool layers. In colder temperatures, this could include a down or synthetic down puffy jacket, although those would typically be worn over the durable layer.

The **durable layer** is what most would consider your regular clothing, like your shirt and pants. They're not necessarily meant to be all that insulating, but they do offer some insulation and protection from convection. They are primarily meant to be durable and protect you and your insulating layers from sharp rocks, sticks, briars, and the like. Cotton duck canvas is a great choice for this, so long as you keep it dry. It is an exceptionally durable material that can take some abuse.

The **wind/waterproof layer** protects you and the rest of your clothing from elements like wind, water, and snow, and prevents them from becoming wet and losing their ability to effectively insulate. In addition, they prevent heat loss through convection by blocking the wind. Think of this as your shell layer. GORE-TEX® is an excellent fabric that's waterproof, windproof, and breathable. If you prefer a more traditional style, a tightly woven cotton duck canvas can be effective. The key is to block wind and water while maintaining breathability so that you don't trap moisture inside.

For warmer weather, your inner wicking layer and durable layer may be the same thing. Your insulating layer may be lightweight and carried in your backpack rather than worn, and only brought out at night when the temperature drops. Your shell layer may be nothing more than a lightweight rain jacket that you have ready to put on if needed.

Shelter Site Selection: The 5 Ws

When looking for a suitable location for a shelter, you should always keep the 5 Ws in mind. You want to be close to the first two but away from the last three.

Wood: Wood is an extremely valuable resource. You'll need it for fire—not just for temperature control but also for making water safe to drink and food safe to eat. Depending on what you have in your pack, you may need wood resources for shelter construction as well. When possible, you want to set up near an area that has sufficient wood resources.

Water: The need for hydration is both crucial and continual. You want to have your shelter reasonably close to a water source. You don't want to have to travel far and spend a lot of time and calories to resupply such a critical resource. Being near water is also beneficial for food prep. Often the wildlife in your area will be near or traveling to the water source for their own needs, and that could mean

CHAPTER 4: SHELTER CRAFT

opportunities for you to get some sustenance. The water source can also be valuable for personal hygiene.

You want to be near a water source, but not so close to it that you're in danger if it floods. Another thing to consider is that cold air sinks down to the lowest area, and those are often the same areas that contain water. Do not set up down in the low ground where the temperature is likely to be colder.

Wind: Wind will sap your body heat via convection rather quickly. If you're in a thick forested area, that will help shield you from the wind. Other terrain and micro-terrain may offer a natural wind break as well. You don't want to set up too low because of the cold air sinking, but you also don't want to set up on top of a ridge where the wind may be howling. A good rule of thumb is to look for something in between that is still close to your wood and water resources.

Widow-Makers: These are dead trees or tree limbs that can fall on you or your shelter and cause serious injury. You should avoid these whenever possible. If they cannot be avoided, but you have the right resources, you can take steps to mitigate the threat. It may be risky to use a saw to take down dead limbs, or throw a line over a dead limb and pull it down, but it also may be necessary to keep the limb from coming down if the wind picks up or a storm rolls in. Sometimes even without those things, a limb just finally decides to let go and falls. For dead standing trees, you may want to go ahead and fell them to add to your firewood supply. Again, the safest bet is to avoid them, but you may be able to take advantage of them if you must.

Wildlife: Avoid setting up on or near animal trails if possible. It's a good idea to know where they are for trapping purposes, but it's not a good idea to set up on one. Wildlife become more active at night and might bump into you at the worst time. This is another reason to not set up too close to your water source. The animals in that area may be moving to that resource at night as well. Some animals may be a welcome sight, while some others could be downright dangerous. Also, take a quick look around where you want to set up and look for "wigglers." Those are snakes, spiders, scorpions, ants, and other bugs. For the most part, snakes in North America will likely get out of your way unless you accidentally step on them or try to handle them. The others are more likely to be a problem. Nothing will ruin your night faster than setting up on a nest of fire ants that you didn't notice at first.

Basic Knots

Before getting into different shelter types, there are a number of knots you should know that could be used to build many of them. With so many to choose from, it can be difficult to know where to start when learning them. I've chosen a handful that I think are great for beginners because they often build on each other. The steps to tying them are familiar, and they have a lot of different applications. These knots are all that are needed for the Rapid Ridgeline and the tarp shelter configurations I mention later in the chapter.

Overhand

The **overhand knot** is a stopper/security knot.

1. Form a loop on the end of the line with the standing end (long end) on top of the working end (short end) as you are looking at it.
2. Continue routing the working end around the line and back through the loop that is formed.
3. Dress it down (tighten) to form the knot.

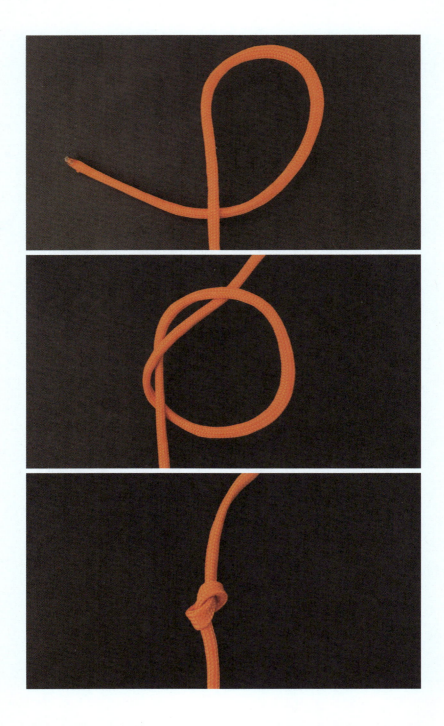

GRAY BEARDED GREEN BERET'S GUIDE TO SURVIVING THE WILD

Fisherman's Knot

The **fisherman's knot** can be used as a joining/bend knot to join two lengths of line together. It can also be used as a binding knot to tie the ends of a single line to form a loop. Both are tied in the same manner, the only distinction being whether you're tying two different lines together or two ends of the same line.

1. Place the ends of the line or lines opposing each other with an overlap.
2. Isolate one end and tie an overhand around the opposite line.
3. Repeat this on the other side. I find it's easiest to just flip the entire thing over when doing this.

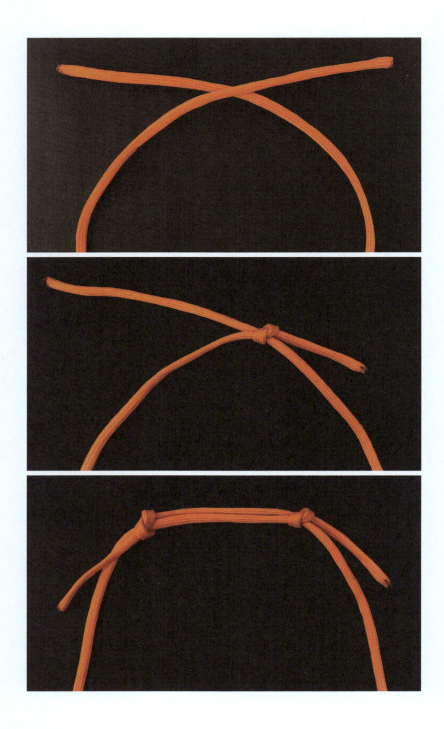

Pulling both lines will cause the overhand knots to dress down into each other and tighten the knot. Essentially, this knot is two opposing overhand stoppers.

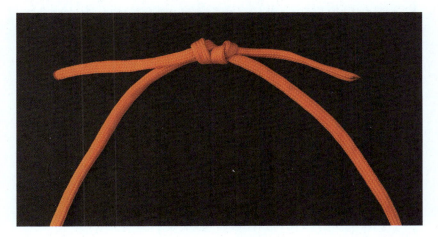

When tied as a binding knot to form a loop, the stoppers can also be pulled away from each other to reduce the size of the loop, earning it the nickname "necklace knot."

Overhand Slip

The **overhand slip** is a simple change to the baseline overhand knot that's used to form a **slip knot**. This is most useful because it's the beginning of several other knots.

1. Leave yourself plenty of length on the working end of the line.
2. Form a loop just like you would when tying a simple overhand.
3. Form a bight from the standing end and route that up through the loop.
4. Dress it down slightly.

GRAY BEARDED GREEN BERET'S GUIDE TO SURVIVING THE WILD

You'll notice that you have a clean side (slip side) to the right, and a dirty side (where the knot is forming) to the left as you are looking at it. Pay attention to where this dirty side ends up, as it will be important for other knots. This is the "tractor" or "mule" that actually holds tension.

Bowline

The **bowline knot** is an extremely useful knot that has several variations and applications. There are other ways to tie it, but I teach it this way because the steps to tying the previous knots are familiar and can also apply to tying the bowline.

1. Start with an overhand slip with the "dirty" side left, clean side right as you are looking at it.

2. Route the working end through the bight, from front (toward your chest) to back (away from you), and fold it back on itself.

3. Pinch and hold the newly formed bight you just made.

4. Continue holding the bight and gently pull tension on the standing end to dress the knot.

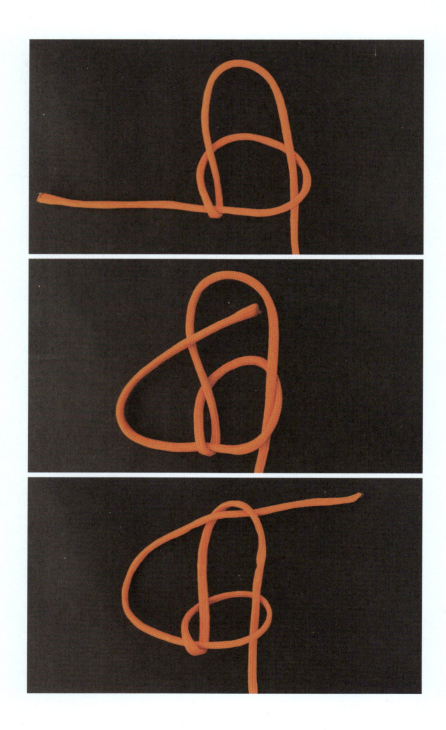

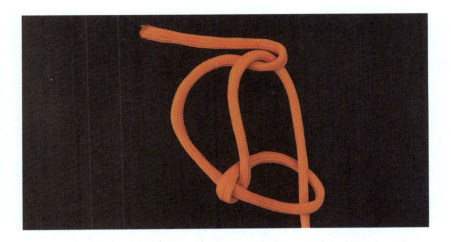

You should have a fixed loop on the end of the line that's large enough to incorporate whatever it is you want to place in the loop. The tail formed by the working end should be to the inside of the loop, not the outside. The standing end should be passing through a small, teardrop-shaped bight with a cross-locking bar (perpendicular) directly above it locking it all down. If properly dressed, the teardrop-shaped bight has not been pulled to the back of the knot, which will negatively affect the tension and function of the knot. The back of the knot looks roughly like a triangle.

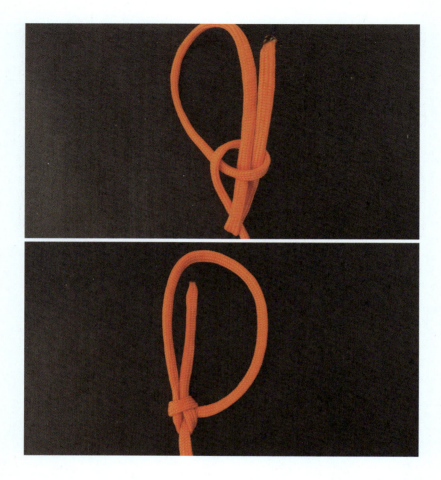

Trucker's Hitch

I categorize the **trucker's hitch** as a specialty knot, because it is a group of knots that work together to form a specific function. In this case, that function is acting as an anchor that provides a mechanical advantage when tightening a line. The very baseline trucker's hitch is nothing more than a slip knot of some form used to create a loop. There are several different knots that can be used to create this.

The standing end of the line needs to be fixed to an anchor point. Let's call that the "far-side anchor," since the trucker's hitch will be tied on the anchor nearest to us, or the "near-side anchor." The rest of these instructions assume that you have the opposite end securely attached to the far-side anchor. Decide where you want the trucker's hitch to be tied, keeping in mind the amount of stretch the line you're using has. Once you begin pulling tension on this, that stretch is going to be removed before everything becomes tight.

1. Begin with an overhand slip. The dirty side (mule) needs to be toward the far-side anchor.

2. Route the working end around the near-side anchor and back through the loop.

3. Tighten the line by pulling back toward the near-side anchor to the desired tension.

4. While holding tension, secure with two half hitches slid tightly against the loop.

Girth Hitch (Lark's Head)

The **girth hitch** is an anchor knot that can be tied on the end of the line, but is rarely used in this context. More often than not, you'll be tying this in the middle of the line or with a premade loop.

1. Place one end of the loop over the desired anchor to form a "window."
2. Route the tails (or the rest of the loop) around the anchor and through the window.

3. Dress the knot down until you have the two parallel wraps with the cross-locking bar.

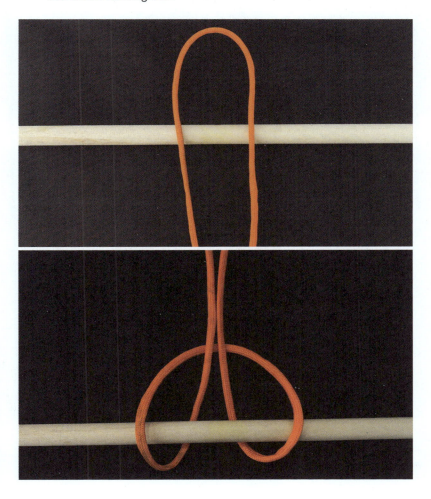

CHAPTER 4: SHELTER CRAFT

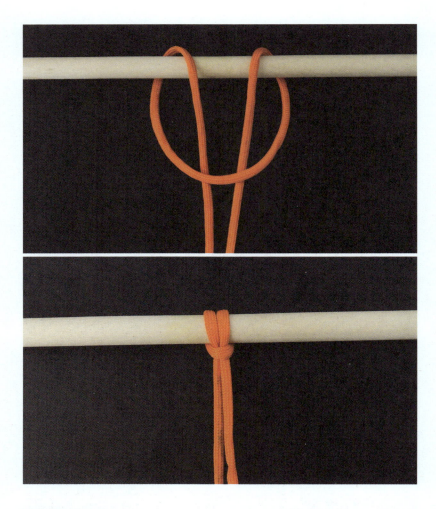

Prusik Knot

Once you know how to tie a girth hitch, tying the **Prusik knot** is easy. Think of it as a girth hitch with additional turns. It uses friction to hold tension on the line that it's tied to. For best results, the Prusik should be used to tie a smaller-diameter line onto a larger-diameter line. When this is not possible, additional wraps that provide more friction can often make up for it. It can be tied on the end of a line, middle of a line, or with a premade loop. In this context, we will be tying it with the middle of the line, which would be the same technique as using a premade loop.

Tying the Prusik using a premade loop is just as simple as tying the girth hitch with the same. The only difference is passing it thorough the additional times to create the desired number of wraps.

1. Place one end of the loop over the desired anchor to form a "window."
2. Route the rest of the loop around the anchor and through the window.
3. Split the first wraps so they are to the outside.
4. Route the next wraps toward the inside of those.
5. Continue this until you have the desired number of wraps.
6. Dress the knot down.

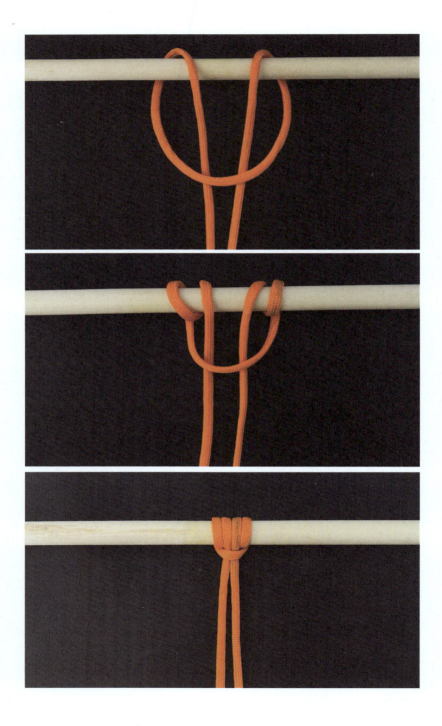

GRAY BEARDED GREEN BERET'S GUIDE TO SURVIVING THE WILD

Remember that the wraps should go from outside to inside, and the lines coming out from under the locking bar last should be in the center.

The Prusik knot is very simple to use. Once fixed to an anchor and weighted, the wraps will tighten around the anchor and hold the tension. This can easily be released by "unlocking" the locking bar with your thumb and repositioning the Prusik wherever needed.

Types of Shelter

Natural Shelter

Finding shelter may not always require constructing anything. Whenever possible, look for natural shelter options that can either eliminate your need to construct something or reduce the amount of work you must do (and therefore reduce the water and calorie loss). If you can find even a partial solution that you can add a little work to make it adequate, that's something you should take advantage of. Some examples of natural shelters are rock outcroppings, as well as downed or hollowed out trees.

CHAPTER 4: SHELTER CRAFT

A couple of things to think about when you locate natural shelter:

- **Do a survey:** Whatever rock outcropping you find has likely been there for an awfully long time. It has also been subject to the environment for that entire time. You don't have any way of knowing the state that it's in when you come upon it. Look for and remove any loose rocks that you can manage. Look for any large flakes above you that could shear off at any time, or large cracks where the whole thing could drop. All of these should be considered widow-makers.

- **Use your senses:** Look, listen, and smell the area to determine if another animal is already using that location for shelter.
- **Rethink fire:** Be incredibly careful about having a fire under the outcropping and heating the rock up. Rock is affected by temperature change, and your fire could be the thing that causes something to break free.

It's rare to find a tree that's perfectly suitable for a shelter, but they can often offer that partial solution. Again, you want to determine if some form of wildlife or wiggler is already using that shelter before you decide to make it your own.

CHAPTER 4: SHELTER CRAFT

The Rapid Ridgeline

The **Rapid Ridgeline** is the baseline for a few different tarp shelter configurations that you should know at the basic level. It's very simple to construct and should be tied and coiled before it ever goes in your pack. That way, when you pull it out of your pack to use, it will be tangle-free and ready to go.

The ridgeline starts with a 25- to 30-foot section of cordage. I prefer paracord for this application because I want it to be a larger diameter than the adjustable loops that are also part of this system. Those are made with #36 bank line (tarred mariners line).

First, make the adjustable loops. Take a 10–12-inch piece of #36 bank line and use a fisherman's knot to make a loop. You want the loops to be about 6–8 inches when complete. You'll need at least two of these. I recommend a third because it gives you an extra loop to use for other purposes, like hanging a light at night.

For the paracord ridgeline, tie a bowline on one end. It helps to stretch the line tight to attach the adjustable loops, so anchoring it between two points may help. To attach the loops, use a Prusik knot. Four wraps are usually plenty, but you can use six if you prefer. Slide all three loops close to the end with the bowline and take down the ridgeline so that you can coil it.

CHAPTER 4: SHELTER CRAFT

You want to **coil the Rapid Ridgeline** in such a way that it's easy to deploy and tangle-free when you need to build a shelter. To do this:

1. Open your hand wide by spreading your fingers and thumb. Place the end with the bowline between your thumb and index finger so that it lays on the back of your hand out of the way.

2. Run the line in a figure-8 manner around your pinky and thumb a few times.

3. Slide the three adjustable loops up so that they can be laid on the backside of your hand along with the bowline. This will keep them out of the way for the rest of the coiling process and should give you enough space to pull the first few coils out to go around a tree for an anchor without having to move the loops.

4. Continue coiling in a figure-8 manner until you're down to about the last four feet of cordage.

187

CHAPTER 4: SHELTER CRAFT

5. Once you have it coiled on your hand, slide the thumb on your opposite hand under the coils and slide the whole bundle off, maintaining control so that it does not come unraveled.

6. Using the tail of the cordage, wrap around the coils to capture them, stacking each wrap next to the other. When you get down to the last couple of wraps, use half hitches so that they stay secure. Bundling it like this prevents tangling when it's bouncing around in your pack, so it'll be ready to go when you need it. You won't be fumbling around with a knotted mess.

To **set up the Rapid Ridgeline**, simply locate two trees or other anchor points that are a suitable distance apart and choose one for the initial anchor point.

Hold the bundle in one hand and insert the thumb of the other into the bowline loop. Pull out an arm's length or more, enough to go around this first anchor. The bowline side is your working end, and the bundle is your standing end.

Place the bundle through the bowline loop to create a running bowline and tighten that against the anchor. Ensure that the Prusik loops are free to slide between anchor points and not inside the running bowline against the anchor.

Holding the bundle in your hand, walk over to the second anchor and the line will feed out easily. Once at the second anchor, tie a trucker's hitch to tighten and secure the ridgeline. This basic method of tying the ridgeline can be improved with a couple of simple modifications.

One improvement is to use a toggled running bowline on the initial anchor. This will give you a quick release on that anchor, rather than having to pull it all back through the loop of the bowline. Just ensure that your Prusik loops are on the correct side of the toggle so that they can still be used and are not trapped on the initial anchor side of the toggle.

CHAPTER 4: SHELTER CRAFT

If you've tied the trucker's hitch before, you'll notice that once you pull tension on the line, it wants to loosen. This can be a problem, as you still need to secure it with half hitches to hold the tension. I learned a particularly useful modification during Robin Sage, which is the Unconventional Warfare phase of Special Forces training. We used the trucker's hitch when rigging resupply packages to be dropped from aircraft by parachute. As you can imagine, the rigging must be extremely tight so that the bundle can survive both the drop and the landing to get there in one piece. Instead of going through the initial loop formed by the overhand slip one time and trying to hold the tension with your fingers, go through the loop a second time, creating a **round turn**. This round turn will roll over and bite down on itself under tension, and will hold itself while you further secure it with the half hitches.

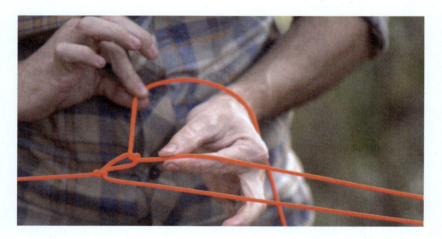

The last modification to the base trucker's hitch that I will recommend is to tie the second half hitch that you're using to secure the round turn on a bight. This bight serves two purposes. The first is to turn it into a quick release for easier take down and recovery of the cordage. The second is to have a useable loop to incorporate into the first grommet (the hole in corners of the tarp, used for tying it up) of your tarp for your shelter. It's important to pay close attention to where you want the first corner of the tarp when you're tying the trucker's hitch so that this bight is in the proper location on the ridgeline and your tarp coverage ends up where you want it to be.

CHAPTER 4: SHELTER CRAFT

Something to Sleep Under

Something to sleep under can be anything that provides overhead cover and protects you from the elements. This can be a tarp, poncho, emergency blanket, rain fly, or an entire tent if you choose. The type of tarp you choose depends largely on the environment and the season of the year. In warmer climates and seasons, you can easily get away with a simple, straight-forward tarp or poncho. In colder environments and seasons, a tarp that also has reflective qualities is a better choice. Many come with a normal side and a reflective side. These are arguably the best choice for all environments. During cooler weather, the reflective side can be oriented to the inside of the shelter to reflect radiated body heat and heat from the fire back to you. In hot weather, they can be reversed so that the reflective side is to the outside of the shelter. This will reflect radiant heat from the sun away from you and your shelter, rather than absorbing it and transferring it to the inside of the shelter.

There are hundreds of different configurations that you could make using a tarp or a poncho for overhead cover. I'm going to narrow that list down to three main configurations—shapes, if you will—that'll work to cover most conditions. Those are the Lean-To, A-Frame, and the Diamond. The main difference between the three, other than the final shape, is the number of sides that are protected from the elements like wind, rain, and snow. Since they all use the same resources to build, the configuration you choose is largely based on the environmental conditions you are experiencing.

Lean-To

The **lean-to** offers protection on one side. Think of it primarily as a warm-weather shelter. This configuration is great for shade and will keep you reasonably dry in warm weather if a quick shower rolls through. It can also be used to block wind from a particular direction if desired. The benefits of this shelter in warmer weather are that it traps the least amount of body heat inside, and it only blocks a beneficial convective breeze on one side. Those same properties are why this shelter is a poor choice in colder weather.

First, establish the ridgeline at the desired height. As a rule of thumb, shelters that are lower to the ground are easier to heat, and that includes the trapping of body heat. Higher shelters allow more heat out and more breeze in. You can even go so far as to "fly" your tarp. Flying your tarp means that none of the sides or corners are in contact with the ground. In other words, none of the sides are completely closed off. This still provides overhead protection but maximizes the escape of body heat and allows you to take advantage of cooler convective breezes in warm weather. Choose the height of your shelter by the desired microclimate you are trying to create.

Once the ridgeline is established, place the bight formed by the half hitch on a bight that is securing your trucker's hitch through the top corner grommet of your tarp. Place a toggle or stake through that bight and pull the toggle tight against the grommet by pulling the standing end of the half hitch on a bight. This will secure the corner of the tarp in place and prevent the quick release from being pulled through.

Next, place one of the Prusik loops through the other top corner grommet of the tarp and toggle it as well. The tarp is tightened along the ridgeline by sliding the Prusik loop toward the anchor point. Tension on the Prusik loop holds it in place.

CHAPTER 4: SHELTER CRAFT

For the bottom corners of the tarp, you can use a girth hitch to secure additional loops in the grommets. They're made by using the fisherman's knot, just like how you made the loops for the Prusiks. These can be prepared ahead of time and left in place. Simply place a stake inside the loop and pull tension. Driving the stake into the ground at a 45-degree angle away from the actual tension will hold best. Repeat this on the other side and your lean-to is complete.

If you want to fly this tarp configuration in warmer weather, rather than staking its bottom corners to the ground, you would tie them higher on a pole or anchor so that the backside is open as well.

A-Frame

An **A-frame** shelter will protect you on two sides, so it offers more protection from the elements. You may choose to use this configuration when it's still a little warmer outside but raining more persistently or heavily. It's still open on two sides, so it still lets some body heat escape and allows for good airflow to take advantage of convective breezes.

It's based on the same ridgeline, except the center of the tarp runs along the ridgeline rather than the top corner or top edge. How you secure it to the ridgeline depends largely on where the grommets in your tarp are. If you have grommets centered on your tarp, you can toggle the grommets to the ridgeline in much the same way as you did before. In this case, you should run the tarp under the ridgeline to prevent water from running down the ridgeline and into your shelter.

If you don't have center grommets, you can simply drape the tarp over the ridgeline and center it. I know what you're thinking: placing the tarp over the ridgeline means that water can now run along the ridgeline and into the shelter. This is true. To prevent this, simply hang a couple of drip lines on either side of the tarp. The water will run down to those drip lines and be directed to the ground rather than to inside your shelter. These drip lines can be as simple as small pieces of bank line secured to the ridgeline with any anchor knot you choose.

Next, stake out the four corners of the tarp to complete the shelter. It's best to choose a corner and stake it off in the desired location. After that, move to the opposite side so that you're on the opposing corner. Pull tension against the opposite corner before staking it off. This will keep it even on the ridgeline rather than pulling to one side or the other. Now tighten the other two corners in this same manner. Remember that staking it directly to the ground will close off two sides. If you want to "fly it" instead, tie the corners off higher on a pole or other anchor.

Diamond

The **diamond**, also known as a plow point or wedge, offers protection on three sides. Think of it primarily as a cold-weather shelter. The three-sided protection traps the most heat and blocks more wind than the others.

This configuration is set up similarly to the lean-to. Secure and toggle the top (front) corner to the bight formed by that second half hitch quick release on the ridgeline. Next, go to the opposite corner, which will be the back corner of your shelter. Pull tension against the top corner that's secured to the ridgeline and stake it off. You may need to raise your ridgeline height to allow for more room inside the shelter. With the front and back corners secured, pull tension to each side of the shelter and stake them down. This will give you a single opening in the front, and the other three sides will be closed off. The diamond is typically not something you'd want to "fly," since it's primarily a cold-weather shelter that's meant to trap heat and maximize protection from the elements.

Something to Sleep On

Something to sleep on can be any kind of mattress pad, hammock, or browse bed that keeps you up off the ground and prevents heat loss from conduction. You never want to lie directly on the ground. This is typically accomplished by creating (or carrying) some sort of insulated mat to lie on.

This bedding or mat can be as simple as a pile of leaves or conifer boughs. It's important that this pile be at least 4 inches thick once compressed. This often means starting with a pile that's upwards of 18 inches thick before lying down on it. Of course, how much it compresses depends on the material you're using. The other challenging part of using material like duff (dried leaves and needles from the forest floor) is collecting it, transporting it to your shelter, and keeping it in one place under you once you get it there. You can build short walls out of stones or logs to define the bedding outline and help keep the duff in place. This could be considered a smaller-scale "leaf crib." If conifer boughs are the more prevalent resource in your area, you can construct a "browse bed" or "bough bed." Neither of these techniques require anything other than natural resources.

To construct the bough bed:

1. Lay boughs in a parallel manner next to each other for the full length of your body.
2. The next layer should be laid perpendicular to the first, creating a crosshatch pattern.
3. Continue alternating each layer as you add more boughs.
4. Ensure that the final layer is a "short run," meaning that it's perpendicular to the length of your body rather than parallel to it. If you end on a "long run," it tends to separate when you lie on it.

Crosshatching in this manner does a few things. First, it creates space between you and the ground. Second, that space also includes "dead airspace" that will be warmed by the body and trapped in the bedding. Third, it provides some comfort due to the springiness of the boughs. Lastly, that crisscross pattern provides great structure that reduces the total amount of boughs you need to get up off the ground.

CHAPTER 4: SHELTER CRAFT

Another technique that works well if you have the resources available is using some sort of bag or bags to build what is called a "browse mattress" or "duff mattress." This is made by stuffing something like a trash bag or contractor bag with duff to create an improvised mattress to lie on and protect you from the ground. Most adults will need more than one bag, so carrying two is a good idea. The bags also solve the challenge of transporting the duff if needed. You can also use a canvas sleeve meant specifically for this purpose.

You may find it best to build your bedding first and then build the shelter around that. This will prevent you from making too small a shelter for the size bed you need. The other benefit is that the shelter is not in your way as you build the bedding. It's less of a problem when using a tarp or poncho, since the size of the poncho and the configuration you use are really going to determine the final size of your shelter. But it's often easier to build the bedding first without having to duck under or go inside your shelter to construct the bed after the fact.

Something to Sleep In

Something to sleep in could be a sleeping bag or blanket that you can use to insulate you. These will trap body heat and help keep you warm and insulated inside your shelter. Once you have your shelter and bedding built, crawl inside and get some good rest. The value of that rest cannot be overstated. It's important for your overall health and well-being, morale, and cognitive function.

CHAPTER 4: SHELTER CRAFT

CHAPTER 5

WATER PROCUREMENT

Water Kit

For your water kit, all you really need are ways to gather it, store it, and make it safe to drink. Typically, a container like a water bottle is used for holding the water, and there are several ways it could be made safe to drink. You can use commercial filters, chemical treatments, or thermal disinfection through boiling.

I use a commercial filter quite often, but hardly ever chemically disinfect it. The number of tablets or amount of the chemical I can carry is pretty limited. They often require a long contact time—that is, how long you must wait after treating the water for it to be safe to consume—in order to be effective. And they tend to leave a taste in the water I don't care for. I'm going to need a fire for so many other things, so I prefer to just use that same fire to boil my water if I didn't use a commercial filter at the source.

I prefer a bottle over a bladder, and I use a single-walled stainless steel water bottle instead of a plastic one. The stainless steel bottle can be placed in the fire to thermally disinfect the water, which is something I can't do with a bladder or plastic bottle. The bladders are also a bit fragile for my taste—I have a pile of them that have holes or leaky valves. Bottles are simple. I can also use a bottle with a nesting cup and lid to give me a few additional options to charr material for my fires.

Sometimes I'll add a cotton bandana or shemagh to this kit. It has a number of uses, one of which is being a pre-filter for my water container when I'm filling it up. Simply place the shemagh over the opening of the container you're using to collect water to filter out debris.

Recommended Water Kit

- 32-ounce, single-walled, stainless steel water bottle
- Stainless steel nesting cup with lid
- Cotton bandana or shemagh
- Commercial filter (optional) like Grayl Geopress or the Sawyer Mini
- Clear plastic sheets (optional for applicable techniques)
- Rubber tubing (if applicable)

Stay Hydrated, My Friends

The average adult will need to consume about one half-gallon (64 ounces/1.89 liters) of water per day to remain hydrated. This need will increase if you're in a hot environment or physically exerting yourself (and if you're in the wilderness, you likely will be). Extremely hot and dry environments like the desert may increase your daily need up to as much as 1–1.5 gallons. Sickness and injury are also factors that will increase your hydration needs. Another thing to consider: if you do have a food source, you'll require additional water to digest it. You should be careful consuming food if you don't have adequate water. Dehydration is more of a threat in the short-term than starvation.

You may not always be able to procure enough water, however, so how little water can you get away with? It really depends on your environment, situation, and activity level. At a bare minimum, if you were to limit activity and stay in the shade or in as cool an area as possible, you might be able to prevent severe dehydration for up to one week on just 1,000 mL (about 4½ cups) per day, assuming there are no other factors contributing to a more rapid loss of water. What that means is, even if you lie around resting all day in the shade of your shelter, you'll dehydrate within a week if you don't consume at least the equivalent of one 32-ounce bottle of water per day. Water truly is life.

A good habit to get into is to always carry at least a full day's worth of water, even in areas with abundant freshwater resources. It's a similar principle to what you learned about collecting fire tinder as you find it. You don't know what resources will be available in an area you haven't been to yet; all you know is what's available now as you find it. Be prepared first, then be prepared to find yourself completely unprepared.

Once you find the next water resource, depending on how far away it was from your last spot and what method you're using to make it safe to drink, you should consider drinking the container of water you already have and refilling it before moving on. This is what I call "filling up the internal canteen." Think of your stomach as another water container. In hot and dry weather where freshwater resources are less abundant, it becomes even more important to hydrate as much as possible at the source, and to leave the source with all your containers full.

Signs and Symptoms of Dehydration

The very first symptom you'll likely experience as you become dehydrated is, predictably, thirst. That's your body's way of telling you that you need to consume more water, and it should not be ignored. It may be coupled with having a dry mouth or lips, but it'll only get worse from there. You may also feel tired, sluggish, and dizzy. Some people may experience painful symptoms like a headache or muscle cramps. Muscle cramps could also be a symptom of heat cramps, which is a an injury that could easily progress to heat exhaustion and heat stroke if not addressed.

Another symptom to look for is the frequency and color of your urine. You'll likely urinate less when you're dehydrated, and when you do it will typically be a darker color than normal. When properly hydrated, your urine should be clear to very lightly colored. Dark yellow to amber-colored urine is a sign of dehydration.

It should be noted that it is possible to over-hydrate, especially with a lack of food—more specifically, the lack of salt (sodium) in that food. You need salt to regulate the water in your body. If you drink too much water without bringing in enough salt, you take the chance of diluting that critical electrolyte to the point that your body can no longer regulate your water intake, resulting in a condition called hyponatremia. This is an extremely dangerous condition that can result in a coma or even death.

Waterborne Pathogens: Not Your Friends

The list of potential waterborne pathogens is extremely long and includes various protozoans, bacteria, parasites, and viruses. In addition to that, in some areas you may need to worry about chemicals and heavy metals. These are microscopic, so it's not possible to determine with the naked eye if a pathogen is or is not in the water source you find. Suffice to say, you should assume all water is contaminated and take the necessary steps to make it safe to drink before consuming it. Just because the water looks clean and clear doesn't mean it is. Vomiting, diarrhea, and fever will all put you at an increased risk for severe dehydration. This is the opposite of what you're trying to do by drinking the water to begin with.

You should always take steps to make water safe to drink if you have the means to do so. If you don't have those means, should you pass up the water resource and not drink it? That's a personal choice that you must make for yourself based on your situation at the time. If waterborne pathogens are indeed in the water, and you consume enough of them that your immune system cannot successfully fight them, you'll likely be sick twenty-four to forty-eight hours after consumption. That sickness will likely result in vomiting and diarrhea, which will make your situation worse once it starts. With that said, how dehydrated are you? If you're severely dehydrated, you could die from that within the day. Is it reasonable to expect that you could make your way out and get home or to seek medical care before that sickness sets in and becomes a problem? Those are some of the things you should consider based on your situation. I personally would not choose dying of dehydration today to prevent my possibly being sick tomorrow.

Procurement: How to Get Your Hands on the Good Stuff

One of the easiest methods of procuring water in abundance is finding a freshwater source. This can be a spring; a stream, like a creek or river; or a pool of water, like a pond or lake. Spring water, as the name suggests, springs up from the ground or through a rock crevice, and can often be safe to drink at the source. It's less likely that the water has been exposed to animal feces or urine, which is a common cause of contamination. This does not mean that it's positively safe to drink, so play it safe. Fall back on the assumption that all water is contaminated and take steps to make it safe to drink when possible.

Water that's flowing is better than water that's stagnant. However, since you're always under the assumption that all water is contaminated and you plan to filter or disinfect it in some way, this is of little concern. You can make either safe to drink. Flowing water often has more natural filtration happening with it flowing through rocks and vegetation as it meanders through the wilds. There's a good chance that it will be cleaner and clearer from the start than a stagnant pool will be, with some exceptions. Again, looking clean and clear is not an indicator that it's safe to drink, but it does usually result in a more palatable experience once the water has been made safe to drink.

How to Find Water

How do you find these freshwater sources? Depending on your environment, a great indicator may be to **look at the terrain and vegetation**. As rainwater falls, it hits the highest point and follows the path of least resistance downhill on its way to the ocean. Traveling downhill is often a good tactic when looking for water. Over time, erosion occurs and cuts the terrain into noticeable "draws" and "valleys," so being able to read that terrain is an extremely valuable skill. We'll discuss terrain features in more detail during chapter 8.

As far as vegetation, plants that grow around water more often are called "water indicators." **Willows, cottonwoods, and basswoods** are great examples. **Cattail** will also often be growing near ponds and pools of water. Learning how to recognize those from a distance can often narrow down your search as well. As a rule, wet areas will often be greener and denser than surrounding areas, since the plants and trees have more water available. The next time you're out in the wilds of your choice, look at the areas around water sources and make a mental note of the terrain both surrounding and leading to them. Also, make a mental note of the unique vegetation and trees around those water resources, build familiarity, and use it to find other water resources later.

Willow

Cottonwood

CHAPTER 5: WATER PROCUREMENT

Basswood

Another key indicator to look for is **animal trails**. All animals need water as well, so they're looking for and using the same sources. Animals are creatures of habit and will often travel using the path of least resistance, so it doesn't take long for them to create a distinguishable trail. The water source is usually a fixed location, with animals from all around the area making their way to it to get a drink. Eventually, trails will begin to converge as they get closer to the water source. When two trails do come together, the point of that V-shaped trail intersection is pointing in the direction of the common resource. Of course, not all trails lead to water, and that common resource could be something else. You'll often have to use more than one natural indicator. If you find a trail that leads downhill, and that trail begins to converge with another one, you're probably onto something.

Freshwater sources may be less abundant in some areas, forcing you to be more creative about finding water. Often, this can be in the form of **rainwater**. If you keep your eyes peeled, you may find a puddle of fresh rainwater available on the ground, in a small concavity in a rock, or possibly even in a concavity in a tree. These may not supply an abundance of water, but they shouldn't be overlooked.

If you have the resources, you can even **build a "rain catch"** to capture rainwater as it falls. You can capture rain in containers, or use a sheet of material like plastic, a tarp, or a poncho. You could dig a hole or trench and line that with the sheet. That could be dug into the ground or carved out of something like a dead log. Anything that

CHAPTER 5: WATER PROCUREMENT

will not leak will capture water. When using a container with a small opening, you can collect more water if you use something like a sheet or bandana to capture it and funnel it into the container. This can also be a function of your shelter during a rainstorm—you can usually catch some of the water as it runs off.

In even more extreme cases, you may have to resort to **dew collection** to find naturally occurring water. When the temperature drops at night, moisture from the air condenses and collects on the grass and leaves. It can be collected with an absorbent material like cotton.

GRAY BEARDED GREEN BERET'S GUIDE TO SURVIVING THE WILD

Vine Water

Water vines are another resource you may be able to find. You need to get somewhat familiar with them to recognize them easily, since there are several vines that could be toxic. The vine from the **wild grape** is a good example of what to look for to access some naturally occurring water. They're rooted in the ground, where they pull moisture to leaves that are often tangled up in the tops of trees. There are two ways you can approach this. One: if you're on the move and find one, you can get a small drink from it as you search for a more significant source of water. When it comes to staying hydrated as best you can, it all counts.

The second way takes more time but can be useful when you're in a fixed location, or if the vines are near your shelter. To take a quick drink, start by cutting the vine with a saw or a knife toward the root of the vine. Don't worry if water isn't exactly gushing out from this cut. It's possible for the vine to be completely dry, but even if it isn't, you won't usually get more than a drip or two because of the capillary action that's happening. This is like holding your thumb against one end of a straw and holding liquid inside it. That liquid is trapped until you release your thumb and open both ends of the straw. The same thing applies to the vine: once you make your second cut several inches higher on the vine (toward the top), it releases that capillary

CHAPTER 5: WATER PROCUREMENT

action and the water that was contained in that section of the vine will flow out. Larger sections of vine will, of course, hold more water. This water does not need to be treated and will also contain trace minerals that are a bit of a bonus.

GRAY BEARDED GREEN BERET'S GUIDE TO SURVIVING THE WILD

This method takes longer but allows you to access more water with the vine. You'll need a container to capture the water.

1. Find a section that's bent a couple of feet up off the ground. Scrape bark off the outside of the section you want to access.

2. Cut a V-notch into the vine to release and channel the water into your container. Some vines can drip water for several hours. Over time, you'll notice that the vine will start to seal itself back off to heal the wound. It will start to turn into a sort of sticky gelatin and shut off the flow of water.

The water in the container should still be good to drink, and this is one exception where there's usually no real need to disinfect it. If you have a lot of these in the area, they can be a sustainable way of maintaining at least a base level of hydration.

Other Sources

On the surface, some areas may seem like they have no water at all. You may hit what appears to be a dry stream bed and have to follow it downstream (downhill) until you find a place where it's either flowing again or, at the very least, trapped in small pools that you can access. However, sometimes looks can be deceiving. There may very well be ground water just below the surface. To access it, you can use a technique called a **seepage basin**. These are sometimes referred to as a sip/seep well or coyote well.

1. Look for sandy areas or a bend in a stream bed, preferably in an area that is shaded.

2. Dig a hole straight down using a digging stick, or your hands if it's soft enough. A lot of times, you'll find water within the first two to three feet. This just depends on where the water table is in that area.

3. Once you find the water, sit back and let it fill the hole you just dug. Although this is technically ground water and some natural filtration has occurred, that doesn't necessarily mean

it's safe to drink as is. It will likely be quite turbid, or cloudy and dirty with sediment.

4. Allow time for the sediment to settle, leaving it clearer and more palatable. The safest bet is still to take steps to disinfect it before drinking, if possible.

This same technique is often used in swampy areas to leverage some natural filtration for particularly nasty water. You can dig a seepage basin on higher ground, about three feet from the edge of the water, and allow that water to be pulled into the basin. It will offer some natural filtration leading to better palatability, but it won't necessarily make it safe to drink. This method can be used on the edge of a pond or lake as well. If you're on a beach, you can dig what is called a "beach well" to access fresh water. Essentially, this is a seepage basin that is dug behind the first line of sand dunes rather than three feet from the edge of the water. If the water in the basin is still salty, simply move farther back.

Now that you know where to find it, what's the best way to gather it? When possible, gather it from a portion of the stream that is fast moving. Again, if not possible, gather it anyway. It's good practice to travel upstream for a bit to look at what may be in the water. That doesn't really have to be more than 75–100 meters. The last thing you want to do is fill up your water when there's a dead animal laying across the stream just a few yards around the corner. You may want to pre-filter with something like a bandana over your bottle to prevent large particles from getting into your bottle.

Tip: When filling from a flowing stream, it's best to face the mouth of your bottle downstream so that large particles, sticks, and leaves can flow around the bottle and go on by rather than into your container, especially if you aren't using a pre-filter. Once it's filled, use your treatment of choice to make it safe to drink. When collecting from a source like a pond or a lake that isn't flowing, it's best to try and collect from only the top few inches of that body of water. This will usually keep you above the sediment that has settled in the water. Another potential advantage is that the sun and its UV rays do have some disinfecting capabilities, but they only penetrate so deep. You're not going to rely on that to make it safe to drink, it just makes it a bit cleaner from the start.

CHAPTER 5: WATER PROCUREMENT

Clarification and Pre-Filtering

Water that could be described as cloudy or dirty is considered "turbid." Clarification is the removal of sediment and solid particles in water to make it—you guessed it—clear. Turbidity reduces the effectiveness of some disinfection techniques, so clarification is often used as a pre-treatment. This can be as simple as giving the sediment time to settle to the bottom and decanting the clearer water from the top. Placing something like a cotton bandana over your water bottle to pre-filter some of the particles as you fill the bottle up is a useful method as well.

Another example of this is making an improvised "**survival filter.**" This is commonly depicted as a water bottle stuffed with various natural mediums like grass, sand, and ground up coals from the fire, or as a large tripod with bandanas suspended on three different levels containing natural materials that are meant to filter the water. It's important to understand that these are not capable of mechanically filtering the water at a small enough micron level to filter out most waterborne pathogens. It's also important to note that ground up burnt coals from a fire are not the same as activated charcoal (carbon). While these will have some adsorptive qualities, they don't have the same surface area as activated charcoal and cannot adsorb as effectively, especially with the limited contact time as the water flows by.

It's worth mentioning again that none of these techniques are capable of making water safe to drink and should be considered steps to increase the clarity of the water *before* making it safe to drink. If you've seen someone drink water immediately after using an improvised "survival filter" and they didn't get sick 24–48 hours later, it's because the water was either not contaminated to begin with or not contaminated enough for them to get sick. The improvised filter had nothing to do with it.

Water Disinfection

The terms disinfection, filtration, and purification are often used interchangeably, and since they are different, this can cause confusion. I like to define them within the same parameters used to describe commercial filters and purifiers. Think of water **disinfection** as the overarching term that describes a variety of techniques for making your water safe to drink. **Filtration** and **purification** are both *types* of disinfection. Simply put, disinfection is a process that removes, renders inactive, or kills waterborne pathogens. Filtration and purification are two techniques that accomplish that at different levels.

CHAPTER 5: WATER PROCUREMENT

Purification and Filtration

Filtration allows fluid to pass through while trapping solid particulates. The pores of the filter are small enough to allow water to pass but not pathogens. A water molecule is approximately 0.000282 microns. Most waterborne pathogens are going to fall within the 0.2 to 10 micron level in size, so this level of filtration is often plenty. This is *mechanical* filtration.

Viruses are an exception as they are much smaller, sometimes as small as 0.03 microns. Most commercial filters that rely solely on mechanical filtration cannot filter viruses. **Purification** takes it a step further by removing, killing, or rendering viruses inert, in addition to bacteria and protozoa. Quite simply, it's just a higher level of disinfection for areas where viruses in the water may be a concern. This is typically accomplished by adding something to the water like activated carbon that adsorbs pathogens and other "strange happenings" in the water.

Most commercial filters that are meant to be portable and packable fall into either the filtration or purification category depending on the technology they're using and whether or not they handle viruses. It's important to research what type of pathogens may be found in the water in your area so that you can make an informed decision on the level of disinfection you need.

The waters get a little muddier (pun intended) when it comes to things like chemicals, pesticides, and heavy metals that may be a concern in some environments. These just are not all that common in backcountry water sources, so they're a bit outside the context of this book. However, if they are a concern for you, research details and claims for your selected filters and use that information to make the best choice for you and your environment.

There are two other common methods for making water safe to drink that are common in a wilderness setting: **chemical and thermal**

disinfection. Chemical disinfection uses chemicals to disinfect the water, while thermal disinfection uses heat.

Some of the most common chemical treatments are either chlorine- or iodine-based. Chlorine-based tablets are water purification tablets that are usually in the form of chlorine dioxide, and are effective against bacteria, protozoa, and viruses. The major drawbacks to these tablets are the contact time. In this case, the contact time is usually four hours. You can thank the extremely resilient Cryptosporidium for that. "Crypto" is a protozoan, and part of its life cycle includes existing in the form of a cyst. This means it has a protective "shell" around it, so it's particularly difficult to kill or inactivate chemically. However, given enough contact time with chlorine dioxide specifically, it will eventually give up the ghost. Giardia is another protozoan with a cystic form, but it's not as hard to kill chemically.

Iodine will handle bacteria and viruses, but it doesn't fully cut the mustard on protozoans. It can handle Giardia but falls short on Cryptosporidium. Iodine simply cannot kill it or effectively render it inactive. On the plus side, the contact time is only thirty-five minutes. The negative? It still isn't necessarily safe to drink. Cryptosporidium is found in every part of the United States and is common throughout

CHAPTER 5: WATER PROCUREMENT

the world. It's probably not a risk you want to take when there are so many other, more effective options.

There are other chemical treatments that are often touted as effective. The two that come to mind are sodium hypochlorite and potassium permanganate. I'd consider both to be improvisations that you use out of necessity and not ones you'd intentionally pack with you for the field. Household bleach (sodium hypochlorite) can be useful in killing bacteria and viruses, but you shouldn't expect it to have any effect on protozoans like Giardia or Cryptosporidium, so it's not something I would recommend when there are other options like chlorine dioxide tablets or boiling that are actually effective.

Potassium permanganate is often suggested as a multifunctional item that's good for fire, water disinfection, and medicinal uses. On the surface, this may appeal to many for those reasons. If it does all that, why wouldn't everyone want to carry it? But if you scratch at the surface and dig in a little deeper, you'll find that it isn't very good at any of that. In reality, it's a gimmicky way of starting a fire, it's not meant for point-of-use water treatment (procuring water from a stream or lake for treatment and drinking immediately), and the "medicinal values" are nothing more than slight anti-bacterial and anti-fungal properties that are good for skin rashes and irritations. Hardly worth carrying in a kit meant for the wilderness.

One of the most effective methods to make water safe to drink is boiling it. Pasteurization could also be considered a form of thermal disinfection since you're using heat to kill pathogens, but it is simply not common in the wilderness. Unless you're carrying a thermometer that you can use to ensure the water was at the correct temperature for the correct amount of time, you'd be guessing it was pasteurized at best. What does 149 degrees Fahrenheit look like in a container suspended over a campfire? It's not possible to know by looking, and your finger is not fine-tuned and calibrated to know what 149-degree water feels like if you were to dip it in. It's true that most pathogens are dead before the water is brought to a boil, but boiling is the only means of determining that the water was brought up to a high enough temperature to be effectively disinfected. In other words, it gives you a positive, reproducible, visual indicator of 212 degrees Fahrenheit (with some variance due to elevation). This is the primary reason for bringing water to a boil, even though most every waterborne pathogen (including bacteria, protozoa, and viruses) are dead in less than a minute at temperatures between 165 and 185 degrees Fahrenheit. By the time the water reaches that full boil, there has usually been plenty of contact time at the actual required temperature to make it safe to drink.

So, what about elevation? It's a fact that the boiling point of water goes down as you go up in elevation. In other words, when you go higher in elevation, water will boil at a lower temperature. Conventional wisdom is to boil water longer at altitude, with the thought behind that being that the lower temperature needs increased contact time to ensure it is effectively disinfecting. This is a chemistry equation, but you can save time by simply researching it on your own. The boiling point does not dip below 185 degrees Fahrenheit until over 14,000 feet in elevation. Conventional wisdom says to boil water for anywhere from 3 to 10 minutes above 5,000 feet. Did you know that the boiling point of water at 5,000 feet is still

CHAPTER 5: WATER PROCUREMENT

over 202 degrees Fahrenheit? That's still well above the necessary temperature to kill most pathogens.

I don't tell you all of this to encourage you to go against the standards set forth by various government agencies. I tell you this so that you can apply some critical thinking to the conventional wisdom and decide for yourself what the correct answer is. In an emergency, or when water is scarce, you might not want to lose that resource to evaporation because you're boiling it way longer than needed. Every little bit counts.

It should be noted that boiling does not do anything for chemicals, pesticides, or heavy metals that may be in water. If anything, it concentrates them since some of the water evaporates during boiling. Again, this is not a common concern in the backcountry, but if it is a concern in your area, boiling may not be the best choice.

Distillation and Desalination

Distillation is a method of purifying a liquid through a process of heating and cooling. To put it simply, "dirty" water is heated up to the point of becoming a vapor (evaporated) and is then cooled to the point of condensation (becoming a liquid again). This process evaporates clean water vapor, separating it from the contaminates, and after cooling and condensing, it is collected in a clean container. You can do this with a method called a **"below-ground solar still."** This system uses heat from the sun to evaporate moisture from the ground and from green plant material (if available). That moisture evaporates and is captured on a piece of plastic where it cools and drips into a collection container. If you have a section of rubber tubing, you can use it as a straw to drink from the container without disturbing the still (just make sure you close or plug the end of the drinking tube). This is a frequently used technique within the survival industry that gets a lot of negative press, the most common being that it is likely a net loss in hydration, meaning you put more water into building the system than you'll gain from the system itself.

Don't be in a such a hurry to dismiss it based on someone else's experience. It depends on several things. First, you must have a sheet of plastic, a container, and a way to dig a hole. Green vegetation is also a plus if it's available. So who carries clear plastic to the woods with them? Well, ignoring that there's always a chance of finding something useful along the way, anyone who plans on making something like this a part of their bigger plan to stay hydrated in an emergency should be carrying the resources needed to make it. Plastic trash bags are useful for more than just this technique. Think of this as a potential supplement in that way rather than a waste of time.

When you build it, look for an area where you expect to find moisture in the ground as well as in the plant material. Remember the locations that were good for attempting the seepage basin? Those are also probably good locations to attempt a solar still because there's a better chance the ground has some moisture in it. Second, don't rely on one single solar still to provide for all your water intake needs. Some produce a little, some produce more, and there are a lot of variables that determine that. Make as many as you have the

CHAPTER 5: WATER PROCUREMENT

resources for and you'll increase your chances of getting enough water. Lastly, it's a slow process that takes time, so don't wait until the last minute to start if this is a method you want to use.

Another thing to consider is that this solar still can distill clean water from contaminated sources. Perhaps you're in a hot area and don't want to start a fire, or you can't get a fire for some reason—you can use this solar still to produce safe drinking water. Simply dig a small trench around the top edge of the still, take the contaminated water, and pour it into the trench all the way around. This water will seep into the ground in and around the still, which will then evaporate, condense, and be captured. This same technique can be used for desalination of ocean or sea water (turning salt water into fresh, drinkable water). It doesn't matter how much moisture is in the ground or the plants if you have a supply of water than you can introduce into the mix.

> ### Tip for the Unexpected
>
> It's probably a result of many of the survival shows out there on television, but for some reason, folks are obsessed with drinking urine. Is urine sterile? Is it safe to drink your own urine? Is it safe to drink someone else's urine so long as it isn't your own? No, on all accounts.
>
> Urine is a waste product. It is not sterile. It contains at least trace amounts of bacteria, worse given any infection. If you apply some critical thinking to this, it's not practical even if you could. First, the more dehydrated you are, the lower the amount of water in your urine and the higher the concentration of wastes, which you will likely use more water to process than you gained. Second, as you get more and more dehydrated, your body will stop producing urine to hold on to the water you already have available in your body. Lastly, the human bladder's capacity is between 500-700mL, which is only about half of what you need per day if you sat in the shade and did nothing to begin with. It's just not a sustainable or sensible method of hydrating, even if it was a good idea to drink it.
>
> Will you die from drinking a little urine? Doubtful. Will you live because you drank a little urine? Also doubtful. With all of that said, you can urinate into the trench around a solar still; it will seep into the ground and the still will

evaporate clean water from it. So if you must drink urine, this is the way to do it. Drink the clean water distilled from urine.

An **above-ground solar still** can also be made by placing green vegetation in a clear plastic trash bag and closing it off. This works best with lush, green vegetation because you're relying solely on the water that is contained therein. Dry vegetation doesn't have much water in it to be pulled out. Place the bag of vegetation in direct sunlight and allow it time to heat, evaporate, and condense again, and it will collect in one of the corners (placing it on an incline helps to collect the water in this way). Tubing is again a plus. The water will likely have a greenish tint to it but be safe to drink. It should go without saying, but so as not to make any assumptions, don't use toxic plants to fill the bag. Also, this will only produce as much water as there is in the vegetation, so it may need to be replenished every day or two. It produces a small amount of water, so never rely on just one to produce your daily requirement. Make as many as you have the available resources for, and they should be part of a larger effort to produce water.

Transpiration

CHAPTER 5: WATER PROCUREMENT

Transpiration is a plant process, and knowing a little about it will allow you to leverage it in an emergency. It's essentially how the plant releases water to the environment. This happens in the stomata, which are pores that are found on leaves and stems. This water can be captured by using what's called a **vegetation transpiration bag**. This is a remarkably simple process that captures moisture as it is released. It also requires something like a plastic trash bag that you can place around a bundle of leaves and stems and secure closed. As the water transpires, it will collect in the lower corner of the bag. This water is drinkable as is and requires no additional treatment. Just like the solar stills, drinking tubes are handy, but not necessarily a requirement. Always make as many as you have the resources for to increase production, and never rely on these techniques as your sole source of water.

Hydrating in Cold Weather

When temperatures drop, water sources will begin to freeze and rain will turn to snow. It's all still useable water, just in different forms, and you may have to melt it to use it. That's just as well, since drinking warm fluids is better for your core body temperature than drinking cold fluids in the winter.

There are some rules of thumb when accessing water in the winter that mostly have to do with fuel consumption—in other words, how much firewood you need to either boil it, melt it and boil it, or simply melt it. Accessing fresh water that's not frozen from a stream or under the ice on a frozen lake or pond is the best practice. It simply needs to be brought to a boil to make it safe to drink. The next best source is ice. Ice will, of course, take more fuel because you must melt it and then bring it to a boil to make it safe to drink. Ice is only as safe as the source of water you got it from. The last choice is to melt snow. Unpacked, fresh snow can be upwards of 90 percent air, so if you were to fill a 32-ounce water bottle with snow, you'd probably only have about 3–4 ounces of water once it melted and you'd have to keep adding more snow to melt until the container was full. It is a source of water but should only be used if you cannot find unfrozen water or ice.

What about eating snow? It's said that it will drop your body temperature and can cause hypothermia. I will say this: it will drop your body temperature slightly, that is true. Will it, by itself, drop it enough to cause hypothermia? Probably not if you're eating it in small amounts like "wetting your whistle" on a walk to gather resources. We've all probably eaten a snow cone or ice cream cone before, even in winter. Small amounts are not any more of a concern than those would be. Now, eating a lot of snow as your primary means of hydration in a cold weather environment with all the other methods of heat loss happening, contributing to lowering your core body temperature? Yes, that is a real concern and should not be done. Drinking warm liquids is always the best bet.

Commercial filters must be protected from freezing and cracking during cold weather. On some filters, these cracks cannot be seen, but they effectively increase the size of particles that can pass through and are no longer safe for use. I often get asked how I protect my filters during cold winters. The short answer is that I don't. In order of efficiency, you've already learned that unfrozen water is more efficient than melting ice, and melting ice is more efficient than melting snow. Those are really the options you're down to in freezing temperatures. Because two-thirds of your options require a fire, you may as well continue using that same fire to boil the water and make it safe to drink. It really doesn't make sense to carry a filter that would only be useful for one-third of your likely options.

CHAPTER 6

FOOD PROCUREMENT

Food Kit

Putting a food kit together has always made me scratch my head. Every time I go out, I pack food if I plan on being out there for any length of time. Even if I don't plan to stay long, I pack some emergency rations just in case. What I usually see is an ensemble of traps packed in a "survival" kit. My question is this: why is it that you can remember to pack traps and snares, but can't remember to also pack some emergency rations to eat? There are no rules that state that you have to trap, hunt, or fish for all your food in an emergency, so don't pack as if there are.

Some people think that real "survival" means making everything out of sticks from the forest because there are no other resources. Why don't you have anything else? If you prepared for possible contingencies, you should have resources available. Improvisation is something we do when we find ourselves with no other option. We don't plan to improvise.

Having said that, you are limited in the amount of rations you can carry, so you should also have a means of procuring food after those rations run out. Think about **multiple traps** being put out to catch smaller fish and game. You aren't actively going hunting for deer or wild turkey. You have no refrigeration and can't eat all of that in one or two sittings, so you'll just waste most of it and draw predators. You're going for the smaller critters and fish that can be cooked and consumed in one sitting.

Actively hunting is not realistic, so don't think you need to carry a gun or a bow to survive—it's the least efficient means of procuring food in your situation. You have too many other things to worry about, and eating is pretty far down on that list. You want to focus on passive means of procuring fish and game. Trapping is the most efficient method of doing this. Once they're in place, traps work for you while you do other tasks. The more traps, the better.

You don't need heavy body-gripping traps like the "Conibear" (one particular brand of body-gripping traps). It's not practical to carry ten of any size of those; they're too heavy, bulky, and awkward. That and even the 110 are too large to catch a lot of the smaller critters you're going for.

You also need to consider what environment you're going into. Life begins at the water's edge: fish, frogs, crayfish, and turtles will be in the water; land animals and birds will be coming to drink water.

You should set up your kit accordingly. Plan to set **traps for land and water**.

I recommend carrying an assortment of traps for land and water. You can quickly set out a small trap line and put that to work before you even break into your emergency rations. You can eat your rations knowing that you're already working on getting more food. Less time spent hungry that way. An assortment of survival snares, rat traps, and yo-yo fishing reels are what I recommend. Add a small packet of peanut butter to that mix and you have a winning combination. Use that to bait your traps—everything loves peanut butter.

If you do catch fish or game, you'll need a way to cook it. Most of the time I can use the **nesting cup** from my water kit to cook with. Depending on the size, you may need to add a bush pot to your kit.

If you're going to actively hunt, do so for fish and frogs at night on the water's edge. A good fish/frog gig that you can attach to the end of a wooden pole made out in the wild is a great addition to your kit and worth the weight.

A good knowledge of edible plants in your area can also supplement your diet well if you take the time to learn them now and are able to positively identify them. What you don't want to do is pack a field manual and try to learn them from a book in an emergency when you're cold, wet, tired, and hungry. That's the wrong way to go about accessing this resource.

Recommended Food Kit

- Emergency rations
- Survival snares
- Rat traps
- Mechanical fishing reels (yo-yos)
- Fish/frog gig
- Small packets of peanut butter

CHAPTER 6: FOOD PROCUREMENT

You can go several days, even weeks, without food, but why would you want to?

In as little as twenty-four hours, you'll begin to see the negative effects of a lack of food. These are psychological in some ways, but also physiological. We're used to eating about three meals per day. That's the fuel our body runs on. Most of us have fat stores and can stand to go a while without some food, but that fuel changeover is not going to feel normal by any means. Physically, you'll feel hungry, and you may feel tired and have little energy to do things. Mentally, you'll likely find it difficult to concentrate or make decisions. After a few days, you may adjust to that and settle into a new "normal," but your brain will quickly switch to being focused on finding fuel to burn. It will occupy nearly every thought.

My first real taste of hunger was during Ranger Training. Food and sleep deprivation were a key part of the "gut check" that comes with that training. We typically had one to one and a half meals per day, and also had an increased physical workload that we had to deal with in spite of that. When I started Ranger Training, I weighed 185 pounds. By the end, I was "tipping the scales" at a whopping 135 pounds. To say I was hungry was an understatement. Nearly every thought of mine centered around food. We all had our different food fantasies, but mine was chocolate and peanut butter. We'd sit in our patrol bases and swap recipes with our buddies and talk about what we were going to eat out of our rations that day. We just couldn't wait for that five-minute window when it was our turn to pull back off the line and eat for the day. When the time came, it was more than enough to eat a full meal. I had it down to a science, and had already been mentally "eating" it for hours.

The often regurgitated "Survival Rule of Threes" says that you can live three minutes without air, three hours without shelter, three days without water, and three weeks without food. Without getting into all the reasons, I personally dislike that statement. I usually don't believe in a "rule" unless it's applicable across the board. Generic statements like that rarely apply in every situation or in every environment, and they're too vague to be all that useful. The only real value it offers is giving a beginner a framework of what needs must be met and in what order, but it's hardly foolproof. Experience will show you that it's very much situationally and environmentally dependent. In this context, the "three weeks without food" part leaves out the fact that three weeks is just the length of time it takes for you to slowly starve to death. There are probably worse ways to go, but withering away to nothing, slowly degrading mentally and physically over a period of three weeks sounds like it's at least near the top of the list.

You need food for fuel. You'll be better off with it than without it physically, mentally, and psychologically. It's going to take time, plus the right knowledge, skills, and resources to procure food in the wild, so it's best to start as soon as possible within the priorities you've established for yourself and your situation. Do you need it more than first aid for life threats, fire, shelter, and water? No, but you'll want it soon after.

Two Methods of Obtaining Food

When it comes to food procurement, you have both active and passive means of doing so. **Active methods** like hunting or fishing may often be a net negative in terms of calorie expenditure versus calories gained. An exception may be hunting a large game animal if you have a weapon capable of taking one down. That comes with a price in other ways, most notably in the processing, preservation, and protection of that food source. It's a lot of work dressing, skinning, and butchering a larger game animal. The meat must then be preserved to prevent spoiling because you cannot eat it all in one sitting. That means you'll have to store it in some way to prevent it from drawing predators and keep them from taking it. Many smaller meals that you can finish in one sitting may be a better choice. Another drawback to actively going after food is that you must be focused on that and cannot accomplish other tasks on your list of priorities. You still must gather and process firewood, you still must collect water, you should still be improving your shelter. You cannot do all of that if you're actively trying to get food.

Passive methods like trapping are a much better choice in this situation. You can set up a line of traps that can work for you while you do other things. Having premade traps is a real time-saver, but there are several primitive traps that can be made to either supplement or take the place of those.

Your food sources can either be land-based or water-based. Obviously, land-based will be animals, and water-based are more likely to be fish. In actuality, the water's edge is probably the best of both worlds since all land animals come to water sources to drink. This is often the best place to try and procure food from both categories. Passive trapping can be used both on land for animals and in the water for fish.

What I call "opportunistic hunting" is an exception. This is nothing more than taking advantage of a potential food source that you see while you're setting up or checking your passive means of procuring food. A great example of this is carrying a rabbit stick as you're setting up your trapline or going to do your daily checks. If you happen to see a small animal like a rabbit or squirrel, why not take a shot at getting it? It's not what you were out there for, but it is an opportunity. Same goes for fishing: why not carry a spear that you can have ready to go if you should see a fish or frog when you're at the water's edge checking on your fish traps?

CHAPTER 6: FOOD PROCUREMENT

Trapping

There are several different traps that have been used over the course of human history. Some are highly effective, some maybe not as much. A trap that is great for one area may not be a good choice for another. With so many different traps out there, how do you know where to start as far as learning them? Like knots, you must narrow them down to what is needed as a baseline, and once you know those, you build on them if desired. It's better to be particularly good at a handful of traps than it is to be mediocre at hundreds. With primitive trapping, the baseline is really understanding what a trap is and how it works.

If you think of it systematically, variations on the baseline are easier to grasp and adapt to different situations. Primitive traps consist of an **action**, an **engine**, and a **trigger**. If you focus on learning and understanding those three key components, you can use your imagination to come up with many and apply them in countless different configurations to suit your needs. Many can even be adapted to be used on land and in the water, which is extremely valuable. Another thing to consider: primitive trapping is illegal in many areas except for actual emergency survival situations, so check your local laws and abide by them. Practicing them is one thing, but using them to trap game while practicing may be illegal.

Your goal is to capture or kill your prey. There are several different actions that accomplish this. Capturing is usually done with a net, cage, snare, hook, or gorge. Killing can be done in several ways as well. This is usually accomplished by blunt force, penetrating trauma, or asphyxiation.

Actions

Cage

A **cage** is used when you want to capture an animal alive. Typically, this is reserved for birds, but that's not necessarily the only prey it can be used for. They can be made with very little cordage, and the rest is natural resources like straight sticks.

Snare

A **snare** is meant to capture at a minimum, but can also kill by asphyxiation (in this case, choking). The goal of a snare is to get a neck catch that results in death, but often you'll get a neck and a leg, a leg, or a body catch that just holds them in place until you get there and have to dispatch them.

Snares can be made of cordage or wire, but wire is the better choice. It holds its shape better and is more difficult for an animal to chew through and escape. As a rule of thumb, if you don't have wire and must use cordage, that type of snare should only be used with a trap that lifts the animal off the ground. This will reduce their leverage and make it harder for them to chew themselves out. Because cordage doesn't maintain its shape like wire, you'll likely have to use small prop sticks to hold it open in a loop. Just take care that they don't interfere with the trap closing when it is sprung.

It's important when making a snare loop to use a locking snare loop. This makes it more difficult for the snare to loosen once it gets tensioned. It's very simple to do. Just make the loop for the slip knot slightly larger than it needs to be to pass the other end through, and twist a second loop into it so that the loop is doubled. This step is less necessary in a lifting trap since the weight of the animal will likely keep the snare tight, but it doesn't hurt and is such an easy habit to get into for making all of your snares.

Deadfall

When selecting a **deadfall** (a heavy object), it should be five times the weight of the animal you intend to catch. It works by asphyxiation, not blunt force—it's not meant to crush or smash them. Once the deadfall is on top of the animal, as the animal exhales, it cannot inhale because the weight of the deadfall is more than its respiratory muscles can overcome. It suffocates because it can no longer breathe.

Deadfalls should optimally be angled at 30–40 degrees. The higher the angle, the greater the chance the animal has to avoid it as it falls. When using a deadfall, ensure that the deadfall comes to rest on a solid surface and not the soft ground, which will reduce its effectiveness. A good practice is to use a large, flat stone as a base.

Engines

The **engine** provides the energy for the trapping action to function. They store potential energy (energy at rest) as they capture the trigger and hold in place. That potential energy turns into kinetic energy (energy in motion) once the trigger is released. This is typically accomplished by the weight of the object like a cage or a deadfall, the weight of the animal, or the addition of a spring pole or counterweight.

Spring Pole

A **spring pole** uses the potential energy of a bent sapling that wants to spring back into place. This is a very effective engine in the spring, summer, and fall. Over time, the poles will lose tension and become less and less springy, so you must check them often. In the winter and in colder areas, these are usually ineffective because the tree will freeze in place or snap.

The spring pole only needs to be strong enough to lift the animal up off the ground. This serves three purposes. First, it keeps constant tension on the action, be it a snare or a fishing rig. Second, it lifts the animal up off the ground, which reduces its leverage and prevents it from chewing out. Third, it reduces the chances of other predators getting to it. With that said, you don't want the spring pole to have so much energy that it launches the animal across the woods or sends it up onto higher limbs to get tangled up.

You want the spring pole to be fast-acting, so take steps to reduce drag and make sure it can spring up free of obstruction. Trim all the branches and leaves off the pole and clear out any brush that it could get caught on.

Another thing to consider when using a spring pole is that there may not be one where you really want it to be. This seems to be especially true when you're using them for fishing. Young saplings may not be available on the banks of the water. When necessary, you can emplace your own spring pole quite easily. You'll need a stick to make a pilot hole, a pole, and a mallet or baton. You'll also need some cordage.

The stick that you use to make your pilot hole should be slightly larger in diameter than your spring pole. Drive this stick into the ground to a depth of two to three feet. After it's driven in, pull it back out and set it to the side. You should now be able to push the bottom of your spring pole into this pilot hole rather easily. To make it more stable, drive the stick you used to make the pilot hole directly in front of it on the side that will receive the tension. Use some cordage to lash the spring pole to this stake to add stability.

Counterweight

A **counterweight** can be used in place of a spring pole. It is most often used in the winter when spring poles tend to freeze and snap. These require a weight and some cordage. The weight is lashed to one end, and the cordage goes up and over a pivot. The weight is lifted and potential energy is captured by the trigger. The pivot can be as simple as a crook in a tree where the branch meets the trunk. Another method of using this is to tie the weight to one side of a beam or horizontal pole that rests on a pivot. The counterweight is then lifted and the weight is held by the trigger. This is often referred to as a "lift pole," but it's just part of a counterweight system.

Triggers

Triggers capture and hold the potential energy of the engine, and once "triggered" by the animal, they release the engine and turn that potential energy into kinetic energy. It may look like there are literally hundreds of different triggers out there, but those are in fact just

CHAPTER 6: FOOD PROCUREMENT

hundreds of variations on a handful of baseline triggers. It's easiest to show you the triggers incorporated into actual baseline traps that use those triggers. This should start putting it all together for you, since you'll be able to recognize the actions and engines that are also involved in each. It's worth mentioning again that there are several different variations and modifications on many of these traps. My goal is to give you one baseline trap to learn with each trigger system and allow you to build on that later.

As you can imagine, the terminology used with all the different variations can be confusing. Many people call the same traps and triggers by different names, so there is certainly no standardization. My terminology is not always what you'd find elsewhere for the same thing. When I decided to take a systematic approach to learning and teaching primitive traps, I had to establish standardization within my system of teaching since none existed.

All trigger components are scalable and should be sized according to the size of the animal you intend to catch or kill. A small animal will have difficulty functioning triggers that are too large. You can refer back to chapter 2 to refresh your memory on the basic notches that are referenced here.

1. Figure-4 Trigger

This trap requires no cordage or other resources from your kit and is an excellent beginner trap. Most commonly, this trap is used as a deadfall. The deadfall is both the engine (weight of the deadfall) and the action (asphyxiation). The trigger is comprised of three sticks: an upright "post," an angled "coupler" stick, and a horizontal stick which doubles as the "bait stick."

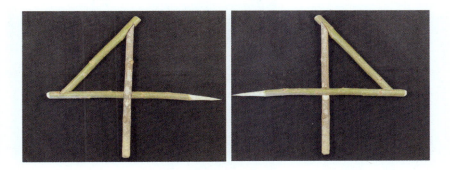

The post should be long enough to fit under the deadfall when the deadfall is at the proper angle. The bottom should be flat so that it sits well on the base. Carve an angle at the top, then carve a **latch notch** a bit more than halfway down the post.

The coupler will typically be the same length as the post. Carve an angle on the bottom end and a **stake notch** just before the top end. This stake notch will correspond with the angle on the top of the post stick. At the top end, cut an angle that corresponds with the actual deadfall so that the deadfall rests securely on that flattened surface.

The horizontal bait stick will be the longest of all three. Carve a stake notch toward the end that will be in the front. That stake notch will correspond with the angle on the bottom end of the coupler. The other end of the bait stick is **pointed** and should extend well under the deadfall, so the animal is as deep into the trap as possible when it releases. Place the trigger together, mark where the bait stick crosses the post, and carve a **square notch** on the bait stick to correspond with the latch notch on the post.

Put the trigger together while balancing the deadfall. The weight of the deadfall will put tension against the notches in the trigger and hold it until the bait stick is released. The bait can be speared or smeared on the point, depending on what you're using. Alternatively, you can split the point and wedge the bait inside the split or tie it on with cordage or wire.

CHAPTER 6: FOOD PROCUREMENT

You can easily replace the deadfall with a cage and capture animals alive with this trigger.

2. Toggle-Release Trigger

This type of trigger incorporates a toggle and cordage. The toggle is typically used at the end of a section of cordage, and is captured and held in place by another stick (usually the bait stick). It's triggered by the animal moving the bait stick, which releases the toggle and functions the trap. There are several different ways this type of trigger can be arranged—horizontal toggle, vertical toggle, horizontal bait stick, vertical bait stick, or several combinations of all of them.

A very popular and useful example of a trap that uses this trigger style is the Paiute deadfall. The Paiute are an indigenous tribe that were historically in the western and southwestern United States. It is a very effective trap that shares some similarities with the figure-4, so it's a great place to start learning the toggle-release trigger.

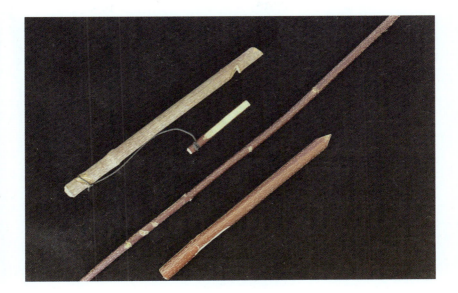

The Paiute trigger is composed of three sticks, a toggle, and a length of cordage. Much like the figure-4, it has a post, a coupler, and a bait stick. The post has a flat bottom that sits well on the base. The top is carved into a wedge or angle. The length is measured in the same way—it needs to be sized so that it sits just under the deadfall with the deadfall at the correct angle.

The coupler is also very similar to the figure-4. The coupler should be as long as the post. A **stake notch** that corresponds with the wedge on the post stick is carved toward the top end of the coupler. At the bottom end, carve a small groove to provide a recess for one end of the cordage to sit in. Tie the cordage in a secure anchor knot.

Measure the length of the cordage by mocking up the trap and marking where you need the toggle to end up. It needs to go past and part of the way around the post stick. Tie off the toggle to the end of the cordage. The knot will not be in the center, but slightly offset to one side. In addition, the toggle may require carving a flat surface to rest against the post, as well as another to rest the tip of the bait stick on.

CHAPTER 6: FOOD PROCUREMENT

Next comes the trickiest part of the entire trap: balancing the deadfall while you set the trigger and capture all the pressure. This can be one of the more frustrating steps, but stick with it as it does take some time. A good practice is to put a stop block under the deadfall so that if it falls, it doesn't crush your hands. This can make it easier to set as well. Wrap the toggle around the post and capture the tension with the bait stick. The bait stick is typically a smaller-diameter stick that is flat on one end and pointed on the other. The flat end rests against the toggle, and the pointed end rests against the deadfall, usually in a small imperfection in the stone or block of wood. The bait is placed on the bait stick as far back into the trap as possible. Alternatively, rather than setting the end of the bait stick into a small recess in the deadfall, it can be angled down to the ground to hold the toggle in place. Disturbing the bait stick will still have the same effect of releasing the toggle.

Like the figure-4, the deadfall can be replaced with a cage to capture animals alive.

3. Opposing Notches Trigger

This trigger is very simple to make and is one of the most useful beginner traps because it is so versatile. It can be rigged to target land- or water-based food sources. The engine for this is typically a spring pole or a counterweight. The action can either be a snare or fishing tackle, depending on what you're going for. The trigger construction remains the same for either.

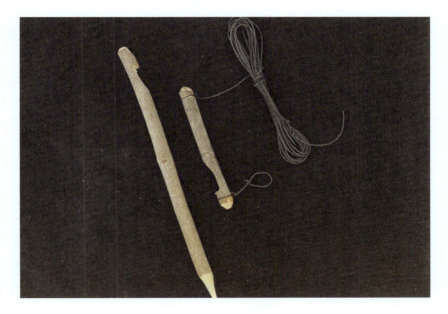

The trigger consists of two sticks: one is a stake, the other is a latch. The stake should be one to two feet long, depending on the conditions of the earth you intend to anchor it in and the amount of weight from the engine you need to hold. If you can make a tent stake, you can make this component. The top portion has a **stake notch** carved into it and the bottom is **pointed** so that it can be driven into the ground.

The latch stick is much shorter, usually only a few inches long. It also has a stake notch carved into one end, but the other end is flat. In addition, it has a groove cut in it to act as a recess for the cordage coming down from the engine and going out to the action.

The opposing notches trigger is easiest to learn in the context of a basic twitch-up snare, which is sometimes referred to as a spring pole snare. We called them "twitch-ups" in the military, so I tend to stick with that terminology; I reserve "spring pole" for describing that type of engine since it's applicable to other traps. Just to be clear, a twitch-up "snare" is used for land since the action is a snare; a twitch-up "rig" could be used to describe it if it were used in the water with fishing tackle. The action is to hook or gorge.

To set the twitch-up, anchor a length of cordage to the engine (in this case, a spring pole). Pull tension on the spring pole so that it's oriented over where you want the trap trigger to be anchored. The cordage should be straight vertically so as not to pull to one side or the other. It needs to come straight down from the anchor point on the spring pole to the stake on the trigger. Drive the stake into the ground.

Tie the cordage around the latch portion of the trigger and leave some excess. It should be tied in such a way that the cordage is still vertical when the engine is pulled down and latched to the stake. The latch will be upside down when compared to the stake, so the notches will oppose each other. This allows one to fit into the other and hold.

Tie a fixed loop into the end of the cordage. This should be rather short. You still must incorporate the action which will add length. This loop allows you to attach different actions to it depending on what you're using it for. Attach a snare for land and a fishing rig for water. If you make a loop in your action as well, it's a simple loop-to-loop attachment that's easy to change out when needed. Pass one loop through the other and girth hitch it. What you end up with will be a square knot.

This snare should be placed at the correct height on a trail to catch what you're going after. A neck catch is best, so always go for that. If you're using wire, it should be easy to mold and hold its shape. Cordage will have to be held open with prop sticks. Once the animal attempts to go through the snare, it will tighten, pull tension against the trigger, and eventually release the engine. The animal will be pulled up off the ground and will either be killed or captured, depending on how it was caught.

4. Split Trigger

The baseline **split trigger** uses no cordage. It's very easy to make many of them rather quickly. The most popular and arguably the easiest to learn is the **promontory peg**. It requires nothing more than a single finger-size stick that's long enough to fit under the deadfall with it set at the correct angle.

The two parts consist of an upper post and a lower post, and the latter of which acts as the bait stick. Making these two components is easy. You'll need to make two cuts, each one quarter of the total length of the stick from either end. This can be done easily with a saw. These cuts should only be cut halfway through the diameter of the stick, and both should be on opposing sides.

The only thing holding the stick together at this point is the grain of the wood, so it doesn't need to be sawed in half. Bend each end away from the other and the stick will break along the straight grain between the saw cuts, leaving you with two identical halves.

For the lower post (bait stick), sharpen the split portion to a point. The bottom of the post will need to be cut at an angle as well, and that angle should match the angle on the lower post (25 degrees). This will allow it to sit on the base at the correct angle.

The upper post simply needs to have the upper and lower ends trimmed at angles that correspond with the deadfall and the lower post, respectively. The lower post will be oriented back toward the inside of the trap so that the bait is as deep inside the trap as possible. The upper post will be angled slightly forward toward the front of the trap. This is important because it orients the weight of the deadfall over the lower post correctly. This trap can be difficult to set at first, but once you get better at matching all the angles, it will get easier. As you might have guessed, the deadfall can be replaced with a cage for capturing animals alive if you prefer.

CHAPTER 6: FOOD PROCUREMENT

5. Captured Knot Trigger

This trigger is not common, but it certainly is unique. The only trap I've ever seen it used for is the **Ojibwa bird snare**, a trap that's meant for open areas, specifically for birds. Rather than relying on bait, it takes advantage of birds' natural instincts to find a high perch to land on. The components are a vertical pole, a horizontal stick that acts as the perch, a snare, and a counterweight that's at least as heavy as the bird you intend to catch.

The pole is driven into the ground and should be higher than the grasses and shrubs around it. At the top of the pole, carve a **square reduction** with a **hole-through**. The hole-through acts as a mortise for the perch. You can either do this on the top of the pole or on a separate stick that's then lashed to the pole. The top of either should be pointed sharply to discourage the bird from landing on that instead of using the perch.

The perch should be a small straight stick. On one end, carve a square reduction that will fit inside the hole-through. This could be considered the tenon in this "mortise and tenon" joint that you've created.

Next, make a snare loop that's roughly the size of the perch. Pass the line through the hole-through. The knot used to make the snare loop should still be on the side toward the perch. Place the perch inside the hole-through to capture the line. This needs to be sensitive since birds weigh very little. Secure the counterweight on the other end of the line hanging down through the hole-through. Ensure that it won't be obstructed by anything on the way to the ground.

When a bird lands on the perch, the perch should fall away, releasing the knot and allowing the counterweight to pull the snare closed. With nothing to push off, the bird cannot easily get away from the rapidly closing snare loop. The counterweight will pull the bird against the post and hold it there.

CHAPTER 6: FOOD PROCUREMENT

6. Step/Treadle Trigger

The **step/treadle trigger** is technically also a toggle-release trigger, but it's different enough for me to consider it a trigger of its own. A basic toggle-release trigger relies on a bait stick being tampered with to release the toggle, whereas the step/treadle trigger relies on the animal stepping on a treadle platform to release the toggle. They are more for trails and taking advantage of where the animal will be walking, rather than using bait.

The best example of this type of trigger is the treadle spring snare. It uses a spring pole for the engine, a snare for the action, and the trigger consists of a toggle that's held in place by a treadle platform and a horizontal support stick.

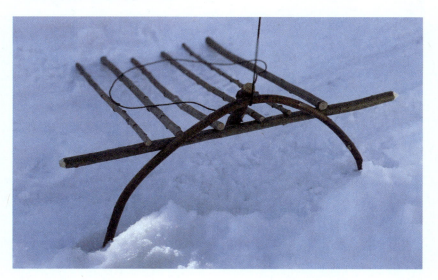

To create the treadle, start by making the horizontal support stick. This can be as simple as a green stick that's flexible enough to drive one end into the ground, bend to create an arch, and drive the other end into the ground. Alternatively, you could use two forked sticks on either side as uprights and lash a horizontal support stick to them.

This support stick should be parallel to the trail and on the edge toward the spring pole.

Next, place another stick along the horizontal support stick on the outside of the arch. It should be longer than the arch is wide. Now take several sticks and place them perpendicular to and on top of the first. These should extend all the way to the other side of the trail so that they must be stepped on by the animal. The entire treadle should be under and inside the arch.

Choose a suitable spring pole on the side of a trail. Tie a length of cordage to the spring pole. Pull tension on the spring pole and mark the location where you will tie on the toggle. The toggle should have a groove in it to recess the cordage. Once you tie the toggle on, use the remainder to tie a large snare loop to cover the treadle.

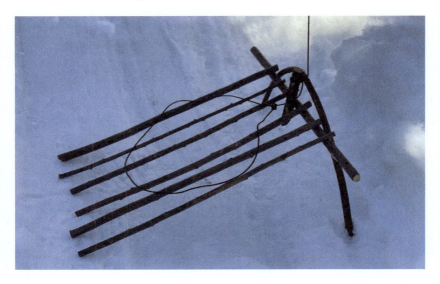

To set this trap, pull the spring pole down and route the toggle over and then under the horizontal support stick. Lift the entire treadle up with the second horizontal stick and capture the toggle and tension with it. The snare should be lying flat on the treadle, as this is meant for a leg catch. It would be difficult to do a neck capture with this setup but not impossible. When the animal steps on the treadle, it will

CHAPTER 6: FOOD PROCUREMENT

drop and release the toggle, and the spring pole will tighten the snare around the animal's leg.

7. Balance Trigger

A **balance trigger** is another trigger that's easy to make. There are a few traps that could be categorized as such, but they all rely on a delicate amount of balance when set. That balance is interrupted—in other words, it is put off balance—to function. A great example of this is the split stick deadfall. I personally dislike that name, since "split" implies that the stick is split with the grain, which is not the case. I have also heard it called the Three Stick Deadfall, but there are several traps that use three sticks for a trigger so that one's not really a good descriptor either. Let us just assume that by "split" they mean crosscut in half.

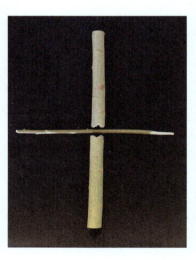

This trigger consists of a single post stick and a horizontal bait stick. The post is crosscut into two pieces on the lower third of the stick. The now upper post should be angled on top to match up with the deadfall, and the lower end should be shaped to allow the bait stick to sit securely inside. The lower portion of the post should be the opposite, with the bottom end being flat to sit securely on the base, and the top end shaped to accept the bait stick.

The bait stick's **pointed** end is as deep inside the trap as possible, and the other end is placed through the recesses in the post stick. The upper post is balanced on the lower post, and the bait stick splits them both. (I suppose I should settle on that being why it is called the split stick deadfall.) The balance is interrupted by any movement on the bait stick, which triggers the deadfall. This could, of course, also be used with a cage instead of a deadfall.

8. Notched Toggle Trigger

The **notched toggle trigger** is also technically a toggle-release, but like the step/treadle, it's different enough to warrant its own category. It consists of an engine, an action, a notched toggle that also acts as a bait stick, and a horizontal support bar that's usually held up by two uprights.

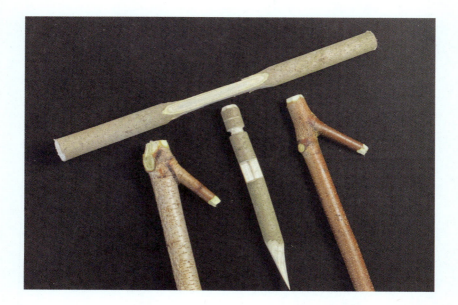

The uprights are stakes that are driven into the ground. The horizontal support can either be lashed to the uprights or held in place by forks in the uprights and oriented in such a way that they keep the horizontal bar from being pulled up. At a minimum, the center of the horizontal support must have a **square reduction** to correspond with and capture the notch in the toggle.

The toggle has a **square notch** carved into the middle that rests on the square reduction of the horizontal support stick. The bottom is sharpened to a point to accept the bait. The top of the toggle is tied to the line that goes up to the engine, where the other end of the line is secured.

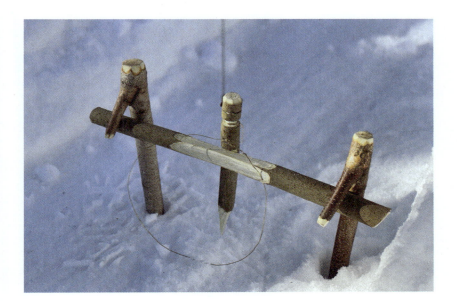

The action can either be a snare, a couple of snares, or a fishing rig, depending on the application of the trap. When used as a snare, the animal should have to put their head through the snare to get to the bait. Interfering with the bait releases the notched toggle and functions the trap. It can be a bit directional since it's easier to release one way versus the other, but once the snare is tight and the animal begins to thrash about trying to get free, there's a good chance it will still trigger.

9. Roller Bar Trigger

The **roller bar trigger** requires two uprights and a horizontal stick that acts as a long toggle. Carve a **saddle notch** toward the top of each upright and **point** the bottom end. The saddle notches correspond with the horizontal toggle stick. Drive these into the ground securely.

CHAPTER 6: FOOD PROCUREMENT

Tie one end of a line to an engine, and the other to the middle of the toggle when the engine is under tension. It's best to have the tension pulling both up and slightly back so that the horizontal toggle sits well into the saddle notches. Leave a loop in the end of the line after tying on the toggle so that you can easily tie on whichever action you choose to use.

On land, this trap is best used along a trail, with the action of the animal putting their head in the snare releasing the roller bar toggle from the saddle notches. This makes it a bit directional as well, but there's still a good chance that the animal thrashing will release it.

10. Arapuca Trigger

The **arapuca trigger** is a unique trigger used for the **arapuca bird trap**. This is a cage trap that relies on the weight of the cage for the engine. It is a complex trap, but it's worth leaning in on the context of establishing a baseline, since the cage can be used in place of most any deadfall. The trap consists of the cage, a vertical post, a Y-shaped coupler, and two trigger sticks.

Making the cage requires several sticks of varying lengths and two lengths of cordage. The sticks should be thick enough to add enough weight to the trap for it to function properly. They also need to be small enough in diameter that they won't cause excessive gaps through which the birds could escape. The smaller they are, the more of them you'll need to complete the cage. Finger-size is usually just right.

Start by placing two sticks down to serve as the base. These should be the longest of all the sticks if they're different sizes. Tie a length of cordage around the top of the first stick, and the other end knotted around the top of the other stick. Repeat for the other end of the same sticks. The cordage should be longer than the sticks to allow for height as you build the cage. Twist these base sticks opposite each other to form an "X" in the middle. Add the next two sticks under the cordage perpendicular to the base sticks, and push them tight against the cordage to take out as much slack as possible. Continue this until you get to the last couple of inches at the top. Fill the gap at the top by placing sticks right next to each other under the cordage. If necessary, trim all the ends of the sticks and ensure the cordage is routed along the inside of the corners made by each layer so that it doesn't come loose. If the cage is loose, you need more layers to make it tight. The goal is to take all stretch out of the cordage, as that tension keeps the cage tight.

The post should be **pointed** at one end and wedged at the other. Drive the pointed end into the ground to the correct height, one that allows the cage to sit at the same angle that a deadfall would.

Next, carve a **stake notch** slightly higher than center on the Y-shaped coupler. This stake notch will correspond with the wedge at the top of the post stick. The bottom of the coupler will be trimmed to an angle that matches up with the trigger sticks before setting.

The trigger sticks will need to be measured so that they extend from the mating surface on the bottom of the coupler to the base stick in the very back of the trap. This trap uses two trigger sticks that extend back at an angle toward opposite corners of the trap, so it can be triggered by either and doesn't rely on the bird being in the center and hitting a central trigger stick.

Place the cage over the post and ensure that it does not interfere with the cage closing completely. Next, lift the front of the cage and place the coupler onto the post. The Y-portion of the coupler will catch the cage's base stick toward the front. The opposite end extends down at an angle of approximately 45 degrees. The trigger sticks are placed in the back corners of the cage and matched up with the bottom surface of the coupler. The trap is now set. Bait should be placed well inside the trap. When a bird jumps on or even bumps one of the trigger sticks, the cage will fall and capture them.

With a working knowledge of all of these different trap triggers, it is possible to adapt and modify them to suit your needs and the resources you have available. An example would be using a split stick trigger as the post, and for that trigger to be released by two strings instead of the two bait sticks.

Principles of Trapping

Now that you know the basic triggers and some baseline traps, let's discuss some commonalities that all traps share. These are principles that need to be applied to all trapping. First, you must trap in a location that you expect an animal to be. You cannot simply place traps at random if there was nothing that led you to believe they were in the area. You're attempting to capture an animal that has free rein over where it travels, eats, drinks, and beds down. To do that you have to place a trigger that will only cover a few inches of that animal's potential route. Animal signs can narrow that down for you. Those would include tracks, feces, dens, burrows, and trails. The use of baits that are attractive to the animal can also alter its daily routine and bring it to the trap itself. Channelization, or "funneling," also alters or limits their route choices and can be used to steer them toward your trigger.

Trapping is a numbers game. You cannot expect every trap to yield a catch every day. Often, even the best placed traps require a two to three day "soak time" before they ever catch anything. My saying for trapping is this: two is one, one is none, ten or more is dinner for sure. I expect my trapping to yield results about 10 percent of the time. If I only have one or two traps out, I should not expect to eat more than once every five to ten days. I would prefer to eat every day, so to increase my chances, I increase the number of traps that are out. The minimum for me is ten traps.

Wild Edibles

In addition to animal and fish food sources, there are a variety of edible plants that you may be able to take advantage of depending on where you are and the time of year. This can be a very challenging thing to teach given the variety of different plant species and their distribution and season. What's available in one area may not even grow in another. This is something that must be learned over time, and as your knowledge and experience increase, your ability to recognize food sources where others would just see weeds also increases.

When it comes to learning wild edibles by yourself, I recommend cross-referencing with at least three different manuals to make sure that you can positively identify them. Over time, they'll become more and more recognizable.

Look at it like this: you can likely walk through the produce aisle at your grocery store and spot common edible plants like carrots, broccoli, cauliflower, potatoes, strawberries, and onions from a distance. That's because they're familiar to you—you've seen them your whole life! Wild edibles are no different, they're just less familiar to you right now. Once you spend time learning the wild edibles in your area, the fields and forests will begin to look like your produce aisle, and you'll start to see edibles everywhere.

Dangerous Plants

Many plants are dangerous for several reasons. Some are contact poisons that will cause an itchy rash if they come in contact with your skin, and some are toxic for consumption. Obviously, you do not want to consume or touch any of these. Rather than spend a lot of time and effort learning these plants, I recommend you focus on learning what plants you *can* eat and always go by the rule of only consuming plants that you can positively identify as edible. Assume any other plant is toxic until you prove it otherwise in your study of wild edibles. By default, that rules out the ingestion of any plant you don't already know as well as any toxic plants. Focus on what you can eat rather than what you cannot.

Backyard Edibles

With thousands of plants out there (the vast majority of them being unfamiliar), and with many dangerous plants potentially lurking somewhere in the mix, how do you start your journey toward learning wild edibles? As a baseline, I recommend starting right in your backyard. Granted, backyard edibles are by no means universal. You may not have these plants in your yard. The specific plants are not what is important in this section. The importance of this section is that you recognize the systematic approach to establishing a foundation of knowledge that you can adapt to your specific environment and build on later. It's not possible for me to give you a list of beginner wild edibles for every environment. What I can give you is one that is applicable to as many areas as possible with quite common plants. It can serve as a template that you can apply to your own situation.

When it comes to learning wild edibles, it's important to first be able to positively identify them. This is not limited to visual cues. There are also clues like preferred habitat and growing season. Think of it in terms of what I call the **"Three Rights"**: is this the right plant, growing in the right environment, during the right season?

Once you can positively identify it, what do you do with it? Is the whole plant edible, or just certain parts? Can it be eaten raw, or does it need to be cooked? How is it best prepared in a field environment? Are there any poisonous look-alikes that you need to be aware of, or is there any other cautionary information about the plant that you should know? This is all information that you should be learning about each plant. It's better to be able to identify a handful of edibles inside and out and know how to use them than it is to be able to simply identify hundreds. All of this is important information to know and include as you learn individual plant profiles. Many wild edible plants can also be considered useful for other priorities, including medicinal. That information should also be included in your plant profiles.

On the subject of "backyard edibles," you must keep in mind that if you treat your lawn, whatever chemicals you put on it are now in these plants. The same is true if you're foraging along roadsides or in public parks. If you plan to consume these items, remember that they are only as good as their source.

Plant Profile Template

The following is the template I use when studying useful, edible, and medicinal plants. I create these plant profiles so that I have a central location for all the information I gain from these studies. I've found that this is the easiest way to learn the specifics of each plant, keep it all organized, and avoid confusion and being overwhelmed with information.

Plant Name: Common *(scientific)*.

It's important when learning to positively identify plants to ensure that you know the scientific name of the plant (not necessarily from memory, but at least in this profile). Common names are often used to describe many different plants and can cause confusion.

Identification: What are the characteristics of this plant that you can use to positively identify it?

What do the flower, seeds, stems, leaves, and root look like?

_____

_____

_____

Include pictures of the flower, leaves, stems, and roots. When possible, you should add pictures that show it in different growing stages throughout the seasons.

Habitat: Where do you expect to see it growing?

_____
_____
_____

Distribution: What areas of the country/world does it also grow in?

_____
_____
_____

Season: During what seasons should you expect to see it growing?

_____

Cautionary Notes: Are there any toxic parts to this plant? Are there any toxic look-alikes that you need to be aware of?

_____
_____
_____

Edible Parts: Specifically list all parts of the plant that are edible. Inedible parts should be listed above under "Cautionary Notes."

_____
_____
_____

Harvesting: When is the best time to harvest which parts?

_____

_____

_____

Field Preparation: How can you prepare this in the field so that you can eat it? You can also list ways you could prepare it in your kitchen at home, if you desire.

_____

_____

_____

Medicinal Value: What other medicinal properties is it known or thought to have? What is the value of that to you in the field? In addition, how should it be prepared medicinally?

_____

_____

_____

Utility Value: What other properties does this plant have that make it valuable for other priorities like fire, shelter, etc.?

_____

_____

_____

Notes: Any other notes you find in your research that you want to have readily available in this plant profile.

_____

_____

_____

CHAPTER 6: FOOD PROCUREMENT

Select "Backyard Edibles" Plant Profiles

This list is by no means all-inclusive. These include my own personal notes and what I feel is important about each plant. You should feel free to use this same systematic approach to learning plants for yourself. If you don't understand my terminology, that's okay. It's more important for you to research each plant and put it into words that *you* understand. Make these profiles your own. This isn't meant to serve as a checklist for you, or be used as a method of identification. It's meant to provide you with an example of how you can turn information gleaned from various courses and books into one systematic and personalized reference that you produce. I used the USDA Plant Hardiness Zone Map as a means of referencing locations where I'd expect to find the plant growing, but you could use any system you want to keep track of that for yourself.

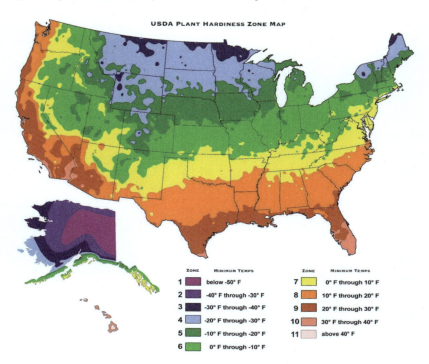

As a note, any information about the medicinal effects of these plants "has not been evaluated by the FDA," may or may not be scientifically proven, and should not be considered medical advice. Do your own research and make your own conclusions about any listed medicinal benefits. Additionally, I am referring specifically to the edibility and preparation of the named species of plant. You may have other species of plant that are similar but have different edibility and preparations. It's especially important to apply this information only to this specific species. This is another reason that common names are not the best practice and scientific names should be specified.

Plant Name: Dandelion *(Taraxacum officinale)*

Identification: Yellow flower, radially symmetrical, with multiple small petals, 1–2 inches wide; brown seeds with white pappus (seed head); basal leaves only, deeply toothed. Leafless, hollow scape (flower stalk) with milky sap; off-white root with white center.

Habitat: Lawns, fields, meadows, roadsides.

Distribution: USDA Zones 3–10.

Season: Spring, Summer, Fall; occasionally Winter.

Cautionary Notes: The stems and seed heads are not considered edible parts of this plant, as they contain sesquiterpene lactones, a phytochemical group that may cause contact dermatitis in individuals who are sensitive to these compounds (rare).

Edible Parts: Basal rosette, leaves, flower bud, flower head, root crown, root.

Harvesting: Flowers are good in late spring whenever they're available prior to going to seed. Leaves are best from early spring to late fall and are less bitter in cool weather. Roots are sweetest from late fall through late winter.

CHAPTER 6: FOOD PROCUREMENT

Field Preparation: Flowers and young leaves may be eaten raw, as well as small amounts of the root. The root should be cooked before consuming larger amounts. All edible parts are good for an herbal infusion (tea).

Medicinal Value: The leaf is high in provitamin A, vitamin B complex, vitamin C, vitamin E, calcium, and iron. The root is high in minerals. The leaf and root are both considered a health tonic for the liver and an aid in digestion. Dandelion may have a mild laxative and/or diuretic effect.

Utility Value: None.

Notes: The red-seeded dandelion (*Taraxacum erythrospermum*) is a similar species. Fall dandelion (*Leontodon autumnalis*) and cat's ear (*Hypochaeris radicata*) look similar but are from a different genus.

Plant Name: Red Clover *(Trifolium pratense)*

Identification: Purple flower, irregular, stalkless head; alternate leaves that are divided, typically in 3 smaller leaflets; leaflets may have a white "V" shape; 6–24 inches high.

Habitat: Lawns, fields, meadows, roadsides.

Distribution: USDA Zones 3–10.

Season: Spring, Summer, Fall.

Cautionary Notes: There's been some debate over the implications of phytoestrogens (plant-based estrogens) on hormone balance within humans. Clover does contain phytoestrogens, so it's important to note if that's a concern.

Edible Parts: Stalks, leaves, flowers.

Harvesting: The leaves are best from early spring to summer. The flowers are best from late spring to mid-summer.

Field Preparation: Edible parts can be eaten raw, cooked, or infused (tea).

Medicinal Value: Infusion is thought to have a mild blood-thinning action.

Utility Value: None.

Notes: There are several other "clovers" within the Trifolium genus.

Plant Name: Yellow Woodsorrel *(Oxalis stricta)*

Identification: Yellow flowers ¼–½ inches wide; alternate leaves that are divided, 3 leaflets that are notched at the tip; stem erect, not creeping, 3–15 inches high; stalks of pods erect.

Habitat: Lawns, fields, meadows, roadsides.

Distribution: USDA Zones 3–10.

Season: Spring, Summer, Fall.

Cautionary Notes: This plant is high in oxalic acid and should not be consumed in large amounts for extended periods of time.

Edible Parts: Flowers, flower buds, seed pods, stems, leaves.

Harvesting: Harvest the leaves and stems from spring through fall. The flower buds will begin to appear in spring right before flowering. The flowers and seed pods can be harvested when available from late spring through summer.

Field Preparation: Flowers are eaten raw; leaves, stems, and seedpods can be eaten raw or cooked.

Medicinal Value: High in vitamin C; cooling; astringent.

Utility Value: None.

Notes: There are other "wood sorrels" with similar characteristics and varied distribution. It's worth noting that any of the other species within the Oxalis genus can be used similarly.

Plant Name: Common Plantain *(Plantago major)*

Identification: Greenish-white flowers on a dense, blunt spike on a long stem; basal leaves only, leaves are entire and mostly egg-shaped with prominent parallel ribs; breaking a leaf in half near the base will often reveal what looks like fine white threads; seed heads start out covered by green seeds that eventually turn brown.

Habitat: USDA Zones 3–10.

Distribution: Lawns, fields, meadows, roadsides.

Season: Spring, Summer, Fall.

Cautionary Notes: None.

Edible Parts: Leaves and seeds.

Harvesting: The young leaves are best and should be harvested from early to mid-spring, but you can still harvest younger leaves from spring through mid-summer. The seeds should be gathered after they've turned completely brown. Although the seeds are edible, they're usually not something you'd bother with in the field.

Field Preparation: The leaves can be eaten raw.

Medicinal Value: Contains vitamins C and K, pro-vitamin A, and the minerals calcium and potassium. Plantain contains substances which are known have wound-healing, anti-inflammatory, astringent, expectorant, diuretic, and antibacterial qualities. Plantains are most useful as relief for insect bites or stings, and can be taken advantage of for minor cuts and scrapes. This can be done by crushing it and mixing it with water before application, or by using a "spit poultice." A spit poultice is made by chewing up the part and mixing it with saliva. Don't worry, the same antiseptic qualities you're leveraging in this plant also work on the germs in your saliva.

Utility Value: None.

Notes: The use of the general term "broadleaf plantain" is often used to describe any plantain species with broad leaves. That could be common plantain or red-stemmed plantain *(Plantago rugelii)*.

Plant Name: Common Burdock *(Arctium minus)*

Identification: Flower is purple or pink, growing in bristly heads in fruit that produces bristly, clinging burs, ½–1 inch wide, stalkless or on short stalks; leaf stalks are hollow; leaves are entire or somewhat toothed and alternating, leaves higher on the plant are typically egg-shaped with lower leaves being egg-shaped; grows 2–4 feet high.

Habitat: Lawns, fields, meadows, roadsides.

Distribution: USDA Zones 4–8.

Season: Summer, Fall.

Cautionary Notes: Contains sesquiterpene lactones, a phytochemical group that may cause contact dermatitis in individuals who are sensitive to these compounds (rare).

Edible Parts: Peeled leaf stalk, peeled pre-flower stalk, root.

Harvesting: First-year plants will grow in the form of a basal rosette. The second year, it will shoot up a stalk. From early summer through fall, the new seedlings have tender, edible roots. The basal rosettes found from spring through late fall have edible tap roots. This tap root is edible from the first-year fall through the second-year spring (when the plant is young prior to shooting up the stalk). The leaf stalk of the basal rosette can be eaten once peeled. From late spring to early summer when it is a pre-flowering second-year plant, you can harvest the pre-flower stalk and eat it once peeled. The roots are going to be extremely difficult to harvest.

Field Preparation: The leaf stalk and pre-flowering stalk can be eaten raw or cooked once peeled. The root should be cooked. It can be eaten raw, but it will make you gassy due to a high inulin content.

Medicinal Value: Root is considered a healthy tonic that contains vitamins B1, B6, B12, and E, plus the minerals manganese, copper, iron, and zinc. The roots are thought to be a blood purifier, digestive aid, and good for chronic skin conditions like psoriasis. The leaves have antimicrobial properties that can be leveraged as a treatment for wounds and for dry, scaly skin.

Utility Value: The fibers from the stalks can be used for cordage and basketry.

Notes: Greater burdock *(Arctium lappa)* looks similar but is much larger. The flowers are 1–1.5" wide and grow on long stalks. The leaf stalks are solid and deeply grooved. It grows 3–8' tall. It is worth noting that it can be used in the same way. Burdock is cultivated in Asian cultures and referred to as "gobo."

Again, this is just a sampling of my notes on a few plants that are abundant, easy to identify, and maybe growing in your backyard as well. Grab a blank journal and a camera and use this template for your own plant studies. You'll be surprised at how quickly you can learn useful, edible, and medicinal plants when you approach them systematically like this. Remember to only consume what you can positively identify and assume everything else may be toxic until proven otherwise through your own studies. Remember, it's better to know a handful of plants (and how to use them) really well than it is to barely know and merely be able to identify hundreds.

CHAPTER 7
FIRST AID IN THE WILDERNESS

First-Aid Kit

The most common causes of death in the backcountry may surprise you. Most think of starvation or exposure, but that's not really the case. Statistically, the biggest killer in the backcountry is cardiac related. Often this is a result of diet, age, fitness level, and preexisting conditions coupled with physical exertion that the person may not be used to. Many of these folks are probably aware of their condition and already seeing a doctor for it. Aside from prescriptions, there isn't much you can carry in a wilderness medical kit that will stop something cardiac related. It's simply outside the scope of things a layperson can prevent. The exception would be people who are certified in CPR. The application of CPR in these instances is certainly valuable, although carrying an AED (automatic external defibrillator) everywhere may not be.

The second biggest danger is drowning. This is often the result of underestimating the current during a water crossing, or a loss of footing causing someone to "fall into the drink." Being a strong swimmer is a good preventive measure, as is not attempting to cross water in swift currents. Again, not something that goes into a kit or that you can necessarily help in this context.

Third on the list is falls, usually from a height that can cause severe trauma that results in death. This can occur after losing your footing due to loose rocks and dirt, slippery conditions, or just inexperience in that type of terrain. If you happen to frequent that type of terrain, the preventive measure is to train in mountaineering and equip yourself accordingly. That's outside the scope of first aid as well, except for minor falls resulting in mechanical injuries that you may be able to help.

CHAPTER 7: FIRST AID IN THE WILDERNESS

So what type of injuries can we expect to actually be able to handle? What resources should we consider having in our wilderness medical kit to handle them? This kit will be highly variable per individual. It really depends on your skill level and the activity you're planning to do when you go out in the first place. If you're hunting or participating in a sport involving firearms, you may want to pack a complete Individual First-Aid Kit (IFAK) designed for handling gunshot wound trauma. If you have preexisting medical conditions, you'll want to pack prescription meds. If you're allergic to bees, you might pack Benadryl and an EpiPen.

A wilderness first-aid kit typically uses a lot of your other gear to improvise medical gear for common wilderness injuries. That's okay to do as a supplement to having proper gear for what you're trying to address. Again, we don't improvise on purpose, and some wounds are very time-sensitive, so we don't want to improvise at all if we don't have to.

The most common injuries that we can actually do something about in the backcountry are bleeds, breaks, sprains, strains (typically to the lower extremities), burns, blisters, bites, and stings. Since these are the most common, it only makes sense to structure your medical kit around them, so that you have the resources available to handle them if needed.

Common Injuries

Bleeds: We use sharp tools in the wilderness like knives, saws, and axes. Lacerations and puncture wounds can happen very easily. Bleeding can be the most time-sensitive, so while you can improvise a tourniquet with items from your kit, you really shouldn't. You need to carry a real tourniquet because if the bleed is severe enough that you need to use it, you may not have time to improvise.

Aside from the actual bleed itself, you may also have secondary and tertiary dangers like hypovolemic shock and the risk of infection to deal with.

Breaks, Sprains, and Strains: Mechanical injuries to lower extremities are common in the backcountry. Hiking on uneven terrain while carrying a pack often results in injuries to the feet, ankles, knees, and legs. Shoulder and arm injuries are also common, as people tend to reach out to break their fall. These are typically less time-sensitive and are fairly easy to improvise if you have the knowledge, skills, and resources to do so. For me, it's worth carrying at least one SAM splint and a couple of cravats to make splinting and immobilization easier.

Burns and Blisters: Large surface area burns are not common, but smaller surface area burns are much more likely. Something as simple as reaching into a fire to grasp a hot water bottle can result in a burn. I like to carry at least one 4x4" burn dressing and a dry sterile cravat for that purpose.

Blisters are very similar—they're essentially "friction burns." While painful, they are rarely serious unless they prevent mobility or get infected. For blisters, moleskin and molefoam are extremely handy. These provide a protective cover over your blister and reduce friction. A lot of times, this can be the difference between being able to make it out of the wild or not. At a minimum, you can usually make it out more comfortably.

Bites and Stings: There are several things that can bite and/or sting out in the wild. Some are simply irritating, while others can be life-threatening. Be familiar with the snakes and insects in your area and take precautions. Venomous snakebites are rare, but they can be deadly if you cannot get help quickly enough.

Contrary to popular belief, whatever folk remedy you heard isn't going to do anything for you. It'll probably do more harm than good. There is no such thing as a "snakebite kit" that actually works. Your "snakebite kit" is your car keys and cell phone and getting to an emergency room as quickly as possible. For insect stings, they are typically not dangerous unless you're allergic, so if that's you, make sure you have what your doctor recommends in your kit when you go out.

Recommended First-Aid Kit

Bleeds Kit

- Tourniquets (2)
- Clotting agent
- S-rolled gauze (2)
- Pressure bandage

Breaks, Sprains, and Strains Kit

- Moldable splint
- Elastic bandages (2)
- Cravats (triangular bandages) (2)

Burns and Blisters Kit

- Burn dressing
- Dry sterile burn cravat
- Moleskin and molefoam

Bites and Stings Kit

- Car keys and cell phone
- Bee sting kit for those that are allergic

Additional Recommended Items

- Individual First-Aid Kit (IFAK)
- Nitrile gloves
- Trauma shears
- Emergency mylar blanket

Disclaimer

Every wilderness medical class that I teach starts off the same way. I ask the students, by show of hands, how many are Emergency Medical Technicians, Paramedics, Military Medics, Nurses, Physicians Assistants, Nurse Practitioners, or Doctors. Usually, there are a couple of hands that are raised. I immediately follow that question up with this statement: "If your hand was not raised, you will not be after this class, either." The same applies to the information contained in this chapter.

I am in no way certifying you in anything at all. What I teach is a hybrid blend of my own personal medical experience with what I think is most important in a remote wilderness emergency. I'm talking about when Emergency Medical Services (EMS) may be days away and all you have to rely on is yourself or others that may be with you. When the ambulance isn't coming anytime soon, you have precious few minutes to handle whatever life-threatening injury you're faced with. With training, you can hopefully prevent those minutes from being your last. The goal of these techniques is to sustain life until more qualified medical personnel can take over, or to regain mobility so that you can reach a higher level of care.

CHAPTER 7: FIRST AID IN THE WILDERNESS

These methods do not necessarily follow any specific protocol that you may be bound to if you're certified or licensed to practice medicine. They're not meant to be your go-to procedures if EMS or a hospital are just minutes away. They're also not meant to replace formal wilderness medical training. This is very much a "what I would do in this situation if it were me with no other options" scenario. As the end user of this information, you use the following methods at your own risk. It's also important to check your local "good Samaritan" laws and be familiar with them before you apply these techniques to someone else on the trail that you may happen upon. In addition, medical practices are often evolving and changing, so take the time to familiarize yourself with the most current best practices.

If you sustain an injury in a remote wilderness setting, whether by yourself or with someone else, you cannot always rely on Search and Rescue (SAR) or EMS getting to you in time. Chances are you're more likely to need to rely on yourself and whomever you're with, if anyone. For most common wilderness injuries, the same principles apply regardless of whether you're handling them on yourself or another person. Granted, it'll be much easier with a partner, but it can also be done by yourself so long as you're conscious.

It is simply unrealistic or unreasonable to expect you or your buddy to be able to handle certain injuries alone. Some injuries are so severe that your ability to self-rescue is not possible. This chapter will focus more on what *is* possible and what will help you get back on your way to civilization.

Bleeds

Life-threatening bleeds are the most critical and often the most time-sensitive injury you can sustain in the backcountry. Even the loss of as little as 10–20 percent of your blood volume can be dangerous. This is considered **hypovolemia** (low volume), which can quickly progress into **hypovolemic shock** (in this case, the hemorrhagic version that's caused by blood loss). Hypovolemic shock is a life-threatening condition in which your cardiovascular system no longer has enough blood to supply your tissues, resulting in organ failure. We will discuss how to recognize, prevent, and treat shock later in this chapter.

The loss of 30 percent is even more dangerous, particularly in a self-aid situation. At this point, many experience **syncope** (passing out) and are unable to help themselves. If the bleeding has not been stopped before that, blood loss will continue until **exsanguination** (bleeding out).

Once a person has lost 40–50 percent of their total **blood volume**, death is likely to occur even with higher medical intervention. The key takeaways from all of this are that it is extremely important to keep as much blood volume in your system as possible, and a life-threatening bleed must be stopped as quickly as possible to maintain that volume.

CHAPTER 7: FIRST AID IN THE WILDERNESS

So how much blood does a person have to begin with? It's important to know where a person starts so that you know how much blood loss has occurred. It varies by size and gender—larger males will usually have more total blood volume than a smaller female, for example. A 200-pound male would start with roughly 6 liters of blood. If he were to completely sever a large artery, he would take less than a minute to bleed out completely, and he would pass the "point of no return" (40–50 percent loss) in as little as 30 seconds.

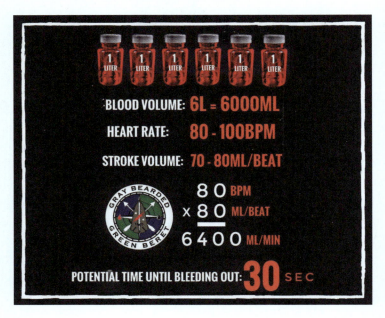

Primary Concern: Stop the Bleed!

I cannot stress this enough: if you have a life-threatening bleed, your primary concern is maintaining blood volume to prevent hypovolemia and exsanguination. If you're by yourself, that needs to be done prior to passing out and being unable to help yourself any longer. This is not the time for improvised techniques.

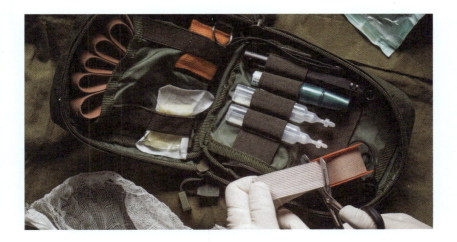

Types of Bleeds

All bleeds are not the same. Certain bleeds are more dangerous than others. Generally speaking, the amount of time it takes to lose blood through a vessel that has been compromised depends on the diameter of the vessel, the degree to which it is severed, and the amount of pressure behind it forcing blood out. In other words, each type of bleed has its own characteristics that can be identified quickly to be handled efficiently and effectively.

Capillary bleeds are a relatively slow oozing of blood and are not typically life-threatening. Venous bleeds can be a larger volume of oozing blood that are typically darker red in color, and can be dangerous depending on the volume. Arterial bleeds are bright red, often spurting, and are the most dangerous.

Moulage make up to represent capillary bleeding

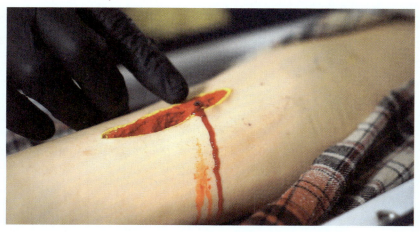
Training arm venous blood flow

Training arm arterial spurting

Location of Bleeds

The location of the bleed is also a factor in choosing what techniques you can use to control the bleeding. In general terms, there are four main areas that you could be dealing with: the **head, junctional areas, torso, and extremities**. Junctional areas are the junctions where the extremities and head meet the torso—the shoulders, groin/hips, and the neck. The torso, or trunk, is medial (closer to the centerline of the body) to the junctional areas. This is your chest, abdomen, back, and pelvis. Extremities are distal (farther from the centerline of the body) to the junctional areas. The appendages (arms, legs, hands, and feet) are the extremities.

This information is important because the type of bleed and bodily location that you're dealing with will often determine the most appropriate intervention.

Interventions

Before getting into the actual interventions, it's important to understand a couple of key things that may be applicable to your situation:

Scene Safety: Always ensure that whatever hazard has caused the injury either to yourself or someone else has been removed, so as to not cause further injury to yourself or others. If you cannot remove the hazard, remove yourself and others away from the hazard.

Body Substance Isolation (BSI): When available, precautions should be taken to isolate you from the bodily fluids of anyone you're helping. At a minimum, gloves should be used (nitrile is recommended over latex due to potential allergies). Depending on the situation, you may want to also include a mask and goggles to further protect yourself.

This is often not a concern when dealing with yourself or your own family members. However, nitrile gloves (while not sterile) are often going to be cleaner than your hands in a field environment and should be used to keep the wound as clean as possible.

Direct Pressure and Elevation

This intervention is used to attempt to stop a **low-volume, low-pressure bleed** that is not typically life-threatening. This intervention is usually appropriate for all areas of the body (head, torso, junctional areas, and extremities).

The wound should be exposed unless clothing is stuck to it. Clothing that's stuck to the wound should not be removed unless completely necessary to assess additional injuries, as it will destroy clots that are already starting to form. If clothing is stuck to the wound, the dressing and manual pressure can be applied over the clothing.

- Apply direct pressure to the wound manually (using your hands or bodyweight), with a dressing between the hand and the wound.
- Position the wound above the heart to allow gravity to help slow blood flow to the compromised vessels.
- Assess to determine the effectiveness after ten minutes. If the bleeding is not controlled by direct pressure and elevation after **ten minutes**, upgrade the intervention to wound packing and pressure dressing (below).
- If the bleeding has stopped, place a bandage over the dressing to keep it as clean as possible. Continue to reassess the wound and change bandages every twenty-four hours if possible.

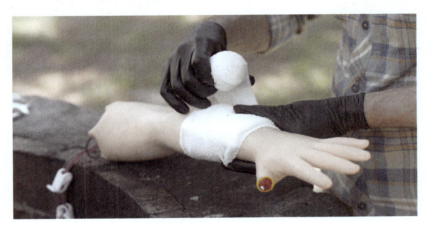

This intervention is usually not appropriate for a high-volume, high-pressure bleed. The exception to this is the application of pressure, usually with the hands or by pressing your knee or elbow on a pressure point (such as a junctional area like the hips), to slow blood flow to an extremity as a "stop gap" measure. In this context, a stop gap is a temporary intervention with the goal of giving you time to handle a more serious injury with a more appropriate intervention.

Wound Packing and Pressure Dressing

If an open wound is big and deep enough, you can pack it with hemostatic dressings. This intervention is usually used for a **medium-**

to high-volume bleed in an **extremity or junctional area** (except for the neck). For junctional areas, since we typically don't carry junctional tourniquets, this intervention would be most appropriate for a high-volume venous or arterial bleed.

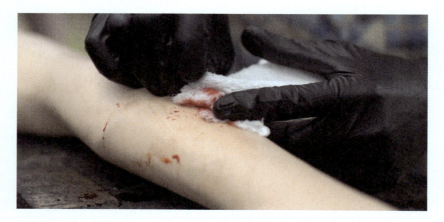

If available, hemostatic dressings can be very effective on extremities and junctional areas. Refer to the most current manufacturer guidelines for indications, contraindications, and proper procedural use and application.

1. Fill the entire void with the dressing, packing it tightly. The goals are to have the dressing directly in contact with the ruptured vessel and to fill the wound cavity completely and tightly. This provides pressure where it is needed to help stop the flow of blood.

2. Any additional material can be placed directly over the wound to provide additional superficial pressure onto the packing.

3. Once packed, apply a pressure bandage over the packed wound using either an Israeli bandage or an elastic bandage. This provides superficial pressure against the wound packing.

4. At this point, you should check the circulation distal to the pressure dressing to ensure you didn't create an unintended tourniquet effect.

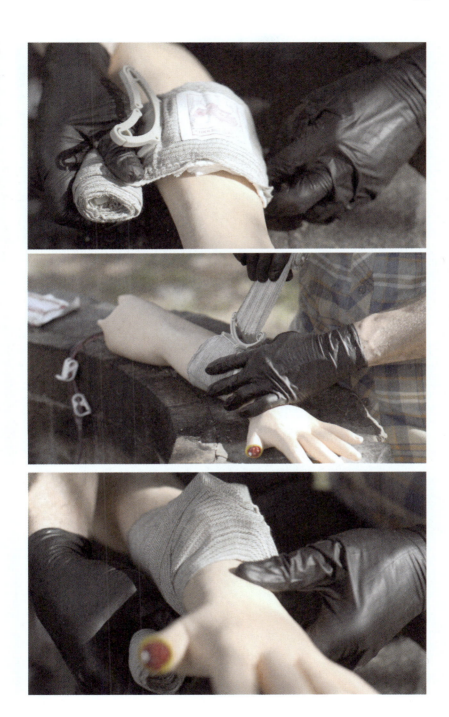

CHAPTER 7: FIRST AID IN THE WILDERNESS

Due to the potential blood loss from a medium- to high-volume bleed, this intervention should be assessed for its effectiveness within **three minutes**. If it's not effective, upgrade the intervention to a tourniquet (for extremities). For junctional areas, manual pressure in addition to wound packing and pressure dressing may be your only choice.

Where Not to Pack: You should not pack the **torso** (into the thoracic, abdominal, or pelvic cavities), as you often do not have enough packing material or solid tissue to "push" against to create the desired pressure, nor should you pack an **open head injury**. Also, wounds to the **neck** are generally not packed due to the risk of compromising the airway. Typically, direct pressure will suffice for a neck wound. An exception would be the carotid artery or jugular vein, in which you may have to weigh the risks of airway compromise against the risk of blood loss.

Tourniquets

Tourniquets are often taught as a "last resort," but this is not always the case. Seeing as you're someone interested in survival, it's good to know the general application.

The tourniquet is the most appropriate intervention for a **high-volume venous or arterial bleed** when time and prevention of blood loss are critical. This may be the first intervention you choose in this case. Knowing how little time you may have to stop a life-threatening bleed, think about how much of that time would be wasted going through the other two interventions to see if they maybe, hopefully work, just to end up using tourniquet as a last resort. Think about the amount of blood loss that will occur. Do not lose a life trying to save a limb.

Direct manual pressure with the hands on the wound, or "dropping" a knee or elbow into a junctional area at a pressure point to slow the flow of blood, are often useful stop gaps that allow more time to apply the tourniquet.

For combat applications (care under fire), placing the tourniquet as high as possible onto a single bone (upper arm or upper leg) is most appropriate, as you may not be able to properly assess the wound location(s) until later and typically have medical evacuation close by.

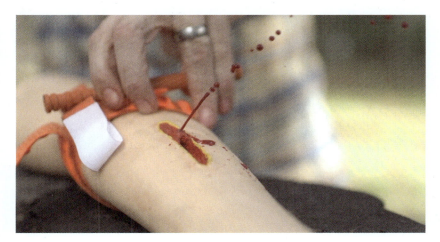

However, for remote wilderness emergencies—without knowing how long the tourniquet may be in place while waiting for rescue or self-rescuing, and often knowing exactly where your wound is located—

CHAPTER 7: FIRST AID IN THE WILDERNESS

it's worth attempting to preserve as much tissue as possible while still stopping the bleeding. For these instances, so long as time permits:

1. Tourniquets should be placed 2–3 inches above the wound, so long as that's not on a joint.

2. Tourniquets must be tightened until the bleeding stops. You should not be able to locate a distal pulse after the application of the tourniquet.

3. If the first tourniquet is not effective at stopping the bleed, place another tourniquet above the first one (closer to the heart). It's recommended that you carry at least two dedicated tourniquets in your kit to prevent having to improvise when seconds count. Record the time that the tourniquet was put in place.

Tourniquets may also be used as a stop gap measure to determine the extent of the injury, and replaced with a more appropriate downgraded intervention if applicable.

Downgrading Tourniquets

This information also goes against the old conventional wisdom out there about tourniquets but is in line with the most current information (at the time of this writing) from battlefield medicine on tourniquet use. The most up-to-date information can be obtained from the Committee for Tactical Combat Casualty Care (CoTCCC).

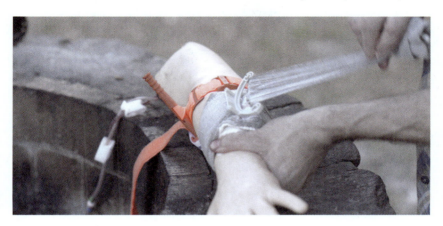

An attempt to downgrade a tourniquet to a wound packing/ pressure dressing may be appropriate **within the first two hours** of tourniquet placement to prevent potentially extensive tissue damage/ loss of limb. If the wound packing/pressure dressing is effective at controlling the bleed, the tourniquet may be removed. If it is not, leave the tourniquet in place. However:

- **NEVER** attempt to downgrade a tourniquet if the person is showing signs/symptoms of shock (listed below for hypovolemic shock). Blood volume is too precious at this point to risk it.
- **NEVER** attempt to downgrade a tourniquet used to stop bleeding on an amputation or a partial amputation. The limb below the tourniquet is already lost (or will be due to the extent of the damage caused by the partial amputation), so there's no benefit to the risk.
- **NEVER** attempt to downgrade a tourniquet after six hours have passed. The limb will not recover after a loss of circulation that long, and the risk of reperfusion injury (release of toxins back into the bloodstream that damage other tissues) is also a concern.

- **NEVER** periodically loosen the tourniquet as an attempt to restore blood flow to the limb and preserve the tissue. Typically, all this results in is periodic blood loss and gradual exsanguination. You either need the tourniquet to control bleeding or you don't, and it should be downgraded in a controlled manner.

Secondary Concern: Hypovolemic Shock

Now that you've stopped the bleeding, your focus should shift to the prevention and treatment of hypovolemic shock from the loss of blood (hemorrhagic shock). Remember that hypovolemia can result from as little as 10–20 percent loss of blood volume, and that can progress into life-threatening hypovolemic shock if steps are not taken to recognize it and prevent it.

How to Recognize the Signs and Symptoms of Shock

Increased Heart Rate: Typically, your heart rate will be greater than 120 beats per minute. This can be determined by counting the pulse at the radial artery. If the pulse cannot be determined at the radial artery, the next step is to try at the brachial artery. If no pulse can be felt at the brachial, move to the carotid artery in the neck.

Decreased Blood Pressure: You probably won't have a blood pressure cuff in the wilderness, so this is something that can be inferred by a weak or absent radial pulse. When you're checking the heart rate initially, this would become evident.

Rapid Breathing: Your breathing rate will typically be greater than 30 breaths per minute. It's very easy to measure this: watch the rise and fall of the chest and count.

Pale, Cool Skin: The condition of your skin, specifically the color and temperature, will be key. In this case, the skin will be pale and cool to the touch.

Cyanosis: This is a bluing (blue color) around the lips and mouth that indicates a lack of circulation.

Altered Mental Status: You could define "AMS" as any deviation from the baseline, but in this case, you're looking for signs of dizziness or confusion that may indicate poor circulation to the brain.

Treating Shock

If you recognize these signs and symptoms, take action to treat the shock.

- Protect the "ABCs" (airway, breathing, and circulation).

- Maintain your core body temperature to keep from getting too hot or too cold. This may require you to build a shelter and a fire, or to use the mylar blanket.

- Make sure you remain hydrated (which also helps with blood volume) by drinking plenty of water.

- Elevate your feet eight to twelve inches off the ground while lying down to help with blood pressure.

Tertiary Concern: Prevent Infection

With the bleeding under control, and preventive measures being taken to recognize and treat shock, the next concern with an injury is **infection**. The wound should be cleaned by irrigating it with water that's as clean as possible. Now you can take time to disinfect the water you'll be using for irrigation by using one of the techniques we discussed in the previous chapter on water. The only exceptions to this are if you don't have the means to disinfect the water, or if you don't have enough water to spare for cleaning because you need it for hydration. If you cannot disinfect the water, use the cleanest possible. The pressure and flow will likely make the wound cleaner than it was. If you need the water to drink and cannot readily resupply it, know that dying of dehydration is a more immediate concern—infection likely won't come until later.

A simple irrigation technique is to hold a full water bottle high above the wound and slowly pour it over the wound. The height of the bottle will increase the velocity of the water flow and make it more effective. Some commercial water filter systems come with a large syringe that's meant to be used for back-flushing the filter periodically. This syringe makes an excellent irrigation tool.

The wound should be irrigated, cleaned, and have fresh bandages placed on it at least once per day while in the field. Of course, this depends on the resources you have available. Remember that cotton material can be cleaned and disinfected by boiling, so you may have to add "cleaning bandaging material" to your list of priorities.

Field-Expedient Wound Closure

Suture kits have no real place in wilderness medicine. It's not a great method of controlling bleeding in the field, unless you happen to be a surgeon who can locate a bleeding vessel and tie it off with no anesthesia. External suturing is meant to close the wound to promote healing, lessen scarring, and prevent infection *after* the bleeding has been stopped. This can usually be accomplished in the field using non-invasive techniques, but it is hardly a time-sensitive thing that's critical for survival. However, with everything else handled, taking steps to promote healing and lessen scarring by non-invasive means may be beneficial.

A simple technique is to use small strips of duct tape to improvise **wound closure strips**. Take small strips of tape and pull the skin's edges close together. Approximate the edges of the wound without overlapping. Alternate the direction of pull on the strips from one to the other to help hold the approximated edges. This is often all that is needed to bring the edges back together to promote healing and keep debris out of the wound. Don't worry about the tape not sticking due to blood. Again, the bleeding should be well under control and the wound should be cleaned before you even attempt this technique. It is not for bleeding control.

Another technique that may come in handy if you have the resources is what I call the sewing technique. This is a more elaborate version of field-expedient wound closure that works well for larger lacerations. Take two pieces of tape and reinforce the edges with smaller-diameter cordage like bank line. Place the cordage on the inside edge along the length of each piece of tape. Roll the tape over the cordage to secure it. Place the two strips of reinforced tape along the edges of the wound and sew the tape closed.

One last note on wound closure in the field: **puncture wounds** are typically not something that you want to close. When a wound has that much depth, it's very hard to clean them properly and there's a good chance that it will get infected. Closing them up can make that even worse. Those are best left open, and you should keep them covered with a dressing and a bandage. Remember that a dressing is in direct contact with a wound, and a bandage is placed over a dressing to keep it in place and protect it.

Breaks, Sprains, and Strains

Typically, breaks, sprains, and strains are non-life-threatening (although there are certainly some dangers with breaks). The issue that's not often thought of (and is sometimes even more dangerous than the break itself) is the loss of mobility. This loss of mobility can force a person to spend the night out in the wilderness without having planned or prepared to do so, and exposure to the elements while unprepared can be catastrophic for them.

A **sprain** is a stretching or tearing of the ligaments that connect two bones together in a joint. A **strain** is a stretching or tearing of a muscle or tendon. Both can be extremely painful and cause a loss of, or limit to, mobility. Both have similar signs and symptoms, and both are handled in the same way.

CHAPTER 7: FIRST AID IN THE WILDERNESS

Sprains or Strains

Signs and Symptoms

- Tenderness
- Swelling
- Bruising
- Pain with movement

How to Treat

For sprains or strains, the **RICES** protocol is most often recommended:

- **Rest:** Resting will take the stress off the injury and prevent further damage.
- **Ice:** Ice will reduce swelling and pain. Apply early and at least three to four times per day.
- **Compression:** This prevents the injury from swelling and provides support.
- **Elevation:** Elevating the joint above the heart will assist in the reduction of swelling.
- **Stabilize:** Taping or splinting the injury will prevent further damage.

Some of this may be difficult to do in a remote wilderness emergency. You have other priorities that you must handle, so you cannot exactly sit back and prop your feet up as if you were back at home. Ice is hard to come by in the backcountry unless you're in a cold area in the winter. However, you should apply the RICES protocol (even if only partially and/or periodically) as time and the situation permit. A cold water bottle may be a good substitute for ice, and when you do rest for the night, you can elevate the injury. Nothing should prevent you from applying compression or stabilizing it.

Fractures (Breaks)

A fracture is a partial or full break in a bone. Besides pain and loss of mobility, it can result in sharp bone ends severing vessels and causing bleeding (internally and externally). There are two types of fractures:

- **Closed (Simple) Fracture:** The bone is broken, but there is no puncture to or open wound in the skin. However, there's still a danger of sharp bone severing vessels if it is not properly immobilized.

- **Open (Compound) Fracture:** An injury where the bone is broken and pierces the skin, causing a secondary wound. This secondary wound can produce a high amount of bleeding and will be at risk of infection. This type of injury often exposes the marrow to the environment, and an infection to the marrow is very serious and difficult to treat. Controlling the bleed is the priority in this type of injury, followed by the fracture.

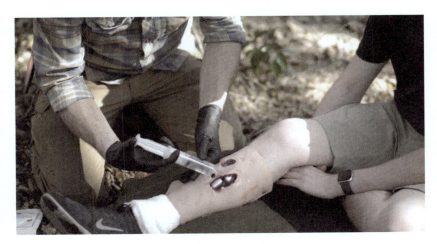

CHAPTER 7: FIRST AID IN THE WILDERNESS

Signs and Symptoms

- Pain and tenderness over a specific site
- Rapid swelling and bruising
- Inability to use the extremity
- Crepitus (grating, cracking, or popping sound)
- Deformity
- Inappropriate movement

How to Treat

Both types of fractures must be immobilized to prevent further injury and regain mobility. Again, for a compound fracture, the bleeding must be controlled first.

Principles of Splinting

Manually Stabilize: When possible, manually stabilize the injury with your hands to prevent further injury while you're applying the splint.

Position of Comfort/Function: Always splint the injury in a "position of function," or the neutral position it should be in when relaxed.

Accessible to Assess/Reassess CMS: CMS stands for circulatory, motor, and sensory. These functions need to be checked both prior to and after applying a splint to ensure that the splint is not interfering with any of them. Check for a pulse below the injury, ensure that the limb can be moved, and that it has feeling in it/is not numb.

Padded: Pad all pressure points, especially where the splinting material meets boney areas.

Rigid: The splinting material must be rigid. When the skeletal system is compromised, the entire framework is no longer stable. Splints are meant to be an artificial framework to stabilize the area.

Adjustable: Use knots that are easy to get out and adjust as needed. This will save time if you notice a change in CMS, or if the splint loosens over time, especially with movement.

Secured Above and Below the Joint/Injury: Splinting should always be done in such a way that the joints above and below the injury are secured and stabilized. This is to isolate and protect the injured area.

What You Need for Splints

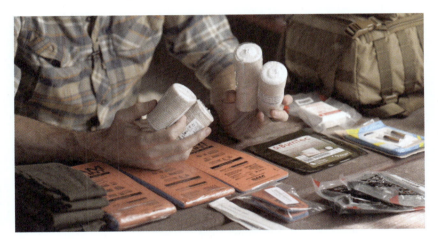

So with all that out of the way, how do we put it into practical application? Splinting really consists of two parts: rigid splinting material that will be used to provide structure, and a means to secure it.

There are several things you can use for rigidity. If you're prepared, you're carrying a **moldable splint** or two in your kit. These are foam-covered, bendable splints that come in a variety of different sizes. In the military, we typically only carried one size and cut them as needed with trauma shears. You can also just fold the excess. These can easily be fitted to a variety of injuries. Other useful common items that may be in your kit are **sleeping pads** (closed-cell foam or inflatable, both work) and a **wool blanket**. You can also use natural resources like **sticks** that can be sourced from your environment.

CHAPTER 7: FIRST AID IN THE WILDERNESS

Securing the splint in place is most easily done with a couple of **elastic bandages** or **cravats** (triangular bandages) if you have those in your kit. Other items you could use are cotton **bandanas** or **strips of cloth**, **duct tape**, or **cordage**—anything to hold the splinting material in place.

The following are several examples that use a variety of different splinting and securing materials. These examples are by no means a complete list of potential injuries or configurations, but they do show the practical application of many different principles.

Types of Splints

Lower Body

Ankle Stirrup: A commercial moldable splint is used for rigidity, and is secured with an elastic bandage to provide some compression rigidity. The splint is secured above and below the injured ankle by capturing both the foot and the lower leg.

1. As with all splints, first check CMS below the injury and ensure the foot is in a position of function.
2. Form the splint into a U-shape by using the uninjured foot and ankle.
3. Apply a C-curve to the upper third of both sides of the splint to provide additional rigidity, and form it to the ankle and leg. Place it over the injury.
4. Secure it in place by wrapping the elastic bandage from the foot to the shin (bottom to top).

CHAPTER 7: FIRST AID IN THE WILDERNESS

Wool Blanket Improvised Splint: In this instance, you improvise an ankle splint using a wool blanket for rigidity.

1. Roll the wool blanket tightly to provide some rigidity.

2. Secure the blanket above and below the injured ankle by capturing the lower leg and the foot.

3. Place the tightly rolled wool blanket in a U-shape under the foot with the foot in a position of function, and bring both sides of the roll up alongside the lower leg. This provides both rigidity and padding. Additional rigidity can be added with a closed-cell foam pad, or by adding sticks sourced from the landscape if needed.

4. Secure the splint above and below the wound using cravats. Ensure that you use knots that are easy to take out so that you can adjust the splint if needed.

5. As always, check CMS before and after application of the splint.

This is an improvised splint, and all improvised splints should adhere to the BUFF Principle: they should be Big, Ugly, Firm, and Fluffy.

CHAPTER 7: FIRST AID IN THE WILDERNESS

Closed-Cell Foam Knee Brace: A knee brace is necessary when you want to add some support to a useable knee injury. If the knee is not useable, you'll want to use the knee immobilizer below instead. This is a very simple brace to make that uses a closed-cell foam pad (your sleeping pad) for rigidity, which is secured in place by cravats above and below the knee.

1. Place the pad underneath the leg, behind the knee.
2. Fold or roll up the sides, place them alongside the knee, and secure them.
3. Leave the front of the knee open. You want to only brace the knee, not completely immobilize it.

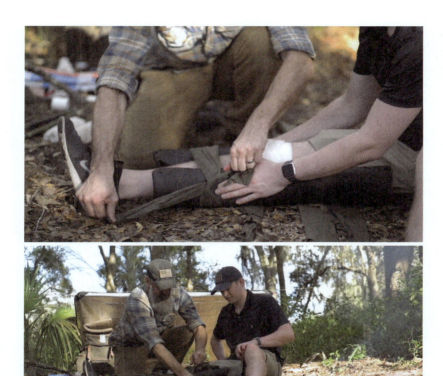

Improvised Air Mattress Knee Immobilizer: This is like the brace above but is meant to completely immobilize the knee due to an injury that renders it useless. This example uses an inflatable sleeping pad rather than the closed-cell foam for rigidity. Secure it with either cravats, cotton strips, duct tape, or cordage. It relies on compression rigidity from the air in the pad, as well as the addition of sticks sourced from the landscape if needed for extra stability.

1. Start with the mattress deflated. Wrap it around the injured knee.

CHAPTER 7: FIRST AID IN THE WILDERNESS

2. Loosely secure it above and below the knee with cravats to allow some room for expansion of the air mattress.

3. Add sticks if necessary, ensuring that the sticks are smooth and do not have any sharp points or edges that can puncture the mattress.

4. Inflate the mattress. This provides padding, compression, and rigidity, and fills all the voids. It is essentially an improvised air splint.

Upper Body

Although they wouldn't necessarily cause you to lose mobility, injuries to upper extremities are still very painful and can make carrying gear that's necessary for your survival that much more difficult. And of course, there is a danger of compounding an injury that you want to avoid.

Sling and Swath: This is used primarily to support and immobilize a shoulder injury. The shoulder is a ball-and-socket joint, so it must be immobilized in multiple directions. The sling is applied to rest the arm in and take some weight off the injured shoulder joint. The swath is then tied around the sling to hold it against the torso and prevent movement. This can be done with two cravats or other cotton material, and can also be done with duct tape rather easily.

1. Start by folding the cravat into a triangle.
2. Tie an overhand knot into the corner so that it creates a pocket. The elbow should sit in that pocket with the rest of the arm inside the sling made by the cravat.
3. Place the other two "tails" over the shoulder and neck and tie them to secure.
4. Fold the other cravat into a long rectangular shape.
5. Wrap it around, capturing the arm and sling, and secure it by tying.

Many other upper extremity injuries can also benefit from applying a sling and swath after applying a splint.

GRAY BEARDED GREEN BERET'S GUIDE TO SURVIVING THE WILD

Humeral Shaft Splint: The humerus is the long bone in the upper arm. To secure it, we must capture above the injury at the shoulder, and below the injury at the elbow.

1. Take a moldable splint and fold it into thirds.
2. Fold a J-shape into the bottom of two of the sections. This is meant to cup and capture the elbow. You can use the uninjured arm as a template for this.
3. Form a C-curve into the upper part of the splint to add rigidity, and mold it to the upper arm.
4. Place the elbow inside the pocket of the splint made by the J-shape. If you have excess that extends above the shoulder, simply fold that back down onto the long portion of the splint.
5. Secure with an elastic bandage from the bottom (elbow) to the top (shoulder). Apply a sling and swath if desired.

GRAY BEARDED GREEN BERET'S GUIDE TO SURVIVING THE WILD

Forearm and Wrist Splint: This is primarily used for an injury to the wrist. It secures the hand and the forearm.

1. Start by folding the moldable splint so that one end can be rolled into a grip that will keep the hand in a position of function. Alternatively, if you have the resources, you can use a shorter moldable splint and something to grip like an elastic bandage.

2. Mold the rest of the splint around the forearm.

3. Secure it with an elastic bandage from the wrist to the top of the splint on the forearm.

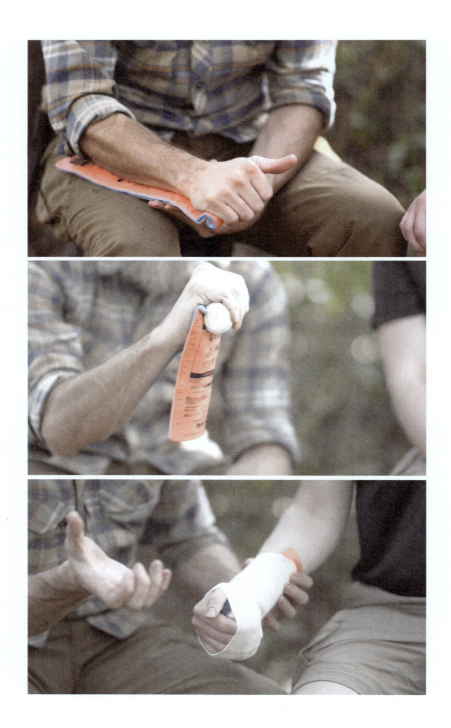

Burns and Blisters

Burns in a remote wilderness setting are usually small and come from spilling hot water, grabbing a hot water bottle from a campfire, or proximity to the flames or coals of a fire. They are typically non-life-threatening. However, large surface area burns can reduce your body's ability to regulate temperature and are highly susceptible to infection.

The two most important things to note with a burn are the total body surface area (TBSA) affected, and the degree of severity (although the latter is less important because it has little bearing on how you will handle it in the field). Typically, in a wilderness setting, you're going to encounter what is considered a **small surface area burn**, which is 10 percent or less of your TBSA. As a rule of thumb, your hand is roughly equal to 1 percent of your TBSA. A small surface area burn will benefit from what is called a "wet dressing," which will be more cooling and soothing on the burn site. This can be achieved with **a dressing that's designed for burns**, or simply by applying **a dressing that has been moistened** with disinfected water.

Large surface area burns (larger than 10 percent of your TBSA) will typically get what is called a "dry dressing." Although wet dressings are more soothing, a person that has lost the integrity of their skin over a large area has also lost the temperature regulation function of that same area. Adding a large wet dressing to that will increase evaporative cooling that they cannot regulate, which can result in hypothermia. At the time of this writing, there has been some research that suggests dry dressings for all, so I will reiterate the need to research the most current information and best practices.

* * *

All burns are extremely susceptible to infection since the skin has lost its ability to be a barrier against the environment. It's very important to clean these wounds well, use dressings and bandages that are as clean as possible, and change them as often as your resources allow.

As far as the degree of severity, the spectrum goes from a "superficial" burn all the way to "full thickness," which involves the tissues underneath the skin layers. A first degree burn is considered superficial, since only the surface of the skin is really affected. Second degree burns may be superficial (but more severe) or "deep partial thickness," meaning some of the underlying layers of skin are affected. Third degree is considered a full thickness burn, meaning all the layers of skin are affected. Fourth degree is a full thickness burn that also affects underlying tissues. These points don't really have any bearing on how you treat burns in the field. Regardless of the degree of severity, it really comes down to TBSA and whether you're going to apply a wet or dry dressing.

Treating Burns

1. When treating a burn, the first thing you should do is remove the source of the burn. That should go without saying.
2. Cool and clean the burn site with cool water or wet gauze.
3. Clean the burn with soap and water. This may be painful, but it is critical to help stave off infection.
4. Cover the wound with the appropriate dressing for the size of the wound, and change that dressing at least once per day.

Preventing Blisters

Blisters, as we noted earlier in this chapter, are essentially small burns caused by friction. They can be extremely painful and at risk for infection, and can make mobility painful, which can hinder your ability to self-rescue. Being able to handle these can at least help you make better time on the way out, and possibly even save you from further issues like infection.

I can remember being in Phase II of the Special Forces Qualification Course, where we were learning Small Unit Tactics. Essentially, it was like going back for another month of Ranger School, which I had already completed. I was wearing a pair of boots that were not as broken in as I would've liked, but that's just how it worked out. My feet were so chewed up I could barely walk. I had open blisters on basically every friction point where my feet touched the inside of the boots—my heels, the tops of my feet, my toes, you name it. I was not able to just go home and get another pair, so I took a knife and cut away every part of the boot leather that touched a blister. Before long I had more holes than I had boots, but the pain and pressure were gone. The running jokes were that every time I walked across a stream, the fish would swim right through my boots from one side to the other, and that I should probably try and just walk on top of the water since my boots were so "holy." I finished that phase with my "holy boots," promptly threw them out, and went back to my older pair.

An ounce of prevention is worth a pound of cure, or in this case, a pound of moleskin or duct tape. **Wear good socks and footwear that's well broken in.** Footwear is "where the rubber meets the road," so this is not a place to skimp. Change your socks often. I like to do a two-sock rotation: the pair that I am currently wearing, plus a pair that's dry or drying to change into whenever necessary. Lightly powdering your feet may also be beneficial, although I don't personally bother with that.

As soon as you start to feel a "hot spot," stop and address it so it doesn't get worse. Protect these areas by taking steps to reduce friction. This can be done with moleskin, molefoam, or improvised with duct tape.

Treating Blisters

If a hot spot does develop into an actual blister, how you handle it depends on whether it's closed or open. If it's **closed**, leave it closed if it doesn't interfere with wearing footwear or cause painful pressure when walking. The skin is still a good form of protection for the new skin underneath that's not quite ready to be exposed to the environment. If you do have to drain a blister to relieve pressure inside your boots, just make a small hole in the bottom of it and massage the fluid out. This will preserve that protective layer of skin over the blister for as long as possible. It will probably fill up again, as your body's natural response is to direct fluid to that area to cool and cushion it and create an environment for better healing. Although I have seen it done, I've never found the need to "sterilize" the needle prior to lancing a blister, or to route a piece of thread under the skin to wick moisture out. Typically, the fluid is pushed out of the small hole I made as I am walking.

If the blister is **open** or gets ripped open, you want to clean it as best as possible and recreate the protective layer over it with resources you have in your kit.

1. Cut away any dead, dry skin.

2. Wash the area with soap and water to help reduce the chance of infection. This new skin is not ready to be exposed to the environment, which is why this is often extremely painful.

3. Recreate the protective layer with either moleskin, molefoam, or duct tape to protect it. Make a donut-shaped cushion around the blister, then cover that with a final layer. Do not apply tape or moleskin directly onto the open blister. This will be extremely painful when you take it off later.

CHAPTER 7: FIRST AID IN THE WILDERNESS

Bites and Stings

Bees

Bee stings are a concern, especially for those that are allergic. If you're allergic, make sure you always have the medications and interventions that your doctor recommends on hand when you're in the wilderness. Anaphylaxis is a life-threatening allergic reaction.

If You Get Stung by a Bee

1. Remove the stinger, as it's still pumping venom into you.
2. Wash the sting with soap and water.
3. If possible, apply cold to reduce pain and swelling.
4. If you are allergic and need it, use your bee sting kit.
5. Continue to monitor for anaphylaxis and be ready to intervene if needed.

Speaking of bees, I'm reminded of a time when I was in Panama for training. We were warned during our in-brief about many dangers of the jungle, including "**killer bees**." What they told us was that if we were stung by a bee, it would release pheromones that attracted the rest of them. If you smashed the bee, it would magnify the release. These bees attacked in massive swarms, so this was a problem you didn't want to have.

Fast-forward to a training patrol along a random ridge line and, of course, we run into some bees. What seemed like dozens quickly turned into hundreds, then thousands, as everyone smacked the ones that were stinging them. Force of habit, I suppose. I quickly dropped my rucksack and dug out my mosquito net. This was a big one that was meant to go over a jungle hammock. I draped it over myself and my equipment and smacked the handful of bees that made it in under the net with me. I remember having to stick my hands in my pockets because they were stinging through the net and my uniform. The patrol was scattering all over. It was controlled chaos with just a touch of attempted discipline. I saw my buddy, a machine gunner, getting stung like crazy but still trying to keep from throwing the machine gun down and running off. This is not something I assumed, as he literally kept saying "I'm going to throw it, I'm going to throw it" over and over as bee after bee stung him. I shimmied my way over to him to get him under the net with me. As the swarm grew, I think we even had three people under that net at one point.

The other thing they told us was that a swarm would chase you, sometimes up to a mile. Even going underwater would not help, as they would just wait for you above. We sat under that net for what seemed like an eternity. Eventually we noticed that the rest of the patrol had scattered and ran off, and we'd lost contact with them. Our first plan was to shimmy down the route we thought they took to catch up, but we realized that would take too long and we'd get further and further behind. So we tightened our ruck straps, and—in a total "on the count of three" moment—we threw the net up and ran as fast as our legs would take us. I'm not even sure our feet were touching the ground as we sailed down this hill. I don't know how far we ran, but eventually we found the rest of the patrol, sitting down in a quick security halt as if nothing ever happened, looking at us strolling in with welts all over. We had finally gotten far enough away from the bees. All's well that ends well—we managed to keep all our gear and not leave a yard sale on the side of the mountain, and my buddy never did throw that machine gun.

Africanized bees (killer bees) are present in the United States. They do tend to attack in swarms and the sheer number of stings and resulting venom can cause severe reactions and death, even if you're not allergic. Other insects that can cause anaphylaxis include the fire ant and the harvester ant.

Scorpions

Scorpion stings are extremely painful, and they can be a problem for people with a history of severe allergic reactions to stings. Fortunately, North America is not home to dangerous scorpions. The most venomous one we'll probably find here is the bark scorpion. Its venom causes severe pain that can be coupled with numbness, tingling, and maybe even vomiting. Often the affected location will go completely numb and become unusable. Certainly not pleasant by any stretch of the imagination, but fatalities are extremely rare. Children, elderly, and adults with compromised immune systems tend to be more susceptible to death from scorpion envenomations.

During the Florida phase of Ranger School, I once leaned my back up against a pine tree during an administrative break and felt something large crawl across the back of my neck. Of course, my reaction was to immediately smack it as hard as I could. I hit this thing against my neck and it simply scurried out from under my hand and moved on like it was nothing, right after it stung me so hard that the neck pain radiated through my molars. It was a Florida bark scorpion, I know this because I saw it scurry off with its dark brown body and tan legs, and it looked exactly like the one that stung me in the neck again a few days later. Lesson learned: look before you lean against a pine tree in scorpion country.

Another lesson I learned both here in the United States and abroad in places like the Middle East is that scorpions like to get into your stuff and just sort of hang out there. Not an issue unless they get inside your rucksack or boots and you don't notice before reaching in or putting them on.

Handling a scorpion sting is very similar to what you'd do for a bee sting.

If You Get Stung by a Scorpion

1. Wash the area with soap and water.
2. Apply a cold compress if possible to help with pain and swelling.
3. Keep an eye out for anaphylaxis.

Spiders

Spiders are other insects that you should look out for. I'm happy to report that I do not have any personal stories of getting bitten by one, but I have seen several brown recluse spider bites firsthand, along with the necrotic damage they can do. The two main spiders of concern here in the United States are the widow (*Latrodectus*) and the recluse (*Loxosceles*).

Widow spiders inject a neurotoxic venom that attacks the victim's nervous system. It causes a condition known as "latrodectism," which causes severe pain, muscle rigidity, vomiting, and sweating. More severe symptoms include chest pain and respiratory distress. The reaction is largely dependent on the amount of venom and the sensitivity of the victim. However, widow bites rarely cause death in humans.

Recluse spiders inject a hemotoxic venom that attacks the blood and tissues. It causes a condition known as "loxoscelism," where the bite presents as a small open sore and the tissue around it begins to die off (necrosis). Often, you won't feel the bite or any initial pain at all. Most bites are minor and do not progress to necrosis.

If You Get Bitten by a Venomous Spider

1. Much the same as a bee or scorpion sting, wash with soap and water, and apply cold to help with pain and swelling.

2. Keep an eye on it to make sure it does not worsen. With spider bites, you may benefit from elevating them to help reduce some of the pain and swelling as well.

3. If the condition gets worse, especially with a brown recluse bite, you should seek medical attention.

Snakes

CHAPTER 7: FIRST AID IN THE WILDERNESS

First and foremost, the information I'm giving you on venomous snakes is specific to North America, where I am from. I understand that you may be reading this on another continent, so I want to make sure this is very clear and you understand that the situation may be slightly different where you are.

Snakebites can be very dangerous, especially if you're in a remote location, and most of what you've probably heard to do is not actually beneficial or recommended.

Some **preventive measures** you can take if you're in an area that has venomous snakes:

- Watch where you step.
- Don't blindly reach into holes or crevices.
- Don't try to catch or handle a snake.

Bites to the lower extremities are typically the result of stepping on or near a snake that has no way of escaping. Bites to the hand are common from reaching into an area where a snake is hiding, or trying to catch or handle them.

If you see a snake, take a couple of steps back and give it room to escape. During colder temperatures, they may not move very quickly, if at all. It's easy enough to just go around them if that's the case. On a particularly cold morning in the mountain phase of Ranger School, the mountainside trail we were using had a rather large timber rattler stretched across it in a desperate attempt to warm itself in the sun so that it could move. There was a long line of us—probably at least thirty-five to forty Ranger students and another handful of Ranger instructors—and we just stepped over it as if it were a stick lying there. The snake didn't even flinch, so it might as well have been.

If You Get Bitten by a Snake

1. Get away from the snake and stay as calm as possible.
2. Remove any jewelry and restrictive clothing around the area because it's going to swell rapidly.
3. Start making your way out of the wilderness.
4. If you have a cell phone and signal, call the closest hospital (or 911) to let them know where you are, what happened, and that you're making your way out. This gives them a heads up that you're coming, and depending on the situation, they may coordinate for an ambulance to meet you. Do not delay movement for any reason.

Like with any other life-threatening injury, immediate evacuation and seeking of qualified medical care is the only real course of action. Not snakebite kits, not sucking the poison out, not constricting bands or tourniquets, not cutting the wound open, not icing it down, not electric shock—none of that. Time and medical care are what you need. The rest is a waste of time and not only delays evacuation in many cases, but also does nothing but cause more damage to the wound. The best snakebite kit is your car keys and cell phone.

You do not need to capture, kill, or even identify the snake that bit you—it's unnecessary. All this does is risk another bite and waste time. Further, even a dead snake can still bite and envenomate someone, so all this does is put people at risk for no reason. The hospital will identify the snake clinically and take the necessary steps.

There have been some studies that show that **positioning the bite** a certain way may help reduce the damage, depending on the type of snake that bit you. Most of the envenomations in North America are from pit vipers (rattlesnakes, copperheads, and water moccasins). Pit vipers have a hemotoxic venom that attacks the blood and tissues.

The bites of the copperhead (*Agkistrodon contortrix*) and water moccasin (*Agkistrodon piscivorus*) affect the tissue in a similar manner. These snakes are closely related, after all. Their bites tend to cause more local tissue damage, rather than systemic, so they should be **positioned above the heart** to minimize that as best you can.

On the other hand, a rattlesnake bite tends to cause both local and systemic damage, so you don't want to hold it above the heart as it will worsen the systemic. A rattlesnake bite should be **held at heart level**.

Holding any of these below heart level will cause the venom to pool in the extremity and worsen local tissue damage.

Coral snakes are an exception. They have a neurotoxic venom that affects the central nervous system rather than the blood and tissues. To prevent that from spreading, it should be **positioned below the heart**. There have been some studies that the **pressure immobilization technique** may be beneficial for a coral snake bite, but more research is needed.

Bites from a coral snake are extremely rare. They don't have the retractable hypodermic fangs that vipers have. They have small, fixed fangs, and deliver their venom with a chewing, grinding motion. Regardless, when you see a snake that you think might be a coral, just leave it alone like any other snake. Don't try to handle it. Just give it space and let it move on.

An important thing to note: the venom of the Mojave rattlesnake is unique in that it is both hemotoxic and neurotoxic. These are found in the southwestern United States, so be aware if you find yourself in that area.

Lizards

What about lizards? There are only two that are venomous in North America, and only one that is native to the United States. The Gila monster is found in the US, and the Mexican beaded lizard is found in

Mexico. The Gila monster is said to produce one of the most painful venoms of any vertebrate. It is about as toxic as a rattlesnake, but it only produces small amounts that are not typically fatal to adult humans. It is best to leave these lizards alone. If you are bitten by one, follow the steps for snakebites.

Medicinal Plants

In the context of short-term survival, medicinal plants can't handle anything that is life-or-death by any means. I usually won't even teach them in basic-level courses for that very reason. It's just not necessary to know to meet your immediate needs. However, I do feel that it is important to establish a solid foundation that can be built on later.

When it comes to medicinal plants, you really only have two things that are important on a very basic level. First, you must know how to positively identify them and know what parts are used for what purpose. This goes back to that systematic approach of learning that we already discussed in chapter 6. Knowing each plant and its uses, inside and out, is more important than just being able to identify a multitude of plants. Second, you have to know how to prepare and use them to make the most of their medicinal benefits. With a systematic approach to learning useful, edible, and medicinal plants already established, what's important to cover here is how to prepare them medicinally. There are many ways to prepare medicinal plants, but I have limited this list to those techniques that can realistically be done in a field environment.

Methods of Preparing and Using Medicinal Plants

Raw: Simply use the desired parts of the plant as is.

Yarrow (*Achillea millefolium*) is very useful as a means of staunching blood flow from a minor wound. Simply place the flowers or leaves in contact with the wound and secure them in place. I will typically just take one of the longer leaves and wrap it around the wound to hold it in place. This isn't yarrow's only medicinal use, but it's what I most commonly use it for.

Poultice: A poultice is a small bunch of plant material that has been ground up and steeped in water, or simply chewed and mixed with saliva (also referred to as a "spit poultice"). The poultice is placed directly in contact with the affected area. A poultice could also be considered a "raw" application of the plant.

Plantain (*Plantago* sp.) is known medicinally as the "master drawing plant" for its ability to draw out impurities in bites, stings, and minor wounds. Typically, I will make a spit poultice by chewing up the leaves of the plant and placing that poultice directly on the affected area. It's very soothing for insect bites and stings, and has antiseptic qualities that promote healing. If you're concerned about the germs from your mouth and saliva, you can grind it up and mix it with a small amount of water instead. Keep in mind that the same antiseptic qualities that make this great for bites, stings, and wounds also take care of anything in your saliva.

CHAPTER 7: FIRST AID IN THE WILDERNESS

Infusion: Infusion is the process of extracting medicinal compounds from plants by soaking them for a period of time in some sort of solvent like water or alcohol. This is typically done with "soft" parts of a plant like leaves, flowers, or needles. Think of an infusion as tea: when used with water, the water is first brought to a boil, and once removed from the heat, the soft parts of the plant are placed in it to steep.

White pine (*Pinus strobus*) can be infused into a beneficial tea that's full of vitamin C. To make it, simply bring some water to a boil and remove it from the heat. Add a handful of green needles and let them steep for several minutes. There are no critical measurements with this, simply add depending on your own personal taste.

Decoction: This is the process of extracting medicinal compounds by boiling and concentrating the plant material, and is typically done with the "hard" or woody parts of a plant like stems, roots, and bark. These denser parts of the plant require a more aggressive approach to extracting the medicinal compounds, so they are placed in the water and boiled down (often more than once) to concentrate them.

Willow bark (*Salix* spp.) is very useful as an analgesic (pain reliever). Make a decoction with bark by filling a container with bark and covering it with water. Bring the entire mixture to a full boil. Continue boiling until half of the water has evaporated away. Cover with additional water and boil it down again to concentrate it. The bark can be strained off and the decoction can be drank. Using medicinal plants for pain relief is not as simple as "take two of these tablets and call me in the morning." You may have to make and drink this decoction for a couple of days before the pain completely subsides.

Wash: A wash quite simply uses the end product of an infusion or decoction that's meant to be used externally to wash the affected area.

Fomentation: A fomentation is the application of hot, moist substances to the body. An example would be soaking dressings or cotton material with the end product of an infusion or decoction that's meant to be used externally, and placing the dressing directly on the wound.

Again, this list is by no means all-inclusive, and the examples given are not the only medicinal uses for these plants. This is meant to help you establish a baseline for knowing how to prepare and use medicinal plants in the field so you can build on this information in the future. This is merely a snapshot of the world of medicinal plants.

CHAPTER 8
MAP READING AND LAND NAVIGATION

Navigation Kit

The baseline for a navigation kit is a reliable **compass**. There are a number of different types, styles, and brands to choose from. Whichever brand you choose, the important thing to know is how to use your compass well. Compasses are most useful for showing direction of travel, reducing lateral drift (our natural tendency to drift one way or the other while walking) by guiding the user to walk a straighter line, and measuring angles between points.

When possible, you should choose items that serve more than one function. I personally prefer the Suunto MC-2 compass because it also has a mirror that I can use for signaling and first-aid applications. The compass should have an adjustable declination feature that allows you to compensate easily for the difference between grid and magnetic north; if it doesn't, you'll be burdened with mathematically converting this angular difference yourself.

Generally speaking, if all you need to do is walk a certain direction to make your way back to civilization, that can be done with nothing more than a compass. However, you still have to know what that direction that is beforehand. If you're lost, there's less of a chance you know what direction that needs to be Compasses work best when paired with a good **map** of the area. The map is used to determine what direction and distance you need to walk to get to where you want to go.

Your "pace count" is what you'll use to measure horizontal distance actually traveled "on the ground." There are a number of ways you can keep track of this, but I prefer to use a good set of **pace beads**. This is a cord attached to your gear with beads on it that are slid up and down to keep track of distance traveled. The principle is similar to an abacus.

Although not required, being able to plot routes and take notes while you're navigating is a huge convenience. I carry a **waterproof notebook** that doesn't get ruined if it gets wet from rain or sweat, and a mechanical pencil. I choose a **mechanical pencil** over one that I have to sharpen as it gets dull because it allows me to make a much more precise mark on the map before measuring the angles and distances that I need to walk.

Last but not least, you may or may not need a **protractor**, sometimes referred to as a "coordinate scale." The scale you need depends on the scale of your map. Protractors are a tool for measuring angles, distances, and coordinates on a map during route planning. Many compasses already have scales on them that can be used to measure distances and plot coordinates, and the compass itself measures angles. If your compass has these features and you know how to use them, you may not need a protractor. If it doesn't, you'll need to add one of these to your kit and learn how to use it.

Recommended Navigation Kit

- Suunto compass
- Map
- Waterproof notebook
- Mechanical pencil
- Pace beads
- Protractor

Map Reading

CHAPTER 8: MAP READING AND LAND NAVIGATION

In my chosen military professions, I relied heavily on my ability to navigate from one point to another in unfamiliar terrain. My team members and I primarily used simple tools like the map and compass. Back then, GPS (Global Positioning System) receivers were very large, clunky, slow, and of course, reliant on batteries. These days, nearly every vehicle and cell phone has a GPS. The map and compass skills of those that once had them are now covered by cobwebs, and they've been dismissed completely by those who never developed them in the first place. While GPS units have gotten smaller, faster, and more prominent than ever, they still rely on two things: signal and battery power.

Many people in the Search and Rescue profession will tell you that too much reliance on technology is often a major contributor to the emergency situations they see. Many lost hikers rely completely on a GPS app on their phone. The danger of this? You have no control over when or where you'll have a good signal, especially in the backcountry. The farther away from civilization you go, the farther you get from cell towers. Even with a signal, you only have so much battery life in your phone or any external battery pack you may also be carrying.

GRAY BEARDED GREEN BERET'S GUIDE TO SURVIVING THE WILD

Cell phones and GPS units are both great parts of any complete navigation plan, but they cannot be all that you rely on. Having low- and no-tech options to fall back on when you no longer have a signal or battery power is always going to be the safest bet. Have a compass and a map of your area, and know how to use them.

Marginal Information

CHAPTER 8: MAP READING AND LAND NAVIGATION

Let's take a deeper dive into all the information given to us on a map, starting with marginal information. There's a lot of important information around the outside (margin) of the map if you know what to look for. There's also a lot of information you do *not* need for basic land navigation purposes, so I'll only highlight the important points.

Map Name: The map is often named after the most prominent and populated area on it. Other times, it may be named for the most prominent terrain feature depicted on it. The date the map was created is also important. Always ensure that you have the most up-to-date and accurate map available.

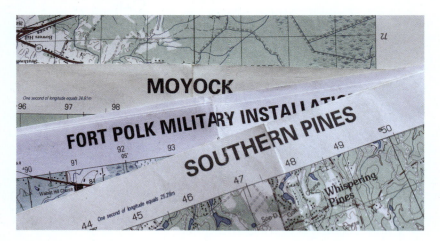

Scale: The scale of the map shows the ratio of a unit of measurement on the map to a unit of measurement on the ground. For example, on a 1:25,000 scale map, 1 inch on the map would be equal to 25,000 inches on the ground. Of course, you'd have to convert that to a more useful unit of measurement for your trek, but that's the idea. Fun fact: the metric system is typically used for maps, since the metric system is a base-10 number system (groups numbers in tens), and map grids are also base-10. The closer that relationship is within the ratio, the more accurate and detailed the map will be. A 1:10,0000 scale is much more detailed than a 1:50,0000 scale.

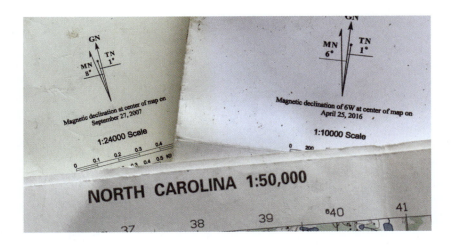

Bar Scales: These are essentially rulers that have already converted map measurements into useful on-the-ground measurements. They have increments that often show meters, feet, miles, and nautical miles.

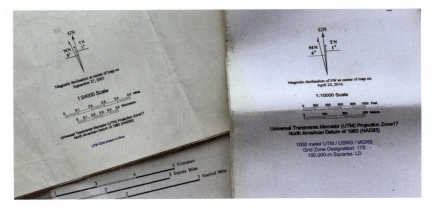

Contour Interval Note: This is an important note that gives the vertical scale between contour lines on the map. This information can be used to determine elevation and relief in each area. It will usually have a number and a unit of measurement. An example would be "10 meters," which means that there are 10 meters of elevation gained or lost between each contour line depicted on the map.

CHAPTER 8: MAP READING AND LAND NAVIGATION

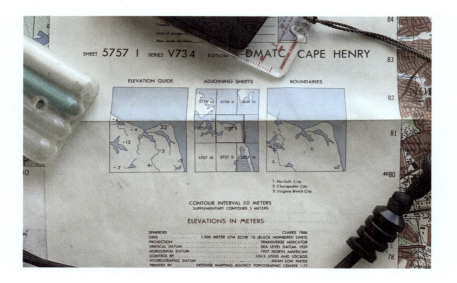

Legend: The legend provides additional information and describes symbols that are used specifically on your map.

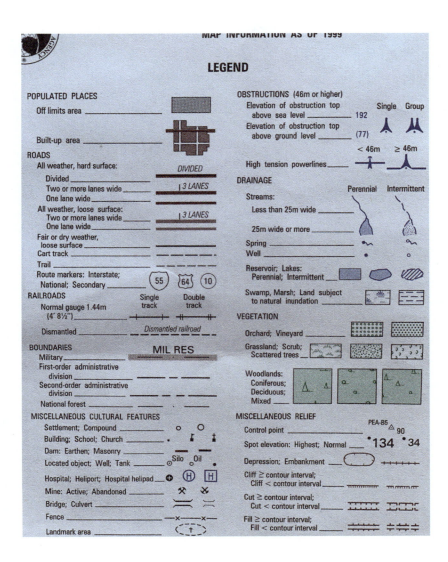

Declination Diagram: It's important to understand that there are three different "types of north" when it comes to maps, and they are rarely the same. The declination diagram shows the angular relationship between true north, grid north, and magnetic north. This information is important for converting them, which we'll discuss later in the chapter. The diagram may or may not also include a note for converting one to the other. If it doesn't, it's worth adding that note yourself for easy reference. Declination does change, especially over time, so reason it's important to have the most up-to-date map available.

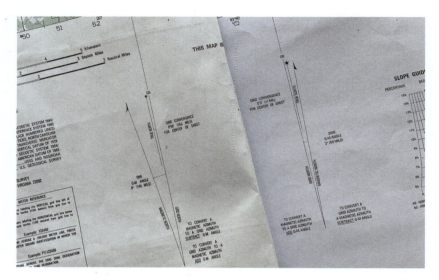

Basic Colors

There are five basic colors on a map, and they are not randomly chosen. The colors themselves give you valuable information, like the location of water, vegetation, roads and trails, and buildings. In addition to contour lines, colors depict the topography of an area, which can be useful for navigation.

Green is used to indicate vegetation like forests, orchards, and vineyards. White is usually used to indicate an absence, meaning the area is not forested and is a clearing or grassland, which is important information to the navigator. Keep in mind that forests are managed and cut from time to time, so it may not always be the most accurate information.

Blue is used to indicate bodies of water like lakes, ponds, swamps, streams, rivers, and creeks. Certain bodies can be there either year-round or intermittently/seasonally. That information will also be depicted on the map. A continuous body of water will usually be depicted as solid, while intermittent or seasonal ones will be depicted with dashed or dotted lines.

Black is most often used to depict man-made features like buildings, roads, and railroads. It is also often used to note political boundaries like state borders and county lines. Usually, a more prominent feature like a county highway would be a solid, thick black line, while a trail through the woods may only be a thin dashed or dotted line.

Red is used primarily for populated areas and major roads. For example, a city may have its political boundary outlined in black, with numerous black buildings within that boundary, but the entire area will be "filled" with a reddish overlay to highlight everything within those city limits. For roads, the black is used up to a certain point, but major roads with multiple lanes and interstates will be depicted in red to differentiate them from smaller roads.

Brown is used for the contour lines that show the topography of the area. Contour lines show both elevation and relief. Many maps use brown for this, especially in the civilian sector. A lot of military maps use a combination red-brown color instead of red or brown so that maps are "red light readable," meaning that using a red filter on a flashlight to read it at night will not drown out the color.

Here's a tip I learned during Special Forces Assessment and Selection (SFAS). We frequently navigated at night, and while I do that less often now as a civilian, I still do it. For quick reference, I would take different colored fluorescent highlighters and trace different points of interest like roads, streams, bodies of water, populated areas, what have you. This highlighted those areas for me during the day, but it proved to be even more beneficial at night. When you use a blue filter on your headlamp or flashlight, the fluorescent highlights glow extremely bright and those key locations really pop out at you. This was extremely valuable to me, as I often needed to navigate as quickly as possible using key terrain while trying to avoid roads and populated areas.

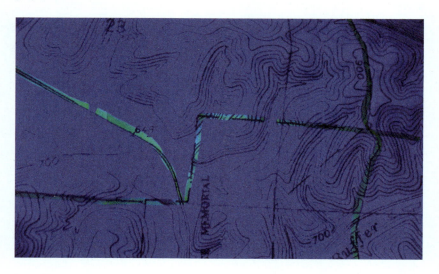

GRAY BEARDED GREEN BERET'S GUIDE TO SURVIVING THE WILD

Terrain Features

Terrain features are extremely valuable reference points when navigating. They give you an idea of the terrain in the area and serve as additional confirmation of where you are on the ground and on the map.

When I first joined the military, I was taught that there are **5 major, 3 minor, and 2 supplementary terrain features**. At some point in my career, the supplementary and minor terrain features were combined into one list.

5 Major Terrain Features

Hill

A **hill** is a point or area of high ground with ground sloping down on all sides. A hill is depicted by contour lines that form concentric circles. If you're standing on a hill, you'll have ground sloping down on all four sides (to your front, behind you, and to your left and right).

Valley

A **valley** is an area of lower ground with ground sloping upwards on three sides (in front/away from you, and two slopes up to the sky). In other words, if you were standing in it, you'd have high ground to your left and right, and the ground would slope upward on the upstream side and downward on the downstream side. These are often linear and usually contain a river or stream bed. The valley "flows" much like a river would: from higher ground downstream to lower ground. A valley is depicted by U-shaped or V-shaped contour lines that "point" uphill to the higher ground.

CHAPTER 8: MAP READING AND LAND NAVIGATION

Ridge

This is a line or stretch of high ground with various elevations along its crest. It's depicted on a map by U-shaped or V-shaped contour lines that point downhill to lower ground. The term **ridge** is often used interchangeably with "ridge line," but they are slightly different. Think of a "ridge line" as a mass like a mountain in its entirety. The mountain is a large grouping of various individual terrain features. An actual ridge is a specific, individual terrain feature within that larger group.

Saddle

A **saddle** is a "dip" or a low point along the crest of a ridge that's normally found between two hills. If you're standing in the middle of a saddle, you'll have two sides of higher ground (the hills) and two sides that lead to lower ground. When looking at the map, you'll notice two separate concentric circles that depict individual hills, with another concentric circle around both (which is lower in elevation than the two hills). The area between the two hills is the saddle.

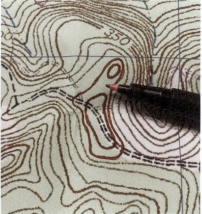

CHAPTER 8: MAP READING AND LAND NAVIGATION

Depression

A **depression** is a hole or low point in the ground that's surrounded by high ground on all sides. These wil often contain water, like a pond. The scale varies, but they're a lot like craters. They're depicted on the map by a contour line that forms a concentric circle, with tick marks along the inside of that line that point toward the lower ground.

 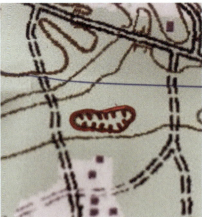

5 Minor Terrain Features

Draw

Think of a **draw** as a valley on a smaller scale, and usually on the side of a ridge. Remember that a valley is a major feature, and a draw is minor. You will still have higher ground on three sides, with one side lower (downstream), and it will still be depicted by U-shaped or V-shaped contour lines pointing up to higher ground, just on a smaller scale. A draw is appropriately named: it quite literally "draws" precipitation out of the high ground and directs it down to the valleys. When rainfall hits higher ground like a hill or ridge, it will follow the path of least resistance downhill until it reaches the valley, and then go on to the ocean. Draws are often the result of, and made deeper by, erosion. This is also why most draws have spurs on both of their sides along the side of a ridge.

CHAPTER 8: MAP READING AND LAND NAVIGATION

Spur

A **spur** is essentially a smaller ridge. It's an area of higher ground along the side of a larger ridge with a draw on both sides. It will have high ground on one side (the uphill side going up to the ridge), and three sides that are lower ground (a draw on each side, and the other low side that leads downhill to the valley). It's depicted by U-shaped or V-shaped contour lines that point downhill to lower ground.

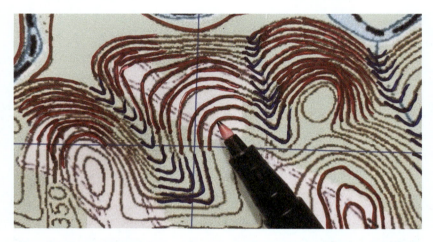

Cliff

Most people are familiar with **cliffs**—a very steep incline, or sheer vertical (even overhanging) drop-off. It's a rather abrupt change in elevation and very dangerous to navigate on or near. A cliff may be depicted by contour lines that are touching each other, or by a single contour line with tick marks pointing to the drop-off.

CHAPTER 8: MAP READING AND LAND NAVIGATION

Cut

A **cut** is a man-made feature that's typ cally seen along a road or railroad bed where people have cut away terrain for progress to be more gradual than following the natural, more dramatic landscape. While driving along an interstate, you've probably noticed where they cut or blasted a path through a hill to build a road. On a map, these are usually depicted by tick marks along the contour lines on the side of a road or railroad. The tick marks point down to the lower ground where the road or railroad is.

Fill

A **fill** is the opposite of a cut. It's a man-made feature in which material has been added to build up a road or railroad bed to make the grade more gradual instead of dropping off with the surrounding terrain. These will be depicted by tick marks along the contour lines, with the tick marks pointing down to the lower ground (in this case, away from the road or railroad bed).

CHAPTER 8: MAP READING AND LAND NAVIGATION

Grid Reference Systems

Finding a location in a developed area is as simple as having the address. It's already laid out with a house or box number, a street or road name, city, state, and zip code. Addresses of specific locations are nothing more than a systematic reference system, so anyone can find any location as long as they know what to do with the specific bits of information that are included.

In the backcountry, there are no house numbers or street signs. This is where **grid reference systems** come into play. Essentially, a grid pattern is overlaid on the area depicted by the map, and that grid becomes the reference point to find all locations within it.

The Universal Transverse Mercator (UTM) is essentially a civilian version of the Military Grid Reference System (MGRS). It's more readily available and more commonly used outside the military, so it's what I base my classes on. For you as the end user they'd both work the same, but since they're different systems of reference they have different coordinate designations. Think of it as MGRS calling one place Maple Street, while UTM calls it Jackson Road. It's the same exact location on the ground, but people are referring to it by different names.

Grid Coordinates

Typically, a "**coordinate scale**" (referred to more commonly as a "protractor") is used to plot or determine the coordinates on a map. It has different scales that are meant to match various, specific map scales that you may be using. To use it, make sure you're using the correct scale. Once you've found the grid square you're looking in, use the smaller increments of the protractor to precisely determine the rest of the 6-, 8-, or 10-digit grid coordinates. Most protractors are not accurate to the 8- or 10-digit grid level, so you must estimate in those cases.

The most important rule you must remember is to **read the map right** (from left to right), **then up** (from bottom to top). This is absolutely critical and bears repeating: always right, then up. Another important note is that each vertical line on the grid, though running north and south, is actually separating east and west, and each horizontal grid line (running east and west) is separating north and south.

As stated before, maps are "base-10," meaning that they are broken down into increments of 10. A grid square within a map is equal to 1,000 meters squared. This is expressed in what is known as a **four-digit grid coordinate**. The first two digits designate the vertical grid line that separates east and west, and the second two digits designate the horizontal grid line that separates north and south.

To put this into practical application, let's imagine you were looking for the grid coordinate 2396. The first two digits (23) are telling you which vertical line to stop at (the 23rd grid line) when reading left to right. The second two digits (96) tell you which horizontal grid line to stop at when reading up. The intersection of those two grid lines is the point that grid coordinate is designating. Four-digit grids are only accurate within 1,000 meters—it simply tells you what grid square you're working in. It's like someone only telling you the city they live in and you having to try to find their house with just that.

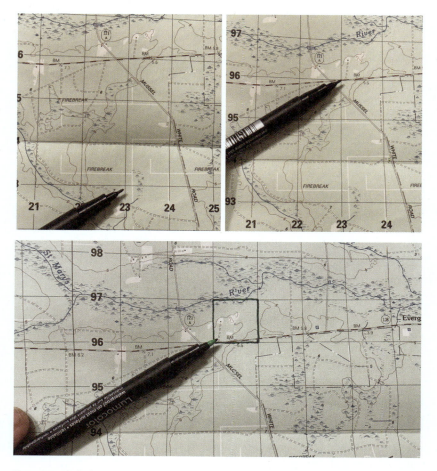

Because it is base-10, each individual grid square can also be further broken down into a smaller 10x10 grid. Having these additional numbers included in what is known as a **six-digit grid** will get you to within 100 meters of your desired location. This is like knowing the city and having it narrowed down to the street name.

Adding to the first example, let's say you're looking for the grid 235 965. At this point I find it best to split the coordinates into halves, so it's easy to identify which are meant to be used together. You would still read right first, then up. The first two digits of each half of the full coordinate are still going to designate the same grid square, but this time we have additional information from the third and sixth digit given. If the original grid square is broken into a smaller 10x10 grid, each square within it is now a 100-meter square. The third digit (5 in this case) tells you that you would read right first to the 23rd grid line, but the actual location you're looking for is halfway across that grid square when continuing to read to the right. The sixth digit (also 5 for this example) tells you that when reading up to 96, the actual location is halfway through the grid square as you continue to read up.

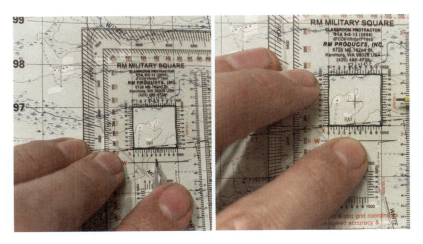

This can sometimes be confusing, but if you remember to use the rule "always right, then up," it'll become second nature. To make it more simple to grasp, what I like to do is use the first two digits of each half to locate the 1,000 meter square I'm working in, and from that point I know that any additional information (digits) given will be further into the square. Once I have identified the grid square, I use the same "right, then up" rule to plot the additional information given within that square.

The same principles apply when given additional digits of information in a grid coordinate. If you were to take one of the 100m squares that were designated by a six-digit grid and break it down into an even smaller 10x10 grid, each square within that would be 10m. Adding to the example, say the grid coordinates are 2352 9658. This time, the fourth and eighth digits are telling you how far to read right and up within one of those 100m squares. This is accurate to within 10m.

CHAPTER 8: MAP READING AND LAND NAVIGATION

If you're looking for a house, think of this as having its actual box number. This is what is most used for land navigation purposes.

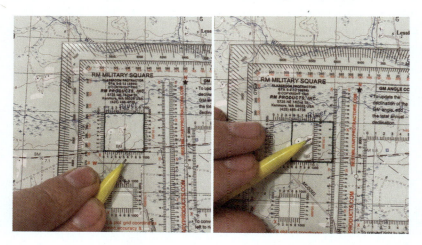

It is possible to further break one of those 10m squares down (again 10x10) into 1m squares and use a ten-digit grid to find it on the map. This would, of course, be accurate to within 1m. This is rarely used in navigation with a map and compass because that level of precision is difficult to put into practical application between plotting points on the map and walking that straight of a line.

Elevation and Relief

Contour lines are used to depict elevation and relief. They are a means of translating the three-dimensional topography of an area onto a two-dimensional map. Contour lines are by no means arbitrary, even if it looks like a cluttered mess of squiggly lines all over the map. These are precise depictions of elevation in each area.

Remember the contour interval note from earlier? It tells you the vertical distance between contour lines. All points along a contour line are the same elevation. If you were to take a snapshot of how those lines of elevation and relief ran along the terrain and place it on the map, you'd have a graphic representation of the terrain in that area.

There are three types of contour lines:

- **Index:** Every fifth contour line is what's considered an index contour. It is depicted by a much bolder line that usually has the elevation of that concentric circle annotated on it somewhere. You may have to follow it around the map a bit to find that index for reference.
- **Intermediate:** These are the contour lines between the index lines. They are set at the actual contour interval. They are solid lines, but not as bold as the index contours.
- **Supplementary:** Supplementary contour lines are used less frequently. They represent an area that is one half of

CHAPTER 8: MAP READING AND LAND NAVIGATION

the contour interval. They are depicted as dashed lines instead of solid.

When using contour lines to determine the elevation of a specific location, the line will fall on the terrain at that specific elevation. Find the nearest index contour line and read that elevation. Using the terrain features, determine whether the point you're looking at is going uphill or downhill from there. Count the intermediate contour lines up or down to the point you want to determine the elevation of. If it's between two contour lines, use half the contour interval for that location.

On a hill, that terrain will usually continue to go higher in elevation within the concentric circle formed by the contour line. The center of that hill, or the summit, is likely higher than the last contour line. The last contour line may read that the elevation is 840 feet. Simply estimate using half the contour interval to determine what the actual elevation is at the summit. If the contour interval is 10 feet, then it's safe to assume the elevation of the actual hilltop is 845 feet (a higher number because the top of the hill is higher ground). The same goes for areas of relief like a depression. The outer rim may be 80 feet in elevation, but with a contour interval of 10 feet, the center or lowest part of the depression would be 75 feet (a lower number because the ground is lower in a depression).

Some areas may have been surveyed and have their actual elevations depicted on the map. The legend will give you more information on the symbols used. Benchmarks, horizontal control points, and spot elevations are common.

Determining Direction

An **azimuth** is used to determine the angular direction from one point to another. Many people use it interchangeably with the term "bearing," but they are not the same. A bearing is based on an angle that is 90 degrees or less within a quadrant defined by a cardinal direction, for example "North 45 degrees West." An azimuth is an angle that is between 0 and 360 degrees as it is measured clockwise from north. Your compass measures an azimuth, not a bearing. That same bearing example would be a 315-degree azimuth. In my opinion, using the terms interchangeably has the potential to cause confusion and should be avoided.

A **reverse azimuth**, sometimes called a "back azimuth," is used to quickly calculate what azimuth you would need to walk to return to where you started. This is a very simple calculation. If your original azimuth was greater than 180 degrees, subtract 180 and you'll get your reverse azimuth. If it was less than 180, simply add 180 degrees and that will take you back. For example, the reverse azimuth of 270 degrees is 90 degrees. The reverse of 45 degrees is 225 degrees.

Converting an Azimuth

As you learned during the section on marginal information, there are three types of north that you need to be familiar with.

- **True North:** A line from any point on the earth's surface to the actual North Pole.
- **Grid North:** Follows along the grid lines that are overlaid on the map as part of the grid reference system. This does not always follow true north because the earth is spherical and three-dimensional, while a map is rectangular (or square) and two-dimensional. If you were to lay the sphere out flat, there would be some declination in the grid. Directions that are taken from the map are **grid azimuths**.
- **Magnetic North:** The north that a compass needle will point to when used. The magnetic north pole isn't the same as true or grid north. Directions that are determined with the compass are considered **magnetic azimuths**. The earth's magnetic field is not at the North Pole, it's in northern Canada.

Declination is the angular difference between true north and either grid or magnetic north. Those are the two types of declination: **grid declination** and **magnetic declination**. The declination diagram in the margin of the map will show this angular difference between the three types of north.

Taking true north out of the equation (it is of little practical value for actual navigation), the **G-M angle** is arguably the most important part of that diagram. It is the angular difference between grid north and magnetic north, and it can be several degrees depending on where you are in the world. What it will also show is whether you have a **westerly G-M angle** or an **easterly G-M angle**.

An easterly G-M angle means that magnetic north is to the east of grid north. A westerly G-M angle means just the opposite: magnetic north is to the west of grid north. Check how it appears on your map. That is important to identify, as it affects how the conversions are calculated.

Here are the conversion formulas for each:

- **Easterly G-M Angles:** To convert from magnetic to grid, add the G-M angle. When converting from grid to magnetic, subtract the G-M angle.
- **Westerly G-M Angles:** To convert from magnetic to grid, subtract the G-M angle. When converting from grid to magnetic, add the G-M angle.

Those two formulas are extremely important and they often get confused, so much so that the military started adding those notes to the declination diagram some time ago. If your map does not already have that information printed on it, I recommend you write it in to avoid confusion. No matter how long I have been doing this, I still second-guess it when I have no notes to refer to.

This information can be used to convert a grid azimuth that was taken from the map to a magnetic azimuth that you can point to with your compass and walk toward. Converting the azimuth ensures you end up at the correct location. For example, say you're working with a map that has an easterly G-M angle of 7 degrees. Using your map, you determine that the direction you need to travel to get from point A to point B is 155 degrees. Since this was taken from the map, this is a grid azimuth. This needs to be converted to a magnetic azimuth that you can now measure with your compass. You're converting from grid to magnetic on a map with an easterly G-M angle, so you subtract the G-M angle which is 7 degrees. The magnetic azimuth you need to travel to get from that same point A to point B on the ground is 148 degrees.

The opposite can also be done by converting a magnetic azimuth that you determine with your compass on the ground to a grid azimuth that you can correctly plot on the map.

One last note on converting azimuths: some compasses have adjustable declination on them. With this feature, you can dial in the G-M angle so that the offset is already factored in. Essentially, it adjusts magnetic north to match the grid north on your map, so you no longer need to worry about converting it. You're probably thinking, "Why didn't you just lead with that?" The answer is because as easy as that is, most people that use it don't understand what it's actually doing for them. If they don't really know what it's doing or how to do it, they'll be at a loss if they must use a compass that doesn't have that feature. If you're using the adjustable declination, make sure to adjust it when you go to a different area with a different declination.

Anatomy of a Compass

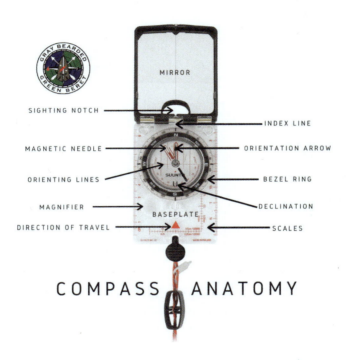

There are many different compass designs, but most share the same basic parts that you'll need to know how to use.

Baseplate: The baseplate is essentially the body of the compass. It will have the **direction of travel arrow**, which indicates the direction the compass should be facing when shooting or measuring an azimuth. You'll also find several different **scales** that allow for measuring distance or using as a substitute for a protractor. Your compass may or may not have a **magnifier**, which is useful for reading small print and doubles as a contingency solar ignition source for fire-starting. It's a relatively weak and small lens, so it works best with charred material.

Mirror: Many compasses have a mirror included. With the baseplate flat and the compass extended out as it should be when taking a reading, it can be difficult to see down onto the compass housing. The mirror is adjustable so that you can view the compass housing and get the reading. The mirror also includes a **sighting notch** that allows for more precise aiming. Most will have one at the bottom hinge between the baseplate and the mirror, and one at the top of the mirror. The lower one is usually the preferred notch to use. The mirror is also great for signaling and for first aid on areas that you cannot see, like your face and your "undercarriage."

Compass Housing: The compass housing itself has several different parts that are important. It has **orienting lines** that are used to align the compass housing with the meridan (vertical) grid lines on a map. The rotating **bezel ring** has an azimuth scale that has degrees marked (usually in two-degree increments). The desired azimuth is lined up with the **index line** at the top of the bezel ring on the baseplate. Many compasses will have a second index line at the bottom of the bezel ring (opposite the direction of travel). This is used to quickly determine the reverse azimuth without calculating. If your desired azimuth is indexed at the top, the azimuth reading that is indexed at the bottom is the reverse.

Magnetic Needle: The needle is the part that points north. It may be a different color, but the side that points north is usually red. This is important to know ahead of time. I've seen many students line up the wrong side of the arrow and walk 180 degrees in the wrong direction. With the chosen azimuth indexed, you have to rotate your body until the magnetic needle is lined up inside the **orientation arrow**, which is a larger arrow (sometimes also red) that's on the actual bezel ring (fixed at 0 degrees north unless you have adjusted declination). The orientation arrow is sometimes referred to as the "doghouse" or the "shed." To use the compass properly, you must "put the needle in the doghouse" or "put red in the shed."

If your compass is equipped with it, you can use the **declination adjustment feature**. This allows you to compensate for a westerly or easterly G-M angle so that your magnetic and grid readings match without conversion.

How to Use a Compass

There are a couple of different ways that you can use your compass. You may have a predetermined azimuth that you want to walk to, so you'll need to input that known azimuth into your compass to "shoot the azimuth" and actually walk in the desired direction. To **input a known azimuth**:

1. Determine the azimuth you want to travel on.
2. Dial the azimuth in by turning the bezel ring until the desired azimuth is indexed at the index line.
3. Keep the baseplate flat, and turn your body until "red is in the shed," or reasonably close.
4. Now that you're facing the right direction, fine-tune it by taking a more accurate reading. With both hands on the compass, extend your arms out as far as you can.
5. Adjust the mirror so that you can see down onto the compass housing and make minor adjustments to ensure the magnetic needle is centered inside the orientation arrow.
6. Look through the sighting notch for a distant aiming point to walk to.

The second way you may use your compass is to actually determine the azimuth of a point you wish to walk to. Essentially, it is the same steps but in reverse. To **determine an unknown azimuth**:

1. Locate the object in the distance with the sighting notch.

2. Keeping the baseplate level and using the mirror to see, rotate the bezel ring to move the orientation arrow to the magnetic needle rather than moving the needle to the doghouse.

3. Take the azimuth reading from the index line on the compass.

Distance

There are two primary methods that are used to determine how far you'd have to walk on a specific azimuth to get from one point to another. Which one you use depends on your route. If you're walking a specific azimuth, you'd use what is called "**straight line distance**." There are two methods you could use to calculate this. Both require that you have the two points marked on your map.

1. Take a piece of paper and place one corner at your starting point.

2. Mark the finish point on the edge of the paper.
3. Use the bar scales on the map to measure the distance in the desired unit of measurement.

The other method is to draw a line between each point. You can use the scale on your compass (depending on the model) or a protractor to measure the distance along that line. To use the bar scale, take the larger reading on the right side of the scale and determine the remainder using the left side of the scale.

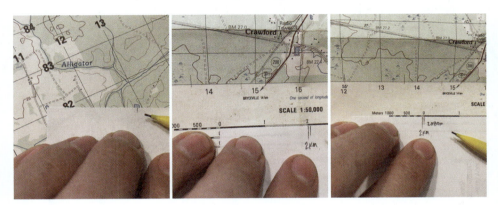

If you're walking along a road or trail, you'd use what is called **"curved line distance."**

1. With the start and finish points marked on the map, place the corner of a piece of paper on the start point.
2. Align the edge of the paper along the road or trail and follow it as closely as possible.
3. Make an index mark whenever the road curves away so that you can turn the paper to follow the curvature of the road or trail. The more precise you are with this, the more accurate you'll be.
4. Once you get to the end, use the bar scales to calculate the total distance.

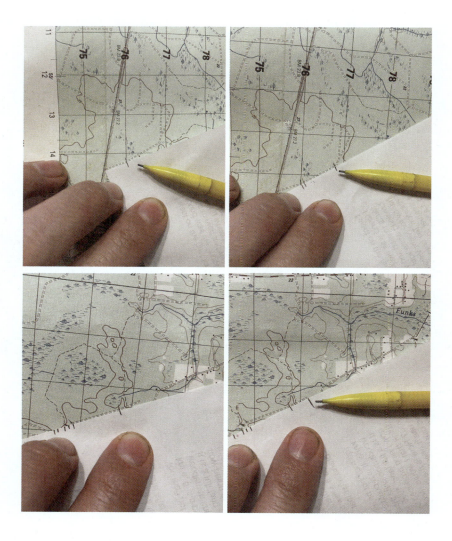

For quick results, you can use a string to try and follow the curvature of the road, or measure the straight line distance and then measure the portion of the string that was used, but I've found those to be fairly inaccurate methods so I don't use them. Using a paper is a much more accurate method in the end.

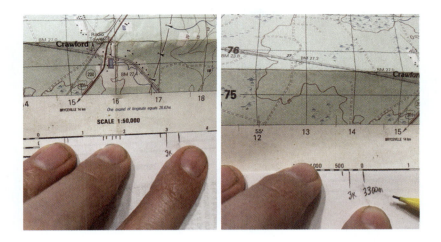

Land Navigation

Different Ways to Get There

Dead reckoning is a technique that uses precise azimuths and distances to navigate from one point to another. For the most part, these are straight-line routes, or a combination of several straight-line azimuths and distances (known as "legs") that get you from one point to another. Typically, you'll use one of two methods (or a combination of the two) when dead reckoning:

- **Distant Aiming Point:** Pick a distinguishable object that's as far off in the distance as possible that lines up with the azimuth you want to travel. Walk to that object (while keeping track of pace, of course). Once you reach that object, take another reading, and look for the next distinguishable object on an azimuth.
- **Leap Frog:** This technique is used when you have someone else with you that you can send out to act as that distant aiming point. Send them out as far as possible and just before they're out of sight, have them stop. Give them any needed directions to move left or right until they are on the azimuth. Once they're

CHAPTER 8: MAP READING AND LAND NAVIGATION

set, they do not move until you get to them (counting pace as you go). Repeat this process as needed.

Terrain association is a technique that uses general directions and follows distinct and recognizable terrain to get from one point to another. It is often quicker and allows for easier movement, especially in hilly or mountainous terrain. Rather than bulldoze on an azimuth from one point to another, through any number of obstacles you might find, this allows you to follow contours and ridges and select easier routes. Often the fauna of an area has already created paths, or at least taken paths of least resistance, along those contours and ridges.

A good navigator will have the ability to use a combination of both techniques on any given route and remain oriented while doing so. This includes: reading the terrain on the map during the route planning portion and recognizing the legs of the route where prominent terrain and ease of movement will allow for terrain association; and seeing where the terrain doesn't really support it and identifying the need for dead reckoning on those legs.

Orienting a Map to the Ground

One of the most important steps when using a map in the field is to first orient the map to the ground. This makes it easier to translate what you're seeing on the map to the ground in front of you. You can orient the map by using a compass or by terrain association. To use the compass, place it on the map with 0 degrees indexed. Use the orienting lines in the compass housing to line it up with the median (vertical) grid lines on the map. Alternatively, you can use the straight edge of the baseplate. Just ensure that the direction of travel is in fact toward the top of the map. The map is now oriented and the terrain you see in front of you on the ground should closely match what you see on the map.

You can also orient the map by using the terrain you see on the ground, assuming they are known terrain features. Orient the map so that it lines up with the terrain on the ground. This is less precise, but very quick and extremely useful when you're navigating more by terrain association instead of dead reckoning.

This step is critical if you're going to use your compass to determine azimuths from the map. It requires precision to be able to get precise directions. This also assumes that you're either using a compass with adjustable declination so that magnetic and grid norths are aligned with each other, or that you're converting the azimuths before orienting the map.

Pace Counts

Navigation is nothing more than walking the answer to a simple mathematical equation. You figure out that answer by measuring the angle and distance on the map. Traveling at a specified angle for a specified distance will get you from your start point to your finish point. All you have to do is walk the answer to see if you got it right. The compass is used to continually measure the angle you're walking. The distance is measured by what is known as a **pace count**. A pace count is the average number of paces it takes to walk a specified distance, usually 100 meters. To simplify, you only count every other step, so you're essentially counting strides.

Uniformity is one key to accurate measurement, so you always want to start from the desired point, step off with the same foot first, and only count every other step on the opposite foot. For example, I will always step off with the right foot and only count steps taken on my left foot. Counting strides rather than steps cuts the counting you have to do in half. Another key to accuracy is replicating actual field conditions as much as possible when determining your pace count. You should include flat, uphill, and downhill sections in your pace course (a short course used to determine pace count). Another variable that you should consider for best accuracy is carrying a similar load to what you'll be carrying in the field. Heavier loads often translate to shorter steps and therefore higher pace counts. Lighter loads tend to do the opposite.

- You'll want to walk naturally with the prescribed load on flat terrain for a measured 100m course. Record that number.
- Walk uphill for 100m and record that.
- Lastly, walk downhill for 100m and record that.
- Average the sum of those three numbers. That's a fairly accurate average pace count through varying terrain with a similar load to what you're going to be carrying. Remember that pace count.

Now, when you're actually out navigating, you'll count every other step until you reach your pace count and know that you have walked 100m. Keep track of this by using your **pace beads**. They have nine lower beads that measure 100m increments, and four upper beads that measure 1,000m (kilometer) increments.

- Every time you hit your 100m pace, drop a bead down and start your 100m pace count over again.
- Once you hit 1,000m, drop one of the upper beads down, slide all the lower beads up, and begin again for the next kilometer.
- Continue until you get to where you are going.

This is extremely important because there's a good chance you'll lose count, and it's not as if you can just go back to the beginning and start over if you've already traveled a few kilometers.

Navigational Aids

There are some extremely useful aids that make navigation that much easier. They are safeguards that not only speed up navigation, but also prevent you from becoming hopelessly lost. These should be part of every route plan, every time.

When you look at your map, determine what area you're going to be traveling through and "box" yourself in using linear features like roads, trails, and streams. You may even have some very prominent terrain features like ridge lines to use. Essentially, you're using these to make a box around your area and if you never cross these boundaries, you're never outside of that box. Even if you get temporarily disoriented, you'll know roughly where you are, which will make it easier to find yourself using an **escape azimuth**. You use an escape azimuth to get out of trouble. When you're boxed in like this, provided you haven't crossed any of your navigational aids, you know that you can walk a specific azimuth and eventually reach one of them.

Determine what your **baseline** is. The baseline is the feature "behind you" in your direction of travel that you have no reason to cross. In other words, if you run into that, something is very wrong. On the opposite end of the corridor you are creating, establish what is known as a **backstop**. This is a prominent feature on the far end of your route that you also have no reason to cross, and if you do, you've gone too far. Next, determine what you're going to use as **handrails** that would be to your left and right as you travel. Like handrails, you can follow closely by them (or on them) to go the desired direction and keep from going outside the box.

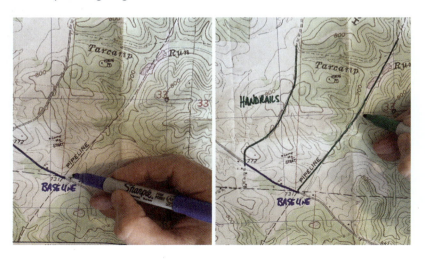

CHAPTER 8: MAP READING AND LAND NAVIGATION

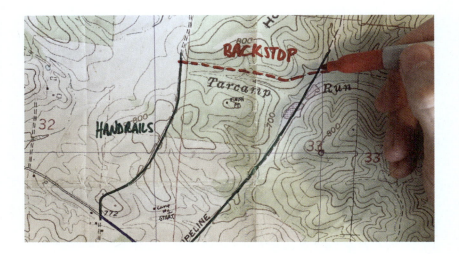

If there are large obstacles or terrain within this corridor that you want to avoid altogether, you can use a technique called **deliberate offset**. Rather than going straight to the point, you deliberately choose to offset one direction or the other to go around the obstacle or area. This will lead you to what is referred to as an **attack point**—a point that is offset from the actual point you're traveling to. You then navigate from the attack point to the actual desired location.

You may find that you run into obstacles that weren't planned when you were dead reckoning, and not accounted for when you were using terrain association or any of the previously mentioned navigational aids. You must be able to get around them, but you still need to keep track of the azimuth and distance you're walking to prevent getting lost. This can be done using the **detour bypass method**. This is used to precisely box around the obstacle and get back on course.

Once you reach the near side of the obstacle:

1. Stop your forward pace count and add or subtract 90 degrees from your original azimuth to make a right or left turn to go around.

2. Walk on that temporary azimuth as far as necessary to clear the width of the obstacle. You need to keep track of that distance with a separate pace because you haven't made actual forward progress on your route with this leg.

CHAPTER 8: MAP READING AND LAND NAVIGATION

3. Make another 90-degree turn to put you back on the original azimuth, and walk until you've cleared the length of the obstacle. This pace is forward progress on your original route, so it's added to the primary pace count.

4. Next, make another 90-degree turn and travel the same distance you traveled originally to clear the width of the obstacle. It needs to be the same so that you end up on the far side of the obstacle directly in line with your original azimuth. This pace obviously does not count as forward progress.

5. Once you've finished boxing around, simply pick up your original route and continue to walk.

These navigational aids really speed up the process. I used them often during SFAS when I had very little time to move relatively great distances as part of the assessment and selection process. I would quickly establish my backstop, baseline, and handrails, quickly assess the terrain in the box that I created, and choose a deliberate offset to an attack point closer to the actual point that I needed to find. I could take one quick compass reading, put it away, and run toward the attack point, "bouncing" off the handrails if I drifted into them but always moving forward. I usually used the intersection of my backstop and handrail as an attack point because there was no way of mistaking it. From the attack point, I used dead reckoning to precisely navigate to the actual point I was looking for. I covered the bulk of the distance very quickly, which saved time, and I only had to take my time precisely navigating a couple hundred meters at the end to find the points.

Route Planning

Here's where we put all this information together into practical application. There's an old saying: "Plot twice, walk once." I don't know who said it originally, but I've found that it holds true. Taking the time to carefully measure angles and distances, and then double-checking them for accuracy, is extremely important. Any mistake you make here can translate to kilometers of calorie expenditure on the ground or getting completely lost. I like to take my time ensuring everything is correct, so I develop a **route planning log** that I can refer to as I'm navigating. This log can have any information you want on it, but mine usually has **a leg number, azimuth, distance, and remarks**.

As a reminder, you should establish your navigational aids to box yourself in before setting up the rest of this route plan.

It's best to read the terrain, look for potential obstacles, and develop multiple legs to get you from one point to the other. Straight dead reckoning on a single azimuth through whatever you run into out there is not always the best choice. The easiest way to eat an elephant is one bite at a time. Break your route into smaller legs so that if you make a mistake, you don't have to backtrack as far to get back on course. Select prominent features that are unmistakable on the map and on the ground to use as checkpoints for each leg. Don't try and change your azimuth at random—there must be something that lets you know you got to where you need to be to change direction and maintain accuracy.

Calculate your azimuth by using a protractor on your map and converting it to a magnetic azimuth that you can actually walk, or by using an expedited technique where you use the compass as a protractor. If the compass has adjustable declination and it's set, you can disregard the conversion from grid to magnetic.

1. Orient the map to the ground.

2. Draw a line from the start point to the next checkpoint, or just use the straight edge of your baseplate. Make sure the direction of travel is correct.

3. With the edge lined up between points, rotate the bezel ring to "put red in the shed." Move the bezel ring, not the map. The map must remain stationary and oriented.

4. With the "needle in the doghouse," the azimuth you need to walk is now indexed at the top of the baseplate.

Now, measure the distance between the points and record this information in your route planning log. Lastly, look at the map information like the streams, roads, and terrain features that you'll be traveling through on that leg. Put notes in the remarks section of your log so you can refer to them. For example, your first leg may be 38 degrees for 500m to the top of a prominent hill. At a minimum, you'd want to note what terrain feature is the finish point for that leg (remember that this should not be an arbitrary finish, there should be something identifiable there). During that leg, you might cross a stream once at 200m and again at 450m. Put those notes in your remarks section. These are used as progress checks along each leg and give you something close to fall back on if you make a mistake at some point. Continue this process for each leg of your route.

Locating Unknown Points

I think of navigation as a preventive priority. The ability to effectively navigate from one point to another to keep from getting lost to begin with is arguably the most important aspect of all of this. A close second is the ability to quickly determine where you are if you do get lost so that you can navigate your way back. There are three very important tools you should learn to really round out your navigation skillset. All three have to do with determining the location of an unknown point using triangulation techniques.

Intersection: An intersection is used to determine the location of an unknown point in the distance by using two or more known points close by. These points must be known on the ground, as well as on the map. From these points, you can triangulate the location of the unknown point in the distance. For example, maybe you see a hill in the distance but are not quite sure which one it is on the map.

1. First, orient the map to the ground and mark the location of the first known point on the map.

2. From that location, shoot an azimuth to the unknown point in the distance and record it.

3. Move to the next known point and shoot another azimuth from there to the unknown point.

4. Repeat this process if you have additional known points. The more you have, the more accurate you'll be, but I have never had to use more than two or three for this to be successful.

5. From the known points on your map, plot the azimuths and draw straight lines extending out toward the direction of the object.

Remember that what you determined with your compass was a magnetic azimuth, so you must convert it to a grid azimuth before plotting it on the map. This is not necessary if you're using a compass for which you've already set the adjustable declination. Where those lines cross on the map is that unknown location. You can now plot a grid to it and develop a route there if you want to.

Resection: A resection is used when the location you're in is the unknown. In other words, you're lost. However, if you can identify two or more locations in the distance that are known both on the ground and on your map, you can use those to determine your own location. Maybe once you got down in a valley you got little disoriented, but you can still see a familiar radio tower and mountain peak (hill) in the distance.

1. From your location, shoot an azimuth to the radio tower and record it.

2. Next, shoot another azimuth to the hill.

3. Now convert those magnetic azimuths to grid, if necessary. However, before plotting them on the map, you need to convert them to reverse azimuths.

4. Draw the reverse azimuth from each known location. Where those two lines cross is your location.

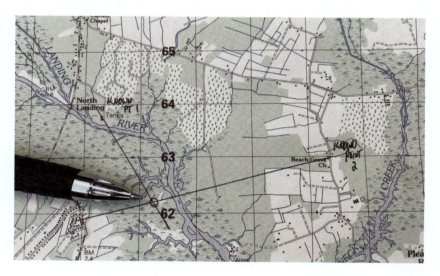

Modified Resection: A modified resection is a little-known but extremely valuable tool. Like a resection, it is used when you're on a road, stream, trail, or other linear feature and you know you're somewhere on that feature, but you're not exactly sure where. If you have at least one known point in the distance that you can recognize on the ground and on the map, you can use the linear feature you're standing on as the second known point.

1. Shoot an azimuth to the known point in the distance.

2. Convert it from magnetic to grid if needed, and then convert it to a reverse azimuth.

3. Plot a line on the map from the known point back to the linear feature. Where the line crosses that linear feature is your location on that road, trail, or stream.

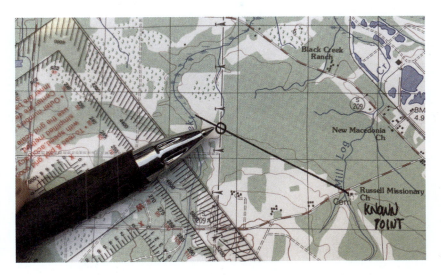

Basic map reading and land navigation skills are arguably some of the most important for the woodsman (or woman). If you can keep from getting lost to begin with, or at least find your way if you do become lost, you can prevent many emergency situations from the start. The other thing I've found is that with the ability to navigate, you can travel safely and confidently anywhere you want in the wilderness, rather than be limited to the marked trails that someone else decided were all you needed to see. Of course, in some places it is illegal to go off-trail, so there's that. But many others are yours to explore. Happy trails, or happy bushwhacking—with nav skills, the choice is yours.

CHAPTER 8: MAP READING AND LAND NAVIGATION

CHAPTER 9

SIGNALING FOR RESCUE

Signal Kit

A good signal kit will give you options to make yourself more visible under a variety of conditions. It's important to distinguish between active and passive methods. **Passive signals** are working for you all the time and require no effort on your part once they're set up. You use them to increase your visibility, but because they are passive, you can continue working on other tasks. **Active signals** require your engagement. These are used when it's reasonable to expect that someone could see them, or when you see or hear someone coming and need to get their attention. They take you away from doing other important tasks, so blindly signaling without an audience does you no good.

In addition, you should be thinking of signals that are good for the **day**, and others that are best used at **night** when day signals may not be seen. Many night signals require a battery, or are only good for single use. Neither of these are good for passive signals that may not even be seen by anyone. Those should be saved for when you are actively trying to get the attention of someone.

Some signals could be considered **universal**, in that they could be used either during the day or at night. These are typically **audible** signals, like a whistle.

Generally speaking, signals should incorporate **color**, **contrast**, **shine**, and **movement** when possible. Choose bright colors like fluorescent orange or blue. These colors contrast well with a variety of natural backgrounds, so they make excellent visual signals. The human eye is naturally drawn to movement, so incorporating that into your signals as well is beneficial. "Shine" could be more appropriately named "reflection," because it is reflecting light towards something or someone.

The best signals will include an **olfactory** element to them, and possibly even leave a **trace** behind so that you can be tracked better if on the move. Signal fires are a great example of this.

Recommended Signal Kit

- Brightly colored tarp (part of the shelter kit)

- Reflective cordage (also part of the shelter kit)
- Signal mirror (may be on your compass as part of your navigation kit)
- Headlamp with strobe function and extra batteries

Before You Leave, Leave a Plan

In this final chapter, I'd like to take this opportunity to commend you for taking the time to learn the baseline skills that are discussed in this book, especially the preparedness skills like being able to fix an injury that may otherwise prevent you from getting home, and learning to navigate so you don't become the next "lost hiker" in the wilderness. With that said, there are some situations that just cannot be helped. If you're injured severely and can't make your way out, or so lost that you cannot locate your precise location, you need to take steps to make yourself as visible as possible so that Search and Rescue (SAR) teams can find you quickly.

The obvious question: is it reasonable to expect that someone is out looking for you? Don't make the mistake of thinking that because you always have your cell phone on you that you can just call for help if needed. Yes, you'll likely have that option and you *should* call for help if you can—there's no questioning the value of that. But what if you don't have signal or battery power to make that call? You cannot rely completely on technology. You must have a no-tech backup plan for when the tech plan fails.

The first step to any emergency signal plan is to leave a detailed plan with someone. Let them know where you're going and how long you expect to be gone. That way, if you don't return on time, someone knows to begin looking for you. Other information you may include is:

- What you're wearing, maybe even down to the footwear so that trackers can identify your footprints.
- What you're driving and what trailhead you're parked at, if any.
- A route plan.
- What day and time you plan to return—be very specific.

Passive Signals

Day

Signal Panel: These are great because they're high visibility and incorporate color and contrast, and if you hang them up in the breeze, movement can be added to that list. A signal panel is usually a large, lightweight, foldable material in bright orange. You don't have to pack a dedicated panel that's only for signaling. If you look for opportunities, you can find other items in your kit that can be useful for this purpose.

In my emergency kits, I always use a bright orange emergency blanket. I can use it for shelter, plus it makes a large passive signal panel. I can use an orange bandana or shemagh (scarf) for my water kit, as bandages, or as a panel in an emergency. I like to wear natural colors for my clothing, but I can also substitute either the bandana or shemagh with an oversized, brightly colored T-shirt that I can put on over everything to make myself more visible. I have an orange backpack that I could choose, or a Signal Joey in my other packs. This is versatile pouch that contains my entire signal kit that I can tie on the outside of my pack. One side is natural colors, and the other is bright orange. If I get into trouble, I can tie it with the orange side out and turn my backpack into a passive signal.

Trail Marking Tape: Trail marking tape is an excellent signal choice that incorporates color, contrast, and if you leave a long tail that can flow in a breeze, movement. This comes in a roll that's easy to pack in any signal kit. It's useful for marking trails to prevent getting lost as well.

CHAPTER 9: SIGNALING FOR RESCUE

Night

Reflective Tape: You've probably seen this before on a road construction worker's vest. During the day it appears silver or gray, but at night when light hits it, it glows brightly. It has also been incorporated into items like running shoes and jackets.

Reflective Tacks: These thumbtacks have reflective material on them like the reflective tape. They're used by hunters to find their way to a tree stand when it's dark out. They are extremely useful in a signal kit because they're multi-directional and glow brightly when light hits them. They're excellent for marking trails as well, so you don't get lost at night.

Reflective Cordage: There are some cordages on the market that incorporate a reflective thread or threads in them. You may have seen something like this on a guyline for a tent to keep you from tripping over it at night when you're moving about your campsite. You can also get paracord with this reflective quality built into it. That's extremely useful to use on your shelter because it becomes a passive emergency signal that increases the chances of you being seen.

Multicolor Signal String: This is a multifaceted signal that I developed when I first got into the survival industry. I was looking for a way to make a passive emergency signal that was effective both during the day and at night. It started with a 25–30 foot line of paracord—the same length as the Rapid Ridgeline I use for my shelter. The paracord is bright orange and reflective. I took three brightly colored bandanas (red, blue, and orange) and installed some small grommets in the corners with a simple grommet kit. The grommets were used to fasten each bandana to the line of paracord. By design, this was meant to be strung up high above the shelter to increase the chances of being seen at a distance. The orange reflective paracord was a passive day and night signal, the three different colored bandanas acted as panels to provide both color and contrast, and because only two corners of each were attached, they would flow in the breeze and give movement to the signal. This system incorporates all the characteristics of a good signal: color, contrast, movement, and shine (reflection). It was meant to be the center of a larger "signal circle."

CHAPTER 9: SIGNALING FOR RESCUE

Making a Passive Signal Circle

The **signal circle** was another system I developed early on. The shelter itself, which is where most of your time would be spent, should be marked by the multicolor signal string. In order to increase your chances of being seen at a greater distance, you should branch out from that central location and leave passive signals that could be seen by someone walking by even if they didn't see your shelter location.

From the shelter, you can travel out in all directions and mark a tree with orange trail marking tape secured by a reflective tack. This makes for an excellent day and night passive signal. Set these up in a 25-meter circle around your shelter, and then out to 50 and 100m. If time and resources permit, this could easily be expanded. This greatly increases the chances of being found because your footprint in the area is so much larger.

Active Signals

Day

Signal Mirror: A signal mirror can be seen for miles. You can use a dedicated signal mirror or the mirror on your compass if it has one. To aim the signal mirror, extend your arm in front of you and make a V-shape with your index and middle fingers. Reflect the sunlight onto that "V" and use it as a sighting window to direct that reflection to the person or object you're trying to signal. This incorporates color, contrast, movement, and shine.

Signal Flag: Movement can help with the visibility of your signal. It may be beneficial to make a flag by attaching a brightly colored panel to a pole that you can source from the landscape that can then be waved to get someone's attention. This incorporates color, contrast, and movement.

Night

Chemical Light: These are small lights that have a capsule inside them. When you snap the capsules, they'll glow for a few hours. Some color choices are brighter than others. Many of these are difficult to see, so I recommend making a **"chem buzzsaw"** to really increase their visibility and add movement. You can make a buzzsaw with one light, but three lights makes it more visible and effective. Take a length of cordage (about 3 feet) and tie it to the chemical lights. Hold the end of the string and twirl the chemical lights to create a larger circle of light. Remember that these are a single-use item, so this should be reserved for active signaling.

Strobe: This can be a strobe function on your headlamp or a dedicated strobe. The headlamp option is not nearly as bright, but it does provide additional function since you can use it primarily as a light source for working or navigating at night. A dedicated strobe is extremely bright and can be seen a lot farther away. Both take batteries, so neither is a good option for passive signaling and should be saved for active signaling attempts.

Audible Signals

Whistle: When it comes to whistles, always choose the loudest possible one you can find. The better the noise carries, the farther away someone can hear you. There's some debate about using a whistle that has a "pea" in it (like a referee whistle), or using a "pea-less" version. The bottom line is this: both are loud, and both can be heard in many circumstances. A pea-less whistle may be a better choice in water because water tends to bind on the pea and cause a potential loss of function. However, pea-less whistles lack the audible contrast that the rattling pea provides and can sometimes be drowned out by heavy winds. No single signal should be relied on completely, so remember that this is just part of a larger signal plan.

Metallic Objects: Banging a bush pot or metal water bottle can be an effective improvised signal in the woods. The sound of metal clanging is not normal and could get someone's attention.

Signal Fires

One of the most effective signals is a fire, and you're likely already using it to accomplish other priorities. A fire and its smoke can be seen day or night. What really sets it apart as an outstanding signal is that it also has an olfactory aspect to it. Even when it cannot be seen, the smoke can be smelled from a long way off. It also has the element of a trace (coals and ash) that's left behind even if you're moving to other locations trying to make your way out or looking for an area with better resources.

It's universally understood that three of anything, evenly spaced, is a distress signal. That is why I place three large Xs evenly spaced across the back of my emergency blanket. That differentiates it from another orange tarp in the woods—it's meant to signal distress.

The same is true when I'm using a fire for signaling. Three evenly spaced fires send a much stronger message than a single fire that could be dismissed as a simple campfire of someone out enjoying themselves in the wilderness. An efficient way to use your existing fire as a standby emergency signal is to have your main fire going that you're using for other tasks, and build two more fire lays evenly spaced on either side, but don't light them. If the opportunity to signal arises, transfer the fire from the main fire to the other two and you'll quickly have three fires going to signal for rescue.

Smoke Generator

Smoke generators are excellent tools for signaling. They are constructed from the landscape and although they take a little time and effort, they're extremely effective signals. To build one:

- Make a tripod about six feet high.
- Lash a platform on the underside about halfway down.
- Build a fire lay complete with tinder on the platform.
- Cover the top half of the tripod with green conifer bows or other green vegetation. This serves two purposes: the green vegetation keeps the fire lay and tinder dry, and it also produces thick smoke when the fire is lit under it.

Start by building one in an area that is highly visible, and then as time permits, build another two. Remember that three of anything, evenly spaced, is a universal distress signal.

A variation you could do on this structure is building a second platform about six inches underneath the first. Pack this lower platform with tinder and use the upper platform for the fire lay. It takes a little more work and resources, but it incorporates significantly larger amounts of tinder so the fire lay is almost sure to light.

Having an effective, redundant signal plan can make all the difference in being found quickly or being forced to continue exposed to the elements. Your signals should not be an afterthought, nor should they be stuffed away somewhere you cannot easily get to if the opportunity to get someone's attention presents itself. The moment you realize you've gone from recreation to an emergency, get your signals out and be ready to use them. You may have a very narrow window of opportunity to catch someone's eye and get the help you need.

CLOSING THOUGHTS

The forest has a way of making us feel like we're home. The artificiality of the life we've created for ourselves at home in our towns and cities all melts away if we let it. Cars give way to hiking boots. We ditch lawn mowers and pristine landscaping to take a look at the chaotic and random beauty that only Mother Nature can create. The noise of sirens and smell of exhaust fumes are replaced by the sounds of birds and crisp, clean mountain air We gladly trade our ranking in the rat race for endless opportunity, adventure, and exploration in our wilds of choice. The "Joneses" we were keeping up with are nowhere to be found out here.

There's a reason the Outdoor Recreation industry is so vast, and so many people flock to the wilderness on the weekends with what precious little vacation time they have each year. Human beings need the wilds. We need the simplicity. Wake up, drink water, eat, explore, stare into the campfire and just be, rest, repeat.

In the words of the late Horace Kephart:

> *"It is one of the blessings of wilderness life that it shows us how few things we need in order to be perfectly happy."*

I'm fortunate to know this feeling well—I've essentially made a living chasing it at every opportunity. One of my goals is to urge others to head out into the wilds of their choice and enjoy that same feeling for themselves. It's true that the vehicle I use to convince people to get off the couch and go outside is encouraging them to learn wilderness skills, but the underlying reason is that I want them to feel this simplicity and sense of being where they belong. That feeling can only be made better when shared with family and friends.

I want to close by encouraging all of you to make time to go out and enjoy our natural areas. The National Parks and State Parks are treasures that should be on every bucket list. Even if it's just a small forest close to home, I hope you'll take more time to go out and enjoy it. Take your family and friends, unplug, practice wilderness skills, go for a hike, sit around a campfire and roast some marshmallows.

Lastly, don't let anyone else define your outdoor experience for you. Mother Nature will meet you where you are, and how you do it isn't the important thing. In this industry, there seems to be a desire to define things—this is survival, this is bushcraft, that's camping, etc. None of that really matters in the grand scheme of things. If you want to go out and practice survival skills, bushcraft skills, primitive skills, or go car or RV camping, that's your experience to have. Just go do it, take your family and friends, and enjoy it. I promise it will be more memorable than a weekend on the couch watching other people live their lives on a screen.

Go find out what that outdoor experience means for you.

Mango Publishing, established in 2014, publishes an eclectic list of books by diverse authors—both new and established voices—on topics ranging from business, personal growth, women's empowerment, LGBTQ studies, health, and spirituality to history, popular culture, time management, decluttering, lifestyle, mental wellness, aging, and sustainable living. We were recently named 2019 and 2020's #1 fastest-growing independent publisher by *Publishers Weekly*. Our success is driven by our main goal, which is to publish high quality books that will entertain readers as well as make a positive difference in their lives.

Our readers are our most important resource; we value your input, suggestions, and ideas. We'd love to hear from you—after all, we are publishing books for you!

Please stay in touch with us and follow us at:

Facebook: Mango Publishing
Twitter: @MangoPublishing
Instagram: @MangoPublishing
LinkedIn: Mango Publishing
Pinterest: Mango Publishing
Newsletter: mangopublishinggroup.com/newsletter

Join us on Mango's journey to reinvent publishing, one book at a time.